2 TONE

Before, During, & After

By
Lee Morris

Media House Books

Dedicated to John Bradbury, Ranking Roger, Saxa, Rico Rodriguez, George Webley, Jah Jerry Haynes, Francis Brown, Gary McManus, Paul Tickle, Tommy McCook, Bo Peep, Winston Wright, Mark Hughes and Cedric Brooks.

First published in 2020 by
Media House Books

© Media House Books 2020

ISBN 978-1-912027-55-2

Original cover design by Marten Sealby

Introduction

By Lee Morris

If you haven't listened to 2 Tone then you haven't lived - that is what I tell people. The whole movement began as an idea from the one and only Jeremy David Hounsell Dammers.

Unfortunately, I'm not old enough to have been around during the heyday of 2 Tone but I've had the music in my life from a very early age thanks to my parents. Whilst I was at school, I never took an interest in any of the music of the day but prefered to play my CDs of The Specials, Madness, Bad Manners and The Selecter to death and when MP3 players came about, I risked our computer's life by downloading song after song from Limewire!

As I got older, I decided to go and watch some of the bands that were the soundtrack of my childhood. The first gig I went to was at the Manchester Apollo where The Specials were playing their second reunion tour in 2011 and I was blessed to see 6 out of the 7 originals on the same stage. I have since seen Bad Manners, The Selecter, Madness and The Beat but unfortunately none of them in their original forms. As a collector of records, it became a mission of mine to try and see how many musicians I could get to sign my Dance Craze LP. I say "my LP" it was actually shamefully stolen from my Dad's collection! I have managed to meet many of the names that feature in this book and each meeting has been a pleasure and I often wonder what the 8 year old me would have thought about meeting all the people from the bands that have given me so much pleasure over the years.

I wanted to try and cover each band in detail and then update the story. I've always been fascinated by Where Are They Now stories and found it interesting to see what all the 2 Tone musicians got up to afterwards. I've tried to go beyond 2 Tone and discuss the bands in full, rather than just focusing on one period of their history. A lot of people are unaware that the label ran for seven years and there were bands signed to the label long after the breakup of The Specials in 1981. I've always been disappointed that 2 Tone books seem to omit the bands that were signed from 1982 onwards and my aim is to give those bands some column space and finally get some recognition for the part they played in the 2 Tone story. Hopefully this book has helped to make up for that previous neglect.

I'd like to thank Andy Pringle for making this project happen, my parents Steve and Jane as if it hadn't have been for them, I wouldn't be alive to write this book and also to every member of The Specials, The Selecter, The Beat, Madness, The Bodysnatchers, The Swinging Cats, The Higsons, The Apollinaires, The Friday Club and JB'S Allstars because if it wasn't for them this book wouldn't need to be written.

Lee Morris

51 Albany Road - where it all started

The Beginning

Every story has to begin somewhere and this one begins in India on May 22nd 1955 with the birth of Jeremy David Hounsell Dammers, or Jerry Dammers for short. Contrary to popular belief he was not christened Gerald Dankey. After spending his formative years travelling around with his parents (his father was a reverend), the family settled in Coventry in 1965. As a teenager, Dammers was made to sing in the church choir and took piano lessons before he gave them up as he hated them! As he grew up, he became a hippy and ran away from home when he was 15, ending up on John Lennon's island off the coast of Ireland. It was home to The Diggers, who used it as a commune, with Dammers and his friend ploughing the fields. They would be given a bowl of flour and water for their trouble though he'd soon had enough and became a skinhead upon his return to Coventry.

Dammers left school with an Art O-level and attended Nottingham Art School for a year before he enrolled at Lanchester Polytechnic, Coventry. He felt that the degree was pretty irrelevant and spent most of his time on campus making cartoons. This is where he met Horace Panter, he was in his second year and befriended Dammers. They worked together on one of these films with Dammers doing the animation and Panter providing the reggae influenced soundtrack. Dammers graduated but never picked up his degree at the graduation, later putting this down to his hatred of privilege.

Aside from art, Dammers had a love of music which stemmed from the first time he saw The Who perform *My Generation* on the television. He first discovered Prince Buster whilst listening to his brother's records and after he'd listened to *FAB-ulous Hits* he was hooked, from his skinhead days he'd already taken a keen interest in reggae but this was when his love of ska began. Dammers then ventured into the local music scene and played with Coventry music legend Ray King before he joined The Cissy Stone Soul Band which was a soul covers band. By 1977, punk had exploded and Dammers started to write his own songs but couldn't persuade the band to play any of them. After he'd kicked up a fuss and played the keyboards with his elbows during a gig, Dammers was asked to leave so decided he was going to form his own band to play the songs he was writing.

Dammers had grown up in Coventry, a city that was devastated by the Second World War. The city had seen a generation of immigrants come over after the War to work and help rebuild the country. By the late 1970s, racial tensions were growing in the UK and organisations that fuelled the flames, such as the British Movement and the National Front, were out recruiting. They were dark days and with increasing unemployment, what else was there to do but try and form a band? Dammers had wanted to form a band since he was 10, after he'd watched The Who on television.

Dammers had a vision and inspired by Tamla Motown, he also wanted to form his own record label, 2 Tone. He wanted the label to have a definitive sound, something that people could identify and be the equivalent to Tamla. He'd been fascinated by the label in the 1960s and he wanted to do something similar. He wanted to incorporate punk and reggae and create a new sound. He also designed some artwork for the label. The artwork saw a black and white man in a suit and a hat, named Walt Jabsco. Jabsco was based on a photo of Peter Tosh that had appeared on a Wailers album. The wheels were now in motion.

The Specials

Jerry Dammers was serious about forming his own band and set about putting it together. He'd been friends with Neol Davies for a few years, having played in Nite Trane with him, and he let Dammers record some demos on his Revox tape recorder. Dammers had always wanted to incorporate reggae into his music, he'd recorded a reggae soundtrack for one of the cartoons he'd produced at the Poly. He became friends with Horace Panter, who played bass on the soundtrack.

Dammers finally took the decision to form his own punk-reggae band in 1977, The Automatics were born, not The Hybrids as has been claimed. Horace Panter (bass), Neol Davies (guitar), Silverton Hutchison (drums) and Tim Strickland (vocals) made up the rest of the band and they began rehearsing. After a few rehearsals, Dammers decided he wanted a more authentic reggae sound and replaced Davies with Lynval Golding, who'd been playing with Ray King's band Pharaoh's Kingdom. Davies has since said; "One day I found out about a rehearsal that I wasn't supposed to know about and I went anyway, opened the door and there was Lynval!"[1] Golding was a Jamaican Windrush immigrant who played rhythm guitar and he provided the authentic reggae sound that Dammers was trying to nail.

The band continued to rehearse and Golding, with the help of his friend Desmond Brown, taught Dammers how to play reggae on the keyboards.

The Automatics played their first gig in October 1977 at the Heath Hotel, Coventry supporting Leamington punk band The Shapes. The gig saw Dammers playing his organ on the dancefloor with his back to the audience as the stage was too small! By now, he'd penned Little Bitch, Do The Dog, Dawning of a New Era and early versions of Nite Klub and Too Much Too Young, all of which had an airing at the gig. They played the venue again two weeks later, this time headlining while Coventry punk band Urban Blight supported. Dammers continued to try and perfect his band and kept watching numerous bands in Coventry, scouting the talent in them. Roddy Radiation and The Wild Boys were one of the bands and one night Dammers and Horace Panter went to a gig but left after a few songs seemingly unimpressed. They also watched punk band Squad, who had built up quite a following and the lead singer Terry Hall was quite a character. He'd been known on occasion to perform a full set with his back to the audience!

After Dammers had seen Squad play in Birmingham, he decided to approach Hall to join the band. Tim Strickland had never been convincing as the singer, he could usually be seen on stage reading the lyrics from a sheet of paper, so was replaced by Hall, with Dammers inviting him to the next rehearsal.

As 1978 began, The Automatics continued to hone their craft playing in and around Coventry including Tiffany's Ballroom twice in January, firstly with Steve Hooker & The Heat and then supporting Ultravox, this being Terry Hall's first gig. The settled line-up now consisted of Jerry Dammers (keyboards), Terry Hall (vocals), Horace Panter (bass), Lynval Golding (rhythm guitar) and Silverton Hutchison (drums). They were gaining momentum and a reputation around the city, managing to secure a residency at Mr George nightclub on Monday nights while they continued to rehearse at the Heath Hotel. Neville Staple, a friend of Silverton Hutchison's, had started hanging around with the band and soon became one of the roadies. This period saw Pete Waterman become the band's manager, he was the resident DJ at Mr George and knew some of the band from when they would play truant from school and hide in his record shop!

Later in the year, Waterman managed to secure studio time in London to record some demos for a princely sum of £600. A date was set and the band were due in a studio in the heart of Soho, London. Dammers was drinking in The Domino, Coventry the night before the recording session and approached Roddy "Radiation" Byers, asking him if he fancied joining them in London to play lead guitar on the demos. Radiation drunkenly agreed, thinking that Dammers was spinning a yarn and went home to bed. He was awoken in the morning by somebody banging on his front door, it was then that he realised Dammers was serious! He threw some clothes on and dashed out of the door to the waiting taxi rather hungover!

The Automatics -
Roddy Radiation and Terry Hall
(Pic. Gillian Flanagan-Jones)

Pete Waterman travelled down to London with them to oversee the recording of the demos, which he later tried to tout around the record labels but ultimately received no takers. A tape was also sent to John Peel at Radio One but this also amounted to nothing. When Roddy Radiation joined the band, he added his punky guitar playing which would later set them apart from the other 2 Tone bands. This style helped the band combine a hybrid of punk and reggae and this is evident on those early recordings. The recordings remained on the shelf until they were released in 1993 on the album *Dawning of a New Era* credited to The Coventry Automatics AKA The Specials. Waterman soon ceased to be the band's manager, legend has it that he'd tried to get them to do dance moves on stage!

After Waterman's departure, Jerry Dammers became acquainted with Chris Gilby, manager of The Saints, who paid for more demos to be recorded in London. These also proved fruitless and Gilby ended his association with them after they'd supported The Saints at The Marquee, London. Dammers then befriended Mike Horseman, a DJ in Birmingham, who helped them get some support slots in the city. This soon led to a residency at the Golden Eagle, Birmingham and they quickly garnered quite a following in the city.

The Automatics supported Sham 69 and Steel Pulse amongst others. Meanwhile, Dammers had heard about Johnny Rotten leaving the Sex Pistols and had the idea to travel to London to ask him to join The Automatics as singer. He didn't end up meeting Rotten but did manage to pass on some demo tapes to Steve Connolly (Roadent), a Clash roadie originally from Coventry. Roadent passed the tapes onto The Clash's manager Bernie Rhodes who liked them and after much discussion, Dammers managed to persuade him to give them a support slot on their 1978 On Parole Tour. The Automatics were originally booked for a few shows but after Joe Strummer was impressed, they were booked for the whole tour.

They were originally getting £25 per night, something that soon stopped when The Clash found out, incensed, they demanded that Rhodes doubled the amount. The Clash tour led to the band changing their name, becoming known as The Coventry Automatics as there was already another band called The Automatics. The name was soon changed to The Special AKA The Coventry Automatics before eventually being shortened to The Special AKA.

The Clash tour was a learning curve for the band, as they didn't go down too well with the punk audiences, being regularly spat at and pelted with beer cans and bottles. Horace Panter later said they "began the tour as civilians and finished the tour as a proper band"[2]. During the tour, Neville Staple joined the band after he'd been jumping on the stage at soundcheck and toasting over some of the songs.

Staple was well known on the Coventry music scene thanks to his involvement with the Jah Baddis sound system. Despite the mixed response on the tour, the band impressed Bernie Rhodes and he let them rehearse in his studio before deciding they needed some experience, sending them to France in November.

This trip is now part of Specials folklore and led to the song *Gangsters*. It began with Bernie Rhodes hiring a van for all the equipment and driving the band down to Dover for the ferry. Once they reached Dover, Rhodes told them to load the equipment onto some trolleys and on to the ferry. Meanwhile, he drove back to London in the van! Once they reached Calais, the first problem arose when Silverton Hutchison was immediately deported due to his Barbadian passport. The second problem was that the van which Rhodes had organised to take the band and their equipment to Paris was too small to fit all the equipment and the band. The white members decided they'd have to hitch-hike as Neville Staple and Lynval Golding assumed that France had similar racial problems to England and that no one would pick them up.

Eventually, they all got to Paris, including Hutchison who had sorted his passport and returned, and were staying in one of the city's hotels. Unfortunately for them, The Damned had recently stayed there and smashed it up. The owners of the hotel confiscated the band's guitars and demanded they pay up for the damage caused by The Damned! Eventually, the owner of the venue where they were playing came to an arrangement with the hotelier and the guitars were returned! Jerry Dammers later put the French ordeal down in words and this became *Gangsters*.

Shortly after leaving France, Dammers decided that the hybrid between punk and reggae wasn't working and suggested they mixed punk with ska instead. Ska could be played a lot faster than reggae and it could be mixed with the punk energy that the band had. Dammers also decided they needed an image that would set them apart and he dragged the band to a local charity shop to get them kitted out, he opted for suits, loafers and button-down shirts which had been popular with the Mods in the 1960s. He also made them get their hair cut. Lynval Golding was particularly unimpressed as he saw ska as "old man music" but was eventually convinced that this was the way to go. After playing a few shows, they found that mixing ska with punk was much better and well received by the audience, it helped that this new sound was a lot easier to dance to. This is when it really started to take off, though the change in musical direction led to the departure of drummer Silverton Hutchison, who left as he didn't want to play ska music.

Shortly after Hutchison's departure, Dammers was given £700 by Jimbo O'Brien, a local businessman, and they headed into the studio to record their first single. There was just one problem - they needed a drummer! Luckily, Dammers had been sharing a flat with John Bradbury, a local lad who worked in Virgin Records and was in Transposed Men with Neol Davies. Bradbury was asked to play on the record on the day of the recording and remained in the band from then on.

Gangsters was a reworking of the 1964 Prince Buster song *Al Capone* and the screeching sound of a car from the original is sampled at the beginning of the track. The original contains the opening words; "Al Capone knows don't argue!" which was changed to; "Bernie Rhodes knows don't argue!" - for obvious reasons!

Although the lyrics are original, the tune is borrowed from Prince Buster's hit, he isn't credited on the record but Dammers once commented that he always received royalties. While trying to perfect *Gangsters*, they used up the budget so they didn't have another song to put on the flip side! Luckily, John Bradbury knew where they could get a song and after Lynval Golding suggested it, Neol Davies provided *The Kingston Affair*, a track that Davies, Bradbury and a trombonist called Barry Jones had recorded in 1977, the song was renamed as *The Selecter*. Dammers asked Davies to overdub a ska guitar onto the track and the job was complete.

The record was finished and Dammers approached Rough Trade, asking them if they'd be interested in distributing the single. After hearing the tracks, they agreed to press 5000 copies of the single and these were hand stamped by various members of the band in Jerry Dammers' flat! Dammers then enlisted the help of The Damned's manager, Rick Rogers, who liked the band's sound and became the manager.

The record was popular, receiving rave reviews in the music press and airplay from John Peel on Radio One. The band also tried to capitalise on the release by playing every gig they could, with Rick Rogers securing two weeks worth of gigs in London. The plan was to have as many journalists as possible at the first week of gigs so they would write reviews for the music press and by the second week everyone would want to see them. This is basically what happened and their popularity soared during this period. People were beginning to take notice.

They also supported a number of prominent bands including UK Subs, The Damned and Gang of Four and by May, the single had sold out and the band were featured in all the usual music newspapers such as *NME, Melody Maker* and *Sounds*. With the single taking the country by storm, the band were being courted by a number of major record labels and this only seemed to intensify when their first Peel session was broadcast on May 29th, where they recorded versions of *Gangsters, Too Much Too Young, Concrete Jungle* and *Monkey Man*. Interestingly, John Bradbury was absent from the recording and the percussion was provided by Neville Staple.

Offers soon came in, even Mick Jagger turned up at a gig hoping to sign them to his label but walked out when he heard *Little Bitch* as he thought it sounded similar to *Brown Sugar* by The Rolling Stones! Dammers and the rest wanted one thing, a deal that would allow them to distribute singles on their own 2 Tone label, not just their own but other bands too. The label that finally got them to put pen to paper was Chrysalis, although they were initially wary of giving them their own label, they agreed to it as they didn't want to lose out on signing them. The deal that was struck saw 2 Tone being allowed to record ten singles a year, with an obligation that at least six of them would be released. The Special AKA themselves were signed up to a five album deal and *Gangsters* was re-released, this time in a black and white sleeve featuring Walt Jabsco.

Dammers had designed the Walt Jabsco logo himself, basing it on a photograph of Peter Tosh from *The Wailing Wailers* album, and it was named after an American bowling shirt he owned. The logo is now synonymous with the music and label and has become almost as famous as the bands themselves. It would appear on every 2 Tone release until 1982.

Dammers had originally come up with the name 2 Tone after the material that was used to make the suits that skinheads wore, he also took inspiration from a black and white checked sticker from his bike when he was a child. He has since claimed that he was unaware of the racial side to using the name 2 Tone but hasn't got a problem with people making that connection. The label contained socialist and anti-racist ideals and the band wanted to use it to release their own music as well as music by other like-minded bands. Dammers wanted it to be different from any other record label in the fact that no band would be subject to a contract and any band that recorded on the label could leave after one single.

Gangsters continued to perform well and it entered the charts at the end of July at No.74 and by early August, they were invited on to the BBC's *Top of the Pops*

Jerry Dammers and John Bradbury
(Pic. Gillian Flanagan-Jones)

and for the first time, the wider public were exposed to the movement that was starting to sweep the nation. The single rose to No.41 that week and by the time they appeared on the show again, it'd hit No.8. The Special AKA had arrived and the meteoric rise was evident for all to see. By September, *Gangsters* had peaked at No.6 and remained in the charts until October and unbelievably, had sold 250,000 copies by the beginning of September, achieving silver status. It also ended up as the biggest selling independent single of 1979.

After the success of *Gangsters*, the band went into TW Studios to start recording their debut album. They decided to record their live setlist at the time which contained a mixture of covers and originals penned by Dammers. Elvis Costello asked to produce it, he was a fan and had been spotted at numerous gigs. Costello even featured on *Nite Klub* bashing a tin tray! Chrissie Hynde also featured on *Nite Klub* singing backing vocals, she was a friend of the band in the early days. Hynde doubles up with Terry Hall on the line "girls are slags" in the song - just in case you were wondering! The album also contained classics such as *A Message To You Rudy* which featured the veteran Rico Rodriguez on trombone, and his friend Dick Cuthell on cornet. Rico had played on the original recording back in 1967 when Dandy Livingstone released it and they were delighted when he agreed to play on their version. This was released as the second single in early October, credited to The Specials featuring Rico, leading to another *Top of the Pops* appearance where they were introduced by Jimmy Savile!

Dandy Livingstone has since spoken fondly of The Specials for covering the song, he once commented at a gig with Neville Staple; "I'd like to thank The Specials for covering the song and making me a lot of money!". The addition of Rico and Dick Cuthell is noteworthy as they leant their brass to other songs on the album and eventually became honorary members, joining The Specials on tour thereafter.

Other Dammers originals on the LP included *Do The Dog, (Dawning) Of A New Era, Little Bitch* and *It Doesn't Make It Alright,* the latter a song about racism, which Roddy Radiation has said is his favourite Specials song.

Radiation also chipped in with one of his own, *Concrete Jungle,* where he performed lead vocals. It had been written when he was still with The Wild Boys. It has since been said Costello told Dammers to sack him, thankfully The General ignored this advice.

One of the highlights on the LP is *Monkey Man,* a cover of a Toots & The Maytals song but brought into 1979 with a faster beat and a sublime spontaneous toast by Neville Staple who was on his way to Banbury Cross! The album also contained *Stupid Marriage,* a little ditty about someone breaking a window and saw Neville Staple as his alter-ego Judge Roughneck and

Chrissie Hynde performing some heavy breathing, while *Too Much Too Young* was a six minute long song about contraception. *You're Wondering Now,* a cover of an Andy & Joey song, closed the album, which is still regarded as a masterpiece.

Sandwiched between the recording of the album, another Peel session took place on October 15th where they recorded versions of *Rude Boys Outa Jail, Rat Race* and *Skinhead Symphony* for broadcast a week later on the 22nd. This version of *Skinhead Symphony* is one of their best recordings and is far superior to the live version that later emerged. *Specials* was eventually released on October 19th to critical acclaim although bizarrely received less favourable reviews than *Live In Manchester,* a bootleg that'd been doing the rounds for weeks before! The album went straight in at No.4 and remained in the charts for a total of 45 weeks, eventually dropping out in September 1980!

A backstage shot with Rico, Rex Griffiths, Horace Panter and Trevor Evans (Pic. Gillian Flanagan-Jones)

In retrospect, the album is still looked upon very favourably and regularly featured in lists of popular and influential albums and the most well thought of album of all the 2 Tone releases. Most of the material on it is top quality although it is let down by the long studio version of *Too Much Too Young*, it had yet to become the 2 minute live version that would top the charts - but more of that later!

With 2 Tone sweeping the country, the album's release coincided with the start of a 40 date tour with Madness and The Selecter, billed as The 2 Tone Tour. The tour has gone down in 2 Tone folklore since and it soon became apparent how much it had been sweeping the nation. Usually at a gig, the support bands will have a few people watching but the venue will rarely be packed out so early. However, on the 2 Tone Tour the venues were packed out for the first band onwards, The Selecter would usually go on first, followed by Madness and then the headline act would be The Specials. The tour commenced in October and saw 2 Tone take over the country, with riotous gigs taking place all over the country and most of the time people forgot the problems that were going on around them and danced. Unfortunately, occasional gigs were marred with violence but most of the time, the gigs were a joyous occasion for all involved. One of those gigs that wasn't joyous occurred at Hatfield Polytechnic where a group claiming to be the Hatfield Anti-Fascist League stormed a fire exit and began to slash the audience. It was a pretty horrendous night but thankfully this type of thing was not a regular occurrence at the gigs.

The end of 1979 saw The Specials record a live show at the Colchester Institute for the BBC's *Rock Goes To College*, which was aired in January 1980. The band performed *Specials* almost in its entirety, including a shorter and angrier version of *Too Much Too Young* and also some new numbers including *Rat Race, The Skinhead Symphony* and a version of *Madness*. The success continued into 1980 and the band set off on their first European tour which commenced

in Paris on January 11th, the tour also took in Brussels, Berlin, Sittard and Amsterdam. The start of the tour coincided with the release of a live EP, *Too Much Too Young*, which had been recorded a few months prior at Tiffany's, Coventry. The record featured a live version of *Too Much Too Young*, a song about contraception and a slower and longer version had previously appeared on the album, as well as versions of *Guns of Navarone, Long Shot Kick De Bucket, Liquidator* and *Skinhead Moonstomp*. The latter three tracks appeared on the 'B' side under the name *Skinhead Symphony* and prominently featured the fantastic horn section of Rico and Dick Cuthell.

The EP hit the charts at the end of January, entering at No.15, whilst the band were in the midst of their first North American tour. By February, the EP had reached No.1 though The Specials were in Vancouver supporting The Police. It was quite an achievement, less than 12 months before, they had borrowed some money to record their first single and had visions of setting up their own record label. Now, they were number one in the charts, their record label had literally sweeped the nation, with people not just listening to the music and attending the gigs, even the fashion had changed, rude boys were seen all over the country and were dressing like their heroes. They continued on the tour of North America until the end of February when they returned to the UK, having been top of the charts for a fortnight in their absence! Despite its success, only snippets of it were aired on *Top of the Pops*, fading out before Terry Hall spat out the final line of "try wearing a cap!". Out of interest, it was the first live release to top the charts since Chuck Berry's *My Ding a Ling* in 1972 which was also recorded in Coventry at the Locarno.

After they'd returned from North America and completed the obligatory publicity for the No.1, The Specials headed back into the studio at Horizon to record their next single. They decided to record *Rat Race*, a song that'd been in the live set for a number of months and had been perfected on the American tour. The song came about when Roddy Radiation had been drinking in the bar at the Lanchester and overheard a conversation between some rich kids talking about the jobs that their families had lined up for them after they'd left university. He felt that the university places would be better off being used by people from less wealthy backgrounds who didn't have jobs lined up. The song has since been, wrongly, referred to as anti-education. It was released in May and the single reached No.6, they later filmed the music video in one of the halls at the Lanchester. The 'B' side was *Rude Buoys Outta Jail*, a composition that'd begun with Lynval Golding playing a tune on the harmonica, Horace Panter then wrote some lyrics and a song was born. Dammers arranged the tune and it was soon knocked into shape and stuck on the 'B' side, credited to Staples/Golding/Gentleman.

Worryingly, Chrysalis wanted a follow up to *Specials* but there weren't any songs to put on it! The musical direction was changing and as time wore on, certain band members had differing ideas of the direction they felt they should take. John Bradbury was interested in releasing a solo single and indulging in his love of Northern Soul. He wanted to record a cover of the Rex Garvey and The Mighty Cravers tune *Sock it to Em J.B.*, the JB reference wasn't lost on the drummer. He secured some studio time and the rest of the band went into the studio to record a cover of the song in double quick time. Despite the original intention of it being released as a JB's Allstars single, it remained on the shelf for the time being. This was quickly followed by the sessions for the eagerly anticipated second album. There would be a difference this time, the first album had been easy to record, they'd perfected those songs over two years. However, nothing was really written for the second album. Also, Dammers wanted to move forward musically, and despite playing ska on the first album, he wanted to move on and adopt a new sound. He'd been influenced by his friend John Shipley, guitarist of Swinging Cats, who was

heavily into muzak. Shipley has since been credited with influencing The General's tastes in music and inspiring the sound that would be present on the eventual album. Dammers got to work writing material for the album but was soon met with difficulty as musical differences occurred between him and the rest of the band. He wanted to move away from the music that had brought so much success and move towards muzak. This caused friction between The General and the rest of the band, Neville Staple wanted to stay true to their roots, whereas Roddy Radiation wanted to experiment with a rockabilly sound and John Bradbury wanted to incorporate a Northern Soul sound. Eventually, a compromise was reached with one side containing music that was more traditional to the Specials sound and the flip side would contain the music that Dammers had been experimenting with. It was intended for the album to be released in July to coincide with a promotional tour but the recording process was difficult and the tour was postponed until the band got some material down on tape.

The songs began to come together and they reflected the changing tastes but also harked back to the past on occasion. Two songs from The Automatics days, *Rock & Roll Nightmare* and *I Can't Stand It*, were dusted off and spruced up with the former becoming *Pearl's Cafe* and the latter included Terry Hall and Rhoda Dakar sharing the vocals. Perhaps the most startling songs were *Stereotype* and *International Jet Set*, both heavily influenced by muzak and although the former was an astute social statement, both songs were far removed from anything they'd recorded prior. The album also saw Terry Hall showcase his songwriting talents for the first time, he penned *Man at C&A*. Dammers added a second verse to it, hence the Dammers/Hall credit. John Bradbury's solo record *Sock it to Em J.B.* was updated with Paul Heskett's brilliant saxophone playing and the other track to feature a saxophone was Roddy Radiation's *Hey Little Rich Girl* with Lee Thompson from Madness making an appearance.

A cover of the 1940s dance number *Enjoy Yourself* (as well as the rather miserable reprise version which featured backing vocals from The Go-Gos) was recorded alongside Lynval Golding's *Do Nothing*, despite being credited to Golding, Dammers wrote some of the words but declined to take any credit. Last but not least came another Radiation tune, *Holiday Fortnight*, which was originally called *Why Argue With Fate* and contained lyrics but Dammers took the words off and left it as an instrumental on the final cut. Radiation has since recorded his own version of the song with the original lyrics set to the original track and is available on his YouTube channel.

The Specials then embarked on a seaside tour of the UK in June but on the first day, Jerry Dammers decided he didn't want to do it and Roddy Radiation's suggestion that Paul Heskett take his place on the keyboards didn't help matters! The band were supported on the tour by The Go-Gos and The Bodysnatchers, the latter being new signings on 2 Tone and the former being an all-girl punk band from the States. The tour saw some of the members at each other's throats, mainly Radiation and Dammers which culminated in an incident on a seaside wall where Dammers alleged that Radiation tried to push him off it! He'd also previously smashed his guitar over The General's organ on stage! The tour is also memorable for a gig in Skegness where after the usual stage invasion, the stage collapsed. Although no one was hurt, it was a lucky escape and the band realised that there could have easily been a fatality. The tour came to an end and they received a call from the American television show, *Saturday Night Live*, to play on the show. After the initial drama of The General refusing to check into the hotel that was provided (he eventually relented) and then refusing to travel in the limousine (opting to travel by taxi!) The Specials appeared on the show and made their mark on the American viewing public with a voracious performance of *Gangsters*, helped in part by them being in a foul mood due to a row just before they took the stage.

After a planned 2 Tone celebratory gig on Clapham Common was cancelled, the band were soon off to Japan for another tour in July. This was only a short one but it didn't pass without incident, when playing in Osaka, Rick Rogers was arrested as standing at concerts was illegal in Japan and obviously after the first couple of songs, everyone was on their feet dancing! Because of this, a second Osaka show was cancelled although the last few shows passed without incident before they headed home. The band hadn't long been home before Lynval Golding was beaten up in the street after some NF cowards had spotted him with two white girls. He'd been on a night out with Neville Staple when the attack took place and his experience led to him writing the song *Why?*, but more of that later! It was around this time that The Specials were approached by Debbie Harry to record a version of *The Tide Is High* with her. However, it didn't end up happening and she ended up recording it with Blondie, resulting in a No.1 in 1981!

The band had started slipping some new tunes into their set, notably when they played the Montreux Jazz Festival in July they played versions of *Stereotype* and *Do Nothing*, as well as *Enjoy Yourself* which had been part of the set for months. Just a few weeks before the release of the LP, *Stereotype* was released as a single, backed by *International Jet Set*. The single was far from commercial although it contained an important message about binge drinking and drink driving. Due to the word "pissed" being used, the controllers at BBC Radio One decided to limit the airplay, not that it mattered, it still peaked at No.6, proving that The Specials were still at the top of their game. Although it marked an incredible change of music direction and was a radical move, time looks back kindly on the single, it still stands up today and continues to be a part of the set played by the current lineup of The Specials. If the fans were shocked by the single, they were about to have an even bigger shock!

The album was due for release in the summer of 1980 but the mixing sessions had overrun, with Dammers producing and mixing it himself along with Dave Jordan, and it was eventually released in October. The album also came with a free pullout poster and a free 7" containing two tracks that they couldn't fit on it, these were *Braggin' And Tryin' Not To Lie* credited to Roddy Radiation and The Specials and *Rude Boys Outta Jail (Version)* credited to Neville Staples AKA Judge Roughneck. The album was released two weeks into the More Specials Tour where they toured to promote the release. It contains very little ska and songs such as *Pearl's Cafe, Holiday Fortnight, Man at C&A* and *International Jet Set* are far removed from their original sound. *More Specials* was successful, reaching No.5 in the charts, but alienated some of the loyal fanbase of rudeboys due to the dramatic musical shift. The Specials no longer seemed angry, something which they definitely were at the time of the first album, but it wasn't just anger, it had a point too and they had something to say. That's not to say that the second album wasn't saying similar things, but they seemed to lose that raw, powerful and angry attitude that had accompanied the first album. *More Specials* was much more relaxed despite some hard-hitting and powerful lyrics. Roddy Radiation has since commented that it would have been wise to do an album in between *Specials* and *More Specials* as the change in direction was far too extreme and would have been better if the change had been gradual. He has been quoted as saying it would be like The Beatles doing *Sgt. Pepper* before *Rubber Soul*. Despite the success of the album, the band were starting to break up and the rows and the differences that'd been brewing during the recording sessions continued to fester.

The album had seen guest appearances from Paul Heskett (Swinging Cats), Lee Thompson (Madness), Rhoda Dakar (The Bodysnatchers) and Charlotte, Jane & Belinda from The Go-Gos. Heskett actually joined the band on the More Specials Tour, playing saxophone on *Hey Little Rich Girl* and *Sock it to Em J.B.* leading to an amusing incident at one gig where he was due on stage for the saxophone solo on *Hey Little Rich Girl* but hadn't made it to the stage as the tour manager had forgotten to wake him up! Heskett had woken up and realised he was due on stage so rushed to the venue and tried to explain to security that he was supposed to be on stage! It led to a hilarious moment when Terry announced to the crowd "and on sax Paul Heskett", the spotlight shone and there was no one there! Thankfully Roddy Radiation stepped in with a fantastic improvised solo. The More Specials Tour almost didn't go ahead when Dammers was seen by a doctor on the first date of the tour in St. Austell. The doctor told him he was overworked but thankfully didn't diagnose glandular fever, which Dammers thought it was. Although some of the new tunes were being played brilliantly by the band, the gigs were marred with violent outbreaks in the crowd. This was nothing new but the violence was becoming more frequent and more vicious and the endless stage invasions weren't helping matters. It'd been a unique part of the show, to invite the audience up to dance along to the last couple of numbers in the set. However, this began to be taken advantage of and the stage would often be invaded just a few songs in and it was causing significant damage to equipment as well as carnage. Some scrupulous individuals also decided to steal anything that wasn't nailed down, Roddy Radiation has said that his hat would be stolen regularly!

The violence gradually got worse as the tour went on, it was bad in both Leeds and Newcastle but the worst of it occurred in Cambridge in early October. The trouble had begun earlier in the day when support band Swinging Cats were on, with a large group of Cambridge United supporters gatecrashing the gig and wanting to fight Coventry City supporters, one idiot even clambered on to the stage to attack lead singer Chris Long. Luckily, before the youth could get to Long, he was thrown off stage by a roadie.

The band quickly left the stage to the confines of the dressing room as continuing was nigh on impossible. It was hoped that the crowd would calm down once The Specials went on stage, although this optimism quickly evaporated when the violence started again just a few songs in. Once the trouble died down, the band started playing again only for the violence to flare once again. This time the band stopped and Terry Hall told the crowd that if the violence didn't stop, then they wouldn't be playing any further. They commenced once again but the tension had been ratcheted up a few knots and Hall had soon started trading insults with some of the troublemakers down at the front. Things turned ugly when they started spitting at the band and things soured even further when some bouncers decided to throw them out. Hall was known for disliking bouncers, even going as far as to throw his tamborine at one at a previous gig, and told them that they were just as bad as the troublemakers. When one of the bouncers told Mr. Hall to keep his gob shut, he took a microphone stand with the intention of wrapping it around his head. Thankfully, the stand was taken off him before he did some damage. Once the youths were thrown out and things had calmed down, the band returned to the stage to complete the set. However, once they returned backstage, the promoter told them that they were the reason for the violent outbreaks during the gig and went to fetch the police! When the promoter returned with P.C. Plod, Jerry Dammers was promptly arrested! Terry Hall was also slapped in handcuffs and both of them were charged with using threatening words and behaviour. This led to them going to court on November 5th where they were convicted of inciting a riot and fined £400 each!

After the tour came to a close, The Specials played a couple of charity gigs in London before taking a well earned break. Meanwhile, Chrysalis wanted to release a single in time for Christmas and after much deliberation, decided on *Do Nothing*, one of the songs from the album.

It was backed by a version of Bob Dylan's *Maggie's Farm* which had been slightly altered to make reference to Margaret Thatcher and The National Front. The single was released, credited to The Specials featuring Rico and the Ice Rink String Sounds, in December, reaching No.4. This culminated in a famous *Top of the Pops* appearance which saw the band don Christmas jumpers and swap bass players with The Beat! The single featured a string synthesiser, which belonged to Paul Heskett, and had been overdubbed by The General but apart from this addition it was the same track from the album.

Following the last tour and the violence that had blighted it, The Specials decided to stop touring and they had a short downtime period into 1981 as everyone concentrated on their own projects. Dammers was busy with the upcoming 2 Tone film, Neville Staple and John Bradbury each set up their own labels, Lynval Golding was producing The People, Roddy Radiation was playing with new band The Tearjerkers, Horace Panter was working on the Barnsley Bill novelty record and Terry Hall was writing songs. It would later transpire he was working on future Fun Boy Three material with Golding and Staple recording a number of demos. By February, the 2 Tone film that had often been talked about was finally released. *Dance Craze* contained live performances from The Specials, Madness, The Selecter, The Beat, The Bodysnatchers and Bad Manners. The Specials performances that were included were live versions of *Nite Klub, Concrete Jungle, Too Much Too Young* and *Man At C&A*. Other performances were filmed such as *Hey Little Rich Girl* and *Sock it to Em J.B.* but ultimately left out of the final cut. Dammers had worked on the film for months before it was eventually released, some sources state that he almost had a nervous breakdown during this period. Despite the reviews at the time not being favourable, it was popular amongst 2 Tone fans and still represents a unique look at the 2 Tone explosion that made its way through the nation in late 1979 and early 1980.

As with all film, it is a time capsule that can be revisited and was re-released for the 40th anniversary on Record Store Day 2020.

By March, Dammers had been working on his next masterpiece and was sure it would be a hit. However, the band were sceptical and the recording process was a nightmare with fallouts occurring and relations were at breaking point. The recording process was particularly fraught with no particular member wanting to play ball, Dammers found himself in a 24-track studio, overwhelmed with it. He decided to go back to basics in an 8-track studio and after hearing the reggae tune *At The Club* by Victor Romero Evans, he approached the producer of it, John Collins, to produce the single. The recording took place in Woodbine Studios, Leamington Spa over a number of days in April, most of the band weren't even talking to each other at this point and Dammers basically had to beg them to record their parts. Roddy Radiation was kicking holes in the studio wall while Lynval Golding stormed into the control room and told them that the brass was out of tune. Eventually, the process was finished and the single was complete, well almost....Dammers decided it was missing something, a flute! Paul Heskett was called in to add a flute at the beginning of the track and that was it. The finished song was *Ghost Town*, and when released it would become the band's most successful and one of the most memorable songs.

Interestingly, another style change occurred while they took some downtime in early 1981, emerging in zoot suits, Hawaiiwan shirts, frizzy hair and The General even sported a ridiculous goatee beard! It's hard to say where the inspiration came from but it wasn't so popular with some of the other members, Terry Hall in particular wasn't a fan of the suits. Meanwhile, The Specials travelled to Europe in April to play some shows and had a new addition to the band, Rhoda Dakar. She'd sung on *I Can't Stand It* and *Pearls Cafe* on the album and Dammers invited her to sing backing vocals for the shows.

Dakar remained with The Specials until the breakup and they also began to play one of her songs from The Bodysnatchers, *The Boiler*, a song about date rape. The European tour culminated in a London show at the Rainbow Theatre which was a benefit held in aid of the unemployed and they topped a bill which also contained Pigbag, The People and Dambala.

The single was released in June and was backed up by *Why?*, a Lynval Golding song, and *Friday Night Saturday Morning,* a Terry Hall composition which contains one of the best organ solos in music history. *Friday Night Saturday Morning* described what Terry Hall saw as his life, describing a night on the town in Coventry. *Why?* had been written after Golding was beaten up by some NF thugs the year before and the song sees Golding on lead vocals with Neville Staple toasting throughout the song with the thought provoking lyrics;

> *"With a Nazi salute and a steel capped boot*
> *A Nazi salute and a steel capped boot*
> *You follow like sheep inna wolf clothes*
> *You follow like sheep inna wolf clothes".*

Surprisingly, there were a number of disagreements with Dammers seemingly getting his way. Hall and Golding were ultimately unhappy with the arrangement of *Friday Night, Saturday Morning* and *Why?* Hall wanted *Friday Night Saturday Morning* to have a pub piano and him singing the words over it rather than the synthesiser that Dammers eventually played. Golding wanted *Why?* to stay true to the original demo recording which didn't contain many instruments. Both are fine tracks, the synthesiser is the best part of *Friday Night Saturday Morning* and the reunited Specials re-recorded *Why?* in the style Golding had intended, in 2014, and it's a pale imitation of the original suggesting that Dammers had it right all along.

Once the single was released, the band threw themselves into live performance again playing a number of benefit shows including one at the Butts Stadium, Coventry in aid of the family of a 20 year old Asian lad who had been murdered in the city.

The Specials were joined by Hazel O'Connor on the day. They also played a free concert in Rotherham and headlined the Carnival Against Racism in Leeds in early July. The Coventry show had actually lost money but Lynval Golding wasn't too bothered about that as he felt that the message had got across, commenting in an August edition of *NME*; "I think since we done that gig in Coventry, although we lost a lot of money, I think it was well worth losing that money for what it's actually achieved. I mean, like before you used to get tension in town. But now, it's like what we've done has actually got through".

Meanwhile, the single was performing well, entering the charts at No.21 before reaching No.2 in the first week of July. One week later, *Ghost Town* found itself top of the charts. This coincided with the riots of July 1981 and it was quite poignant that a song about urban decay, unemployment and growing unrest in the country was at the top of the charts while the country literally burned. A total of 35 towns and cities saw disturbances. Contrary to popular belief, it is NOT a song about Halloween! The song managed to define an era, where some of the country were getting rich quick and earning lots of money, Dammers was talking about what was really happening. While The Specials were touring during 1980, they had witnessed the true effects of Thatcherism, Dammers has since spoken about witnessing old ladies selling their cups and saucers on a street in Glasgow and how something was "very, very wrong". Coventry had been booming in the 1960s with the car industry but by 1981 its unemployment was one of the highest in the country and despite the song being true of Coventry, it's actually about the whole of the UK. For added irony, the band were almost at war with each other but continued to play live gigs, their last UK show taking place in Liverpool on July 24th 1981.

The Specials embarked on a North American tour in August, which had previously been postponed due to The General's health.

The band were joined on this tour by Rhoda Dakar and Paul Heskett. The set list had started to include some of Rico's tunes and also *The Boiler*, a song originally by The Bodysnatchers. The gigs went ahead without incident and the highlight was a gig where they shared the bill with Iggy Pop, The Police and The Go-Gos in Toronto. It was after this particular gig that Rick Rogers ceased to be the band's manager, with Dammers firing him after a heated discussion. The final show The Specials played was at the Bradford Ballroom, Boston on August 27th 1981. The band returned to the UK and the seven went away to concentrate on their own projects again although it all came to an abrupt end. Terry Hall, Lynval Golding and Neville Staple left to form Fun Boy Three, managed by Rick Rogers! Roddy Radiation left to concentrate on his own band The Tearjerkers and after just over two years at the top of their game, it was over. The official word was out in October that The Specials in their current form had broken up and this was confirmed by the release of Fun Boy Three's first single, *The Lunatics Have Taken Over The Asylum* in November, with the original intention of it being a Specials single. The nucleus of a band remained with Jerry Dammers, John Bradbury and Horace Panter who had decided to continue working together to see what came up.

Reunions

In 1993, Roger Lomas was approached by Trojan Records to produce a new album with Desmond Dekker and had the idea of using The Specials as his backing band. Lomas contacted the members and the four that expressed interest were Horace Panter, Neville Staple, Lynval Golding and Roddy Radiation. Panter, Staple and Golding had played with Special Beat since the beginning of the decade. The four were the only members that still lived in Coventry. The resulting album, *King of Kings*, was released in late 1993, credited to Desmond Dekker and The Specials. It only had moderate sales and didn't perform as well as Trojan had hoped.

However it had been noticed by a Japanese promotor who saw the album cover and assumed The Specials had reformed. He contacted Desmond Dekker's agent who rang Lomas to inform him of the interest. The promoter offered the band a tour of Japan, as ska was still popular over there, and Lomas set about trying to convince them to do the tour. They quickly agreed to reform The Specials and began rehearsals. Terry Hall, Jerry Dammers and John Bradbury had no interest in rejoining so Lynval Golding's friend Mark Adams took the role of keyboard player, Adam Birch joined on trombone and vocals, former Selecter drummer Aitch Bembridge on drums and they were later joined by Jon Read on trumpet and the MC Kendall Smith. There were some discussions about what name they would use, Panter and Radiation suggested Specials2 and The Coventry Specials was also briefly used before it was decided to use The Specials. It was felt the name would be stronger business wise and help them get more bookings. Although the band were billed as The Specials, this incarnation is more commonly known as Specials Mk.2.

The tour of Japan commenced in 1994 and was followed by successful tours of America and Europe. They were also capitalising on the so-called "third wave of ska" which had been occurring in America since the late 1980s. They were soon offered a deal by Ali Campbell's Kuff Records in 1995 and went into the studio to record some new material, deciding to record an album of covers, similar to the *Labour of Love* albums by UB40. Roddy Radiation was against the idea but was outvoted by the other members. The first release from the sessions was the single *Hypocrite*, featuring then Prime Minister John Major on the cover. The band performed the new single live on the daytime BBC show *Pebble Mill*, alongside old favourite *Do Nothing*. The album *Today's Specials* was released in May 1996 and was a spectacular failure, the press had a field day in pulling the band to bits and questioned whether they should be using The Specials name for such a release. This album has since been described as *Today's Bollocks* by Roddy Radiation! One of the better songs on the album, *Pressure Drop,* was released as a single and is still played by ska DJs to this day. There was a lot of material recorded in the sessions that didn't make it onto the album, such as a cover of *Johnny Too Bad,* originally by The Slickers. The reason for its exclusion was because Ali Campbell had just released his own version of it!

Without Jerry Dammers in the band, Neville Staple took up the mantle as leader and also became the lead singer, sharing his vocal duties with Roddy Radiation. Dammers commented on the band in 1998; "I'm not at all happy about them using the name. It would be alright if they called themselves The New Specials or something different, but they are using the name without any right."

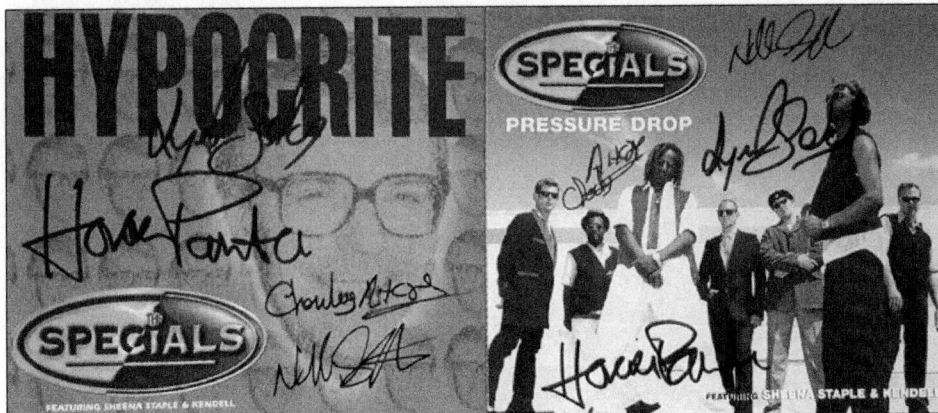

Hypocrite and Pressure Drop singles

2 TONE | THE SPECIALS

In my view, they shouldn't be doing it and it is unfair - especially putting out dodgy albums with that name". [3]

Despite the poor album sales, they continued to play live and toured America again in June and July before returning to the UK to play the Phoenix Festival in Stratford-upon-avon. More American shows followed in the autumn before they played some intimate shows at the Jazz Cafe, London before Christmas 1996.

The band then continued in mid 1997 playing a number of festivals and some members were writing their own songs, which were being included in the live shows. Roddy Radiation was the most prominent songwriter in the band and the rest of the band also wrote some material between themselves culminating in the release of *Guilty 'Til Proven Innocent* in March 1998.

The band were soon back on the road and played all over America and Canada between March and May before they joined the Vans Warped Tour. The Vans Warped Tour had been created in 1995 and was a travelling tour of bands which would play all over America.

The Mk.2. Specials were one of the headline acts and the North American leg of the tour began in June and ran until August. There was barely any time for rest when the band then joined the European leg of the tour. Horace Panter pulled out of the tour and was replaced on bass by Jon Read before the band played across Europe before travelling home in September and after a tour of Japan, the band fizzled out as the members were exhausted, skint and had basically had enough.

However, in 1999, The Selecter recorded three albums of Trojan covers with Roger Lomas and The Specials were approached to record some as well. As they'd split up, Horace Panter, Neville Staple and Roddy Radiation went into the studio along with Neol Davies as Lynval Golding wanted nothing more to do with the band and had pulled out of the project a mere fortnight before it was supposed to go ahead. These sessions led to the albums *Skinhead Girl* (2000) and *Conquering Ruler* (2001), both carrying The Specials name.

By the millennium, attempts were made to try and put The Specials back together for a reunion.

The Specials embark on their 2009 reunion tour (Pic. Wonker)

Simon Jordan, the chairman of Crystal Palace FC, was a big fan and wanted them to reform to play his 40th birthday party. He befriended Terry Hall in the process and set about trying to convince the members one by one to reform and mentions in his autobiography that he put a £1 million contract in front of Jerry Dammers. The reunion was being driven by Jordan and Hall's manager, Steve Blackwell. Meanwhile, Dammers had been working on a track with Horace Panter, Neville Staple, Lynval Golding and Dick Cuthell. The track, entitled *First Victims of War*, remains unreleased as of 2020. The attempts for a reunion in 2004 were ultimately unsuccessful but the talks continued between the members and at one point the idea to re-record the first two albums for distribution in a Sunday newspaper was mooted. Thankfully this idea never came to fruition! Four years later, in June 2008, The Specials appeared on stage together for the first time since 1981 when they were inducted into the MOJO Hall of Fame. Though Neville Staple was absent due to a delayed train!

The Specials later re-formed but without Jerry Dammers, although he'd been involved with early rehearsals, he was thrown out of the band or chose not to be involved depending on which version of events you believe. In the latter part of 2008, Dammers was involved in a war of words with the other six members, claiming he'd been thrown out of the band, whereas the other six stated the door was open should Dammers want to return. The reunited Specials, minus Dammers, performed at Bestival in September where they were billed as Terry Hall & Friends, due to legal wrangles at the time, before news of a 30th Anniversary Tour soon surfaced in December with the band announcing a UK tour to commence in April 2009. For the tour, the band were joined by Nik Torp (keyboards), Tim Smart (trombone), Jonathan Reed (trumpet) and Drew Stansall (saxophone). The Specials also toured Australia and Japan in July and August and after the success of the first UK tour, another one was announced for late 2009, with the band playing in locations they'd missed on the first tour. The band also played Glastonbury, T in the Park and V Festival, with the latter seeing Amy Winehouse guesting on *Ghost Town* and *You're Wondering Now*. After the success of the reunion, the band continued into 2010 playing some American shows and also a number of festivals across the world such as Love Music Hate Racism, Hurricane Festival, Ruisrock Festival and Ibiza Rocks. Neville Staple, Lynval Golding, Roddy Radiation and Jon Read showed their charitable side when they recorded a charity single for the Haiti Earthquake Appeal in April 2010, recording a version of *A Message To You Rudy* with some of the children from Moel Llys Short Stay School, Leicester where Reed was the headteacher. Towards the end of 2010 it was announced that The Specials would play a huge European tour in 2011 and it was hinted that this would be the band's final hurrah.

The Specials embarked on the tour, which also saw them broaden their horizons with the material that they played, a number of songs from *More Specials* made it into the set but at the expense of old favourites such as *The Skinhead Symphony* and *Too Hot*. Reports emerged that they would break up at the end of the tour due to Roddy Radiation's exit. However, they performed a u-turn in November and confirmed they would continue to perform and that Radiation was still a member! They were pretty quiet throughout 2012, playing mainly festivals such as Pinkpop and a short Australian tour. August saw the release of a live album, *More... Or Less The Specials* which contained live recordings from 2009 and 2011. Later in August, The Specials closed the Olympic Games in Hyde Park, London alongside Blur and New Order. This marked Neville Staple's final gig with the band as he left due to ongoing health issues, having been diagnosed with epilepsy. He had missed some shows due to illness over the past year. The Specials saw out 2012 by playing live on BBC Radio 6. This was also the last appearance of saxophonist Drew Stansall, who left the band shortly afterwards.

The band embarked on a tour of America in early 2013, with Lynval Golding taking on Staple's vocal duties and some of the other songs that relied heavily on his input were dropped such as *Stupid Marriage*. Roddy Radiation departed after growing tension between him and Terry Hall. His departure wasn't acknowledged by the band but Radiation released a statement in February 2014 stating he would be concentrating on his own band, The Skabilly Rebels. He was replaced by Matt McManamon for the following gig at the Isle of Wight Festival but his official replacement was Steve Cradock, guitarist with Ocean Colour Scene and Paul Weller, who joined for the autumn tour of 2014. The band also recorded a new version of *Why?* with updated lyrics attacking the Black Power Movement and the EDL. Since the release, Lynval Golding has sung the new lyrics when the song is played live.

The band had been discussing the possibility of recording some new material before John Bradbury passed away suddenly in December 2015 from a heart attack. After some discussions, they decided to carry on without Bradbury, who was replaced by Gary Powell from The Libertines, his arrival coincided with an announcement in February 2016 that the band would be touring North America and the UK later in the year. The tour went ahead in September, with the band taking in the US before heading back to the UK in

October for a month-long tour, culminating in two shows at the London Troxy, the last of which was broadcast live on YouTube. By now, two new songs had made their way into the set, *All The Time in the World* and *Redemption Song* which were, at various times, dedicated to John Bradbury and Rico Rodriquez (who had also died in 2015).

They then performed three co-headline shows with Toots & The Maytals in Leeds, Birmingham and Hatfield in May 2017 and also performed another short tour of the US in June. Then after almost a year off, the band supported The Rolling Stones in June 2018 when they played the Ricoh Arena in Coventry.

Unbeknown to the fanbase, the band went into the studio to record some new material and it was announced in October that they would be releasing a new album, the first to feature Terry Hall since *More Specials*. *Encore* was released in February 2019 and launched at an intimate gig at 100 Club, London, also broadcast live on BBC Radio. Upon its release, the album received a warm response from critics and fans alike, it was soon discovered it was creeping up the charts with the band at war with Busted for the No.1 spot! The album hit No.1 in the first week of its release and the band then toured the UK to promote it and celebrate the 40th anniversary of *Gangsters*. This culminated in four homecoming shows back-to-back at Coventry Cathedral in July.

A new look reunited Specials containing Horace Panter, Terry Hall and Lynval Golding from the original lineup

The Specials are almost unrecognisable in their current form, with more members absent than the ones that remain. They have also undergone a fashion change in recent years, opting for more casual wear than the smart tonic suits that they wore during their heyday. Also, a number of the new album's tracks have made it into the live set at the expense of classics such as *Little Bitch, Hey Little Rich Girl* and *Guns of Navarone*. Their latest album also contains a track, *Ten Commandments*, written by activist Safiyah Khan as a response to Prince Buster's 1967 hit which begins with the lyric "Thou shall not listen to Prince Buster. Or any other man offering kindly advice" which is a surprise after the original band were heavily influenced by him and a number of their songs were covers of songs by the ska legend.

Terry Hall, Lynval Golding and Horace Panter continue to tour as The Specials and are backed by Steve Cradock (guitar), Nikolaj Torp Larsen (keyboards), Kenrick Rowe (drums), Tim Smart (trombone) and Pablo Mendelssohn (trumpet). When Cradock is busy with Ocean Colour Scene and Paul Weller, Jake Fletcher usually deputises. Activist Safiyah Khan has also been joining the band on stage since February 2019, performing *Ten Commandments*. The Specials plan to tour and record more material.

Releases on 2 Tone

The Special AKA vs The Selecter - Gangsters (1979) - Single.

The Specials with Rico - A Message To You Rudy (1979) - Single.

The Special AKA - Too Much Too Young Live (1980) - Single (Live EP).

The Specials - Rat Race (1980) - Single.

The Specials - Stereotype (1980) - Single.

The Specials - Do Nothing (1980) - Single.

The Specials - Ghost Town (1981) - Single.

The Specials - Specials (1979) - Album.

The Specials - More Specials (1980) - Album.

Where are they now?

Jerry Dammers
Keyboards, 1977-1981

The General, the main man and the founder of the whole 2 Tone movement. After the implosion of The Specials in 1981, Dammers continued the band, renaming it The Special AKA and toured as Rico's backing band with the remaining members in late 1981. Away from the band, Dammers was single-handedly running 2 Tone and continued to sign bands to the label, recruiting The Apollinaires and The Higsons in 1982 (producing each band's debut single) though the success it'd seen between 1979 and 1981 was never repeated. Although there was a brief resurgence when he penned the anti-apartheid tune *Nelson Mandela* which reached No.9. Shortly after the release of The Special AKA's album *In The Studio*, which left him heavily in debt with Chrysalis, he threw himself into anti-apartheid politics. Though in between he signed one more band to 2 Tone, The Friday Club, producing their single *Window Shopping*. After JB's Allstars released their final single on the label it was closed down and Dammers formed

Artists Against Apartheid and was heavily involved in politics, campaigning against apartheid and organising a number of benefit concerts.

Dammers continued to be involved with music, producing the band The Untouchables and working on the soundtrack for the film *Absolute Beginners*, contributing the track *Riot City*.

He combined his political work with his music, organising the charity record *Starvation* in 1985 for famine relief. He also recorded *Wind of Change* with Robert Wyatt & The SWAPO Singers for the Namibia independence effort.

With his involvement with Artists Against Apartheid, Dammers helped to organise the Nelson Mandela 70th Birthday Tribute at Wembley, culminating in a singalong of *Nelson Mandela* and he even played keyboards on it. He helped organise a similar concert when Mandela was released in 1990.

He'd also become involved with Red Wedge, a collective of left-wing musicians that toured in aid of the Labour Party. By the 1990s he was regularly DJing with Lynval Golding but also on his own and also ventured into occasional production work, producing the single *Operation Ivy and Don Brennan* in 1994 by Wat Tyler.

He also formed his own band, The Spatial AKA Orchestra in 2006, originally formed as a Sun Ra tribute band but have since played a variety of different music, including Specials covers. He was involved in the efforts to get The Specials back together in 2008 but ultimately didn't take part in the reunion and has not played with his band since.

Dammers continues to DJ around the world and is currently working on new music, he spent much of 2019 touring with Neville Staple for the 40th anniversary of 2 Tone celebrations and is currently living in London with his partner, Jo.

"Sir" Horace "Gentleman" Panter
Bass, 1977-1981, 1993-1998, 2008-present

Sir Horace Gentleman had known Jerry Dammers for years and joined The Automatics in 1977. It was Lynval Golding that christened him Sir Horace Gentleman thanks to his plummy English accent! He remained with The Specials throughout and continued in 1981 when they became The Special AKA. He toured with Jerry Dammers and John Bradbury as part of Rico's baking band in 1981 and also played on the album *Jama Rico* in 1982. Panter left The Special AKA in April 1982 after a fall-out with Dammers and after a couple of years in the wilderness, he joined General Public in 1984 with Dave Wakeling and Ranking Roger. General Public continued until 1987 and after Ranking Roger went solo, Panter played bass on his album and also on the subsequent tour. By 1990, he was working for a transport firm before he joined Special Beat, with Neville Staple, John Bradbury and Ranking Roger, playing songs by The Specials and The Beat. After a three month tour in 1991, Panter quit the band after he'd missed his son's first day at school while he was touring and enrolled on a teacher training course, later qualifying in 1993. Although he continued to work as a teacher, Panter remained active in music, touring and recording with The Specials Mk.2 between 1993 and 1998 and also teamed up with Neol Davies to form the band Box of Blues and could regularly be seen in the pubs and clubs playing locally in Coventry. He has also played with his own band Horace Panter's Uptown Ska Collective in the 2010s. Panter was working as an art teacher in a disabled school in 2008 when he re-joined The Specials for the 2009 reunion tour. Panter remains in the band at present and also moonlights as an artist in his own right, running Horace Panter Art, and has had a number of exhibitions across the UK. He has been married to Clare since 1982 and is still living in Coventry.

Lynval Golding
Rhythm Guitar 1977-1981, 1993, 1994-1998, 2008-present

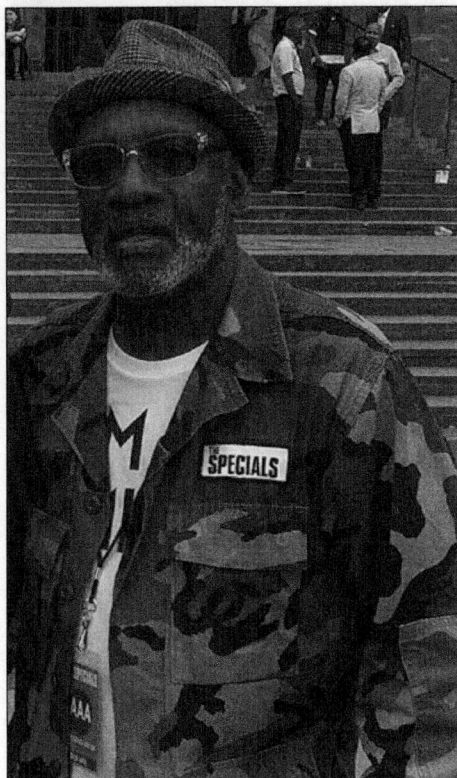

Lynval Golding was playing in Pharaoh's Kingdom with Ray King when he was recruited by Jerry Dammers to join his band. By 1980, he'd written his first Specials song, *Do Nothing*, which reached No.4,

and also contributed the song *Why?* to the *Ghost Town* single in 1981. Golding left the band with Terry Hall and Neville Staple to form Fun Boy Three and released the single *The Lunatics Have Taken Over The Asylum* in October 1981. They recorded two albums and half a dozen singles before they broke up in 1983, clocking up seven Top 40 hits.

Golding later appeared on The Special AKA single *Nelson Mandela* in 1984 and recorded *Pirates on the Airwaves* in the same year with Neville Staple and Pauline Black, credited to Sunday Best. Golding remained friendly with Dammers and worked with him in 1985 on the *Starvation* single and also guested on the Robert Wyatt & SWAPO Singers single *The Wind of Change*.

He then formed After Tonite in 1986, releasing three singles and an album before breaking up in 1988. As well as playing guitar in the band, Golding produced.

He also guested with The Pogues at the Town and Country Club, London in March 1988. By 1990, Golding was DJing regularly in Coventry with Jerry Dammers and also joined Special Beat alongside Neville Staple, John Bradbury and Ranking Roger. In 1993, he reunited with Staple, Roddy Radiation and Horace Panter to reform The Specials.

He remained until 1998, by which time they had recorded two albums. Golding then moved to Seattle with his new partner and became a stay-at-home father, only rarely playing guitar. It was only after an impromptu performance at Glastonbury in 2007, where he joined Terry Hall and Lily Allen to play *Gangsters*, that he got the bug again.

Golding was the main driving force behind the eventual reunion of the band in 2008 and remains in the group to this day. Aside from performing with The Specials, Golding has since guested on a number of recordings by Rhoda Dakar, Roddy Radiation, The Skapones and Pama International amongst others and continues to reside in Seattle with his family.

Roddy "Radiation" Byers
Lead Guitar, Vocals 1977-1981, 2008-2013

Radiation had been performing for years before he was asked to join the band in 1977. He was the only other songwriter in the band, having already written *Concrete Jungle* and also wrote *Rat Race, Hey Little Rich Girl* and *Holiday Fortnight* whilst in the band. In 1981, he formed The Tearjerkers as a side-project but later left The Specials and concentrated on them full time. They released the single *Desire* in 1982 though it failed to chart and he was soon dropped by the label. The Tearjerkers supported Stiff Little Fingers on their 1982 tour but they split in 1986. Radiation went back to his original trade and set up his own painting and decorating business.

He continued to play and formed The Bonediggers, later recording an EP in 1990 and despite being popular in Coventry, they didn't hit the big time and he left in 1993, later forming The Raiders. Radiation reunited with Lynval Golding, Neville Staple and Horace Panter in 1993 to record *King of Kings* with Desmond Dekker after they were approached by producer Roger Lomas to record the album. Radiation toured with The Specials Mk.2 from 1994 until its implosion in 1998 and since 2003 has played with The Skabilly Rebels, releasing a number of CDs, the last being the *Losing Control EP* in 2018 which featured Neville Staple on a re-recording of *Hey Little Rich Girl*.

Radiation re-joined The Specials in 2008 for the reunion but left in 2013.

When he's not touring with The Skabs, Radiation guests with other bands and has guested with The English Beat, The Skapones, Stiff Little Fingers, The AC30s and The Neville Staple Band, playing on their 2017 album *Rude Rebels* as well as during some live performances.

Terry Hall
Vocals, 1978-1981, 2008-present

(Pic. Joe Kerrigan)

Hall joined the band in 1978 and remained until the split in 1981. He was the face of The Specials and famous for his deadpan delivery and apparent inability to smile! Hall sang on most of the songs and even penned a couple while in the band. *Friday Night Saturday Morning* was released on the flip side of *Ghost Town* and he also co-wrote *Man at C&A* with Jerry Dammers for *More Specials*. Hall left in 1981 when he, Lynval Golding and Neville Staple suddenly departed to form Fun Boy Three, shortly after *Ghost Town* had reached No.1. Fun Boy Three enjoyed considerable chart success with singles such as *The Lunatics Have Taken Over The Asylum, Summertime, The Telephone Always Rings* and *It Ain't What You Do*, the latter being a collaboration with Bananarama.

They also released two albums *Fun Boy Three* (1982) and *Waiting* (1983). After a tour of America, Hall suddenly pulled the plug on the band in 1983. Shortly afterwards, he emerged with The Colourfield in 1984. They released a number of singles, with *Thinking Of You* being most successful after it reached No.12 in 1985. They also released two albums before disbanding in 1987.

After a couple of years in the wilderness, Hall re-emerged with Terry, Blair & Anouchka in 1989. The singles *Missing* and *Ultra Modern Nursery Rhyme* were released before the album *Ultra Modern Nursery Rhymes* followed in 1990. Nothing was heard of Hall until 1992 when he collaborated with Dave Stewart to form the duo Vegas where they released an album, *Vegas*. Hall then teamed up with Ian Broudie of The Lightning Seeds to write songs, some of which ended up on their album *Sense* in 1992. The album itself is named after one of the songs Hall had co-written. He then released his first solo album *Home* in 1994, featuring songs co-written with Broudie and Craig Gannon and it also contained his own version of *Sense*. This album was followed by the release of the *Rainbows* EP in 1995, a collaboration with Damon Albarn. It was around this time that Ian Broudie was working with Baddiel & Skinner on the eventual hit *Three Lions*. Hall provided the guide vocal on the track for Baddiel & Skinner to follow when they recorded their parts. Hall's second solo effort, *Laugh*, was released in 1997 and reached No.50 before he faded into obscurity.

Although he did guest on the Gorillaz song *911* in 2001, a song written about the 9/11 terrorist attacks in America.

Hall has suffered from mental health problems which culminated in a breakdown and a suicide attempt in 2003. He was diagnosed with bipolar disorder and given help for his illness. He later released an album with the Dub Pistols in 2007 before he reunited with Lynval Golding at Glastonbury to sing *Gangsters* with Lily Allen, sowing the seeds for the reunion of The Specials in 2008.

Hall had not sung with The Specials since 1981 and rejoined the band for the 30th Anniversary Tour in 2009 and has remained ever since. In his spare time, Hall watches Manchester United, works as a DJ and lives in Islington, London with his wife and children.

Neville Staple
Vocals, 1978-1981, 1993-1998, 2008-2012

Staple was one of the band's roadies before he joined after toasting during the soundchecks. He remained in the band until 1981 when he formed Fun Boy Three with Terry Hall and Lynval Golding. They achieved seven Top 40 hits before breaking up in 1983. Staple and Golding then recorded *Pirates on the Airwaves* with Pauline Black in 1984, credited as Sunday Best. He was also involved with the Ferry Aid appeal in 1987 when they released *Let It Be*. Staple provided backing vocals on the single.

Neville Staple

After a period out of the music business, Staple became the manager of Johnny Zee, a successful Asian singer who came to prominence in 1989.

He later formed Special Beat with Ranking Roger, Horace Panter and John Bradbury and worked as a manager and producer. Staple reunited with some of The Specials in 1993 and they continued to play until 1998 after which he moved to California and performed in the US for a number of years before returning to the UK and forming The Neville Staple Band.

He'd been gigging with his own band for around four years before he joined the reunited Specials in 2008, remaining until 2012 when he left due to ongoing health issues stemming from a car crash in 2011.

The accident had left him suffering from epilepsy and he'd collapsed shortly after a show. Staple has continued to tour and record with The Neville Staple Band and has also recorded and performed with his wife, Sugary Staple, who has released her own solo material as well.

In 2019, Staple played a number of shows to commemorate the 40th anniversary of 2 Tone which included guest appearances from Jerry Dammers, Neol Davies and Roddy Radiation.

Staple is also a regular face at the 2 Tone Village, Coventry and can be seen there regularly opening exhibitions or launching his albums. The Neville Staple Band is now known as From The Specials and they released a new album, *The Rude Boy Returns*, in 2020 where Staple and his band re-recorded some of the songs that appeared on an album of the same name in 2004. This album was exclusively launched at the 2 Tone Village in January 2020 where Staple and his wife, Sugary signed copies of the album for fans.

During the coronavirus pandemic of 2020, they released a limited edition single *Lockdown*.

John 'Brad' Bradbury
Drums, 1979-1981, 2008-2015

Brad had played on *The Selecter* with Neol Davies and Barry Jones in 1977 and has the distinction of being the only person to appear on both sides of the *Gangsters* single. He was familiar on the music scene in Coventry from his time working at Virgin Records and shared a flat with Jerry Dammers. When Silverton Hutchison left The Special AKA, Dammers asked Brad if he'd replace him.

He was known as Prince Rimshot, due to his distinctive drumming style, and Horace Panter has previously described his style as "attack drumming", Brad played his drums like he hated them!

When The Specials imploded in 1981, he remained in the band with Dammers and Panter and they toured Germany as Rico's backing band, also playing on the *Jama Rico* album in 1982. Dammers reverted back to the name of The Special AKA and built a new band around himself, Bradbury and Panter and began to work on a new album which was eventually released in 1984, though the band disbanded soon after. Brad had formed his own group JB's Allstars in 1983, releasing a few singles which culminated in 2 Tone's final single in 1986 with the release of *The Alphabet Army*. This meant that Brad has the distinction of playing on both sides of the first and last 2 Tone single.

'Brad' Bradbury
(Pic. Paulrclarke)

After JB's Allstars finished, Bradbury moved into production working with The Loafers and Maroon Town on various releases. He also worked with Jason Votier, under the name 2 To The Power.

He later played in Special Beat, Big Five and the reformed Selecter before leaving the music business to work as an IT specialist. He remained in that industry until 2008 when he joined the reunited Specials for the reunion tour of 2009. Brad remained in the band until his death in 2015 from a heart attack.

Prior to his death, the band had explored the prospect of recording some new material, which Brad had been heavily involved in. The Specials eventually released a new album in 2019, *Encore* hit No.1 in February 2019 and Lynval Golding was quoted as saying "We are so proud to have produced a great album, the world is divided and here is our album that we feel addresses this. Some of my last words I ever spoke to our late drummer Brad as we worked on song ideas, was we are going to have a number one. Well here it is, this is for Brad"4.

Dick Cuthell
Flugel Horn, 1979-1981

Cuthell was never an official member of the band but played on both albums and most of the singles, usually playing the cornet or flugelhorn. He was friends with Rico, having previously worked on his 1977 album *Man From Wareika*, playing a number of instruments and working on the production. They were firm friends by the time Rico was invited to join The Specials in 1979 and he took Cuthell along with him. Cuthell remained with the band until its breakup in 1981 and continued to work with Jerry Dammers and The Special AKA. Away from The Specials, Cuthell also played trumpet on The Selecter's *Too Much Pressure* in 1980 and worked on Rico's 2 Tone releases, *That Man Is Forward* in 1981 and *Jama Rico* in 1982, playing a number of instruments and also producing both albums. He continued to work with

Dammers, playing on *Starvation*, a charity record for famine relief, and *Wind of Change*, a record for Namibia. Cuthell later played with Madness, The Eurythmics, Roddy Radiation, The Pogues and Fun Boy Three before moving into production. He's since retired from the music business, settling in Lincolnshire, where he remains in quiet retirement.

Rico Rodriguez
Trombone, 1979-1981

Much the same as Dick Cuthell, Rico was never an official member but also played on both albums and most singles. He had played on a lot of the original ska records from the 1960s and had played on *Rudy, A Message To You* by Dandy Livingstone. Rico was the link between the original ska and this new style of music which had been created by Jerry Dammers. He was brought in to play on *Message To You Rudy*, the single was even credited to The Specials with Rico, and he remained in the band throughout. He also played trombone on The Selecter's first album *Too Much Pressure* in 1980 and released a solo single, *Sea Cruise*, on 2 Tone. When The Specials split in 1981, Rico released two of his own albums on 2 Tone, *That Man Is Forward* in 1981 and *Jama Rico* in 1982. He continued to work with The Special AKA, releasing *Jungle Music* in 1982 and also played trombone on their 1984 album, *In The Studio*. Away from The Specials, Rico featured on Paul Young's *Love of the Common People* in 1982 playing trombone and later joined Bad Manners in 1990, remaining with the band until mid-way through the decade. He then joined Jools Holland's Orchestra and performed his own solo shows. He remained friendly with Jerry Dammers and played with his Spatial AKA Orchestra and even said he'd never join The Specials reunion without Dammers' involvement. Although he was no longer able to play trombone in his later days, he still played gigs and sang along with his songs instead and was also awarded an MBE for services to music before his death in 2015 at the age of 87.

Silverton Hutchison
Drums, 1977-1979
After leaving The Special AKA, Hutchison continued to play around Coventry and joined The People in 1980 with Charley Anderson and Desmond Brown. For the 30th anniversary of 2 Tone, he unveiled some of the plaques on the Two Tone Trail and also guested with the band Too Much Too Young at some of the events. Hutchison is still based in Coventry and believed to be working as a van driver.

Tim Strickland
Vocals, 1977-1978
Strickland was the original vocalist in the band but was replaced by Terry Hall in 1978. He continued to work for 2 Tone in promotion until 1984 when he moved to Sheffield and worked for the City Council as a Music Services Coordinator. Strickland has been working at Sheffield Hallam University as the funding development manager since 2000.

Chrissie Hynde
Backing Vocals, 1979
Hynde had befriended The Specials in 1979 and sang backing vocals on *Nite Klub* and *Stupid Marriage*. Her band, The Pretenders were still pretty much in their infancy at this time. Their first album followed in 1980 and she has enjoyed a wide and varied career in music, guesting on UB40's *I Got U Babe* in 1985, INXS's *Full Moon, Dirty Hearts* in 1993 and Frank Sinatra's *Luck Be A Lady* in 1994. Away from music, Hynde has appeared in the American show *Friends* and released her memoirs *Reckless* in 2015 to critical acclaim. She is currently living in London and is a follower of Vaishnavism, a form of modern Hinduism.

Belinda, Charlotte and Jane
Backing Vocals, 1980
Belinda, Charlotte and Jane are perhaps better known as the American punk band The Go-Gos. They toured with The Specials in 1980 and sang backing vocals on *More Specials*. The Go-Gos continue to tour and record to this day despite playing a farewell tour in 2016. They released their latest single *Club Zero* in 2020.

Jane Wiedlin
Wiedlin would later have an affair with Terry Hall and they wrote the song *Our Lips Our Sealed,* a song released by both the Go-Gos and Fun Boy Three. Wiedlin also enjoyed a solo career, which is best remembered for *Rush Hour,* which reached No.12 in the UK and No.9 in the US. She has also turned her hand to acting and has appeared in *Star Trek, Frasier* and *HoneyBee.* She has also voiced one of the Hex Girls in *Scooby Doo,* an eco-goth rock band that occasionally appeared in the show.

Belinda Carlisle
Away from the Go-Gos, Carlisle began her solo career in 1985 and is perhaps best known for the song, *Heaven Is a Place on Earth.* She has continued to be successful as a solo artist and has released a number of successful albums and singles, which have been hits in both the UK and the US. Her albums *Belinda* (1986) and *Heaven on Earth* (1987) both reached No.13 in the US and *Heaven On Earth* and *Runaway Heroes* (1989) both reached No.4 in the UK. She released her autobiography *Lips Unsealed* in 2010 to critical acclaim. Away from music, Carlisle is known for her activism including supporting LGBT rights and forming Animal People Alliance in 2014 which raises funds to train impoverished women to care for street animals.

Charlotte Caffey
Caffey is the only Go-Go to not launch a solo career, choosing to concentrate on songwriting. She wrote some songs for Belinda Carlisle after the Go-Gos broke up. She later formed her own band, The Graces in 1988 who released the album *Perfect View* in 1989 and four singles before going their separate ways in 1992. She continues to play with The Go-Gos, though is semi-retired due to carpal tunnel syndrome. In 2008, she co-wrote the rock musical *Lovelace: A Rock Musical* and some of her songs appeared in the 2018 Broadway musical *Head Over Heels.*

Lee Thompson, Paul Heskett and Rhoda Dakar also guested on More Specials but are covered in the sections for their own bands.

The Selecter

The Selecter began life as a song in 1977, originally titled The Kingston Affair, which was used as the flip side to The Special AKA's Gangsters in 1979, but by then known as The Selecter.

Neol Davies had been playing in various bands around Coventry since the early 1970s, his introduction to music coming at the Holyhead Youth Centre. The youth club was run by Ray King and in the basement anyone could set up their instruments and jam. It was here where Davies first met Charley "Aitch" Bembridge, Arthur "Gaps" Hendrickson, Desmond Brown, Charley Anderson and Lynval Golding. He was also acquainted with John Bradbury from jamming at Warwick University. Davies formed Nite Trane with King in 1974 but after some rehearsals they decided they needed a keyboard player. They placed an advert in the local newspaper and Jerry Dammers turned up and soon joined. They gigged for a year but fell apart after a disastrous two week stint in Tunisia in 1976. After Davies had been a brief member of The Automatics, he set about trying to get his own songs together and began to play with John Bradbury and Kevin Harrison. This fizzled out but after Davies and Bradbury had listened to *Watching The Detectives* by Elvis Costello, they realised he'd mixed reggae and pop in a way they wanted to, and Brad suggested they record a single.

By 1977, Roger Lomas was a producer and had built a studio in his garden and Bradbury suggested they approach him to produce the single. They did and Lomas agreed to be involved. The recording process took around three months as they would only record when they were all available at the same time as Davies and Bradbury still had jobs. As has been mentioned, it was originally titled *Kingston Affair* and credited to The Selecters. The track was eventually finished with Bradbury on drums, the local sweetshop owner Barry Jones on trombone and Davies played guitar, bass and percussion. A publishing deal was signed for the track, but nothing came of it. Not content with just having the single, Davies wanted to form a band to play his songs and formed Transposed Men, named after a comic book on John Bradbury's table! The band consisted of Davies (guitar & vocals), Kevin Harrison (guitar), Steve Wynne (bass), Desmond Brown (Hammond organ) and John Bradbury (drums). By now, Davies had written the songs; *On My Radio, Out On The Streets, Missing Words* and *Street Feeling*. After a few gigs they attracted some interest from Virgin Records but this amounted to nothing, with Virgin eventually turning them down.

31

Jerry Dammers had been playing with The Automatics, now known as The Special AKA, for over a year and was about to record a single and needed a drummer to play on it. Davies has since said; "I had a band with Brad and Desmond Brown called Transposed Men and we did *On My Radio, Street Feeling* and other later Selecter songs. That was going along in 1978 after *The Selecter* track and nothing had happened with it. Then one day Jerry approached me in the pub and asked if he could borrow Brad...bye bye Brad!"[1]. Transposed Men fell apart after Bradbury's departure and disbanded shortly afterwards.

Davies was still working his day job and would go and watch The Special AKA rehearse while he was on his lunch break. "I was kicking my heels, still working in an office which was just around the corner from where The Special AKA would rehearse and I used to go on my lunch break and I used to think 'they're getting really good!'. I used to go back to work and get really annoyed and angry so I wrote *Too Much Pressure* at the office desk one Friday afternoon"[1].

It wasn't all bad news though as The Special AKA used up the budget recording the 'A' side and needed a 'B' side quickly! As Davies has said; "We get to the point where they've recorded *Gangsters* but they've run out of money to record a 'B' side. And Jerry said he had the idea to release the single as a double 'A' side to launch the label. It took me the smallest amount of time imaginable to say yes!". It wasn't unusual for Jamaican releases to have a track on each side by different artists.

The song had remained untouched for two years; "The missing ingredient was a rhythm guitar. So we took the master tape into the studio and I overdubbed the rhythm guitar over the master"[1]. The original title seemed out of place so it was changed to *The Selecter*, with the name coming from the Jamaican "selector", written on Davies' hi-fi amp switch.

After Dammers secured a deal with Rough Trade to distribute 5000 copies, various members of The Special AKA stamped the record sleeves, Davies also joined in and stamped his own version. With the singles having The Special AKA Vs. The Selecter on the sleeve, Davies stamped a unique The Selecter Vs. The Special AKA!

The record now has pride of place in the Coventry Music Museum. The single was released as a double 'A' side and was soon performing well, selling out by the end of May and becoming an underground hit in the process.

John Peel played both sides of the single on his radio show and when he played *The Selecter* he incorrectly stated that it was a song by The Special AKA! Davies was listening at the time and phoned the BBC, managing to be put through to Peel in between songs. He explained the situation and Peel later corrected himself on the show.

Shortly after the single's original run sold out, Dammers managed to secure a deal with Chrysalis for his own label, 2 Tone, and the single was re-released, this time in the black and white sleeve featuring Walt Jabsco. Although he was surprised by the success of the single, Davies was instructed to put a band together to capitalise on it and set about recruiting his members, though he didn't have to look very far.

The first single was re-released in a 2 Tone sleeve

By 1979, Davies was well acquainted on the Coventry music scene, he'd been in Chapter Five with Charley Anderson, Gaps Hendrickson, Desmond Brown and Silverton Hutchison in the mid 1970s and up until recently had been in Transposed Men with Desmond Brown. Also, Anderson and Hendrickson were in Hard Top 22, which also featured Charley 'Aitch' Bembridge and David 'Comi' Amanor.

Also, at the same time there was a radiographer called Pauline Vickers who was singing in Coventry pubs and knew Desmond Brown. Vickers was in a band with Brown, Lawton Brown and Aitch Bembridge.

Should be: One day they were rehearsing at the Wheatsheaf pub when Lynval Golding approached Vickers, Bembridge and Desmond Brown and invited them to a band meeting at Charley Anderson's house. When they got there, Anderson was there with Neol Davies, Compton Amanor and Gaps Hendrickson. It was here where they agreed to meet up at a later date to begin rehearsals as a band at the Binley Oak, Coventry.

The line-up was now settled and consisted of; Pauline Vickers (vocals), Gaps Hendrickson (vocals), Neol Davies (guitar), Charley Anderson (bass), Compton Amanor (guitar), Desmond Brown (keyboards) and Aitch Bembridge (drums). The band, like The Special AKA, were a multi-racial band with Neol Davies being the only white member. Soon after joining the band, Vickers became Pauline Black, partly so no one at work would recognise her if they read the music press and because it sounded definitive. Mrs. Black later changed her name by deed poll in early 1980 and Charley Anderson has since claimed that he gave her the name.

The Selecter began to rehearse in May at various pubs in Coventry including the Golden Cup, and performed their first gig in early July in Gloucester. The band's fashion sense left a lot to be desired and the audience that night witnessed a rather muddled appearance.

Pauline Black and Desmond Brown both sported afros. Charley Anderson wore a beige safari suit and Neol Davies was the only member that resembled anything like their later style with his loafers and sta press trousers.

Shortly after the gig, Davies and his wife Jane told the band they needed an image and suggested a similar style to how The Special AKA were dressing. Jane Davies took the band around various second hand shops and kitted them out.

Next on the agenda was a photoshoot which took place under the watchful eye of John Coles, a 2 Tone legend that photographed all the bands in the early days. The band soon contacted John Mostyn, who'd been involved with booking gigs for The Special AKA, and he secured them their second gig, supporting The Special AKA at the F Club, Leeds!

The Selecter's second gig occurred just a week later on July 10th and the band were still getting to grips with the music and learning the words. Pauline Black and Gaps Hendrickson taped the words to their songs across the front of the stage!

The crowd reacted well and Elvis Costello was even spotted in the audience although he didn't go down very well with Black as he trod on her foot at the bar and didn't apologise!

It was at this gig where she first adopted her now famous trilby hat. She'd been talking to Trevor Evans, a roadie for The Special AKA, in the dressing room before the gig and he suggested she wore one, letting her borrow one for the occasion. The fairytale continued on July 21st when they supported The Special AKA and Madness at the Electric Ballroom, London. It was perhaps a sign of things to come that the venue was packed out long before the headline act had taken to the stage. The Selecter were starting to be noticed and spent the next couple of months travelling the country and gigging to a growing number of people, enhancing their ever-growing reputation.

The Selecter had developed into a proper band in such a short space of time but now it was time to record some material. They were rushed into Horizon Studios, Coventry with a £1000 recording budget from 2 Tone to record a single. Roger Lomas, the producer of the original *The Selecter* track, was recruited to produce it. As was the norm with 2 Tone at this time, the band recorded three tracks; *On My Radio, Too Much Pressure* and *Street Feeling*.

It was decided that *On My Radio* backed by *Too Much Pressure* would be the first single and it was released in October, mere months after the band had been swiftly put together. The single proved popular, an attack on boring radio stations, an irony completely overlooked by the Radio One DJs of the time.

They appeared on *Multi-Coloured Swap Shop* to mime along to the single shortly before their first appearance on *Top of the Pops* on October 18th. The single peaked at No.8 and soon after, The Selecter joined 2 Tone as co-directors, meaning along with the seven members of The Specials, who were already directors of 2 Tone, the seven members of The Selecter also became directors.

As ever, John Peel took an interest in the band due to their association with The Specials and had played both *On My Radio* and *Too Much Pressure* on his radio show. He became a fan of the band after the first single, but preferred *Too Much Pressure*, and was later spotted in the audience on the 2 Tone Tour at the University of East Anglia, Norwich and was impressed.

The band were booked in for a Peel session in early October, recording versions of *They Make Me Mad, Carry Go Bring Come, Street Feeling* and *Danger* which were broadcast on October 22nd. The Selecter had also built up an association with The Beat, having offered the Birmingham band any support slots they wanted. The Beat were happy to be asked and they played a number of Midlands dates with The Selecter in the early days.

As the 2 Tone bug swept the nation, The Selecter joined the 2 Tone Tour, along with Madness and The Specials, which began later on in October. The Selecter were at the bottom of the bill but this tour was different from others because the crowds packed in to the venues to see all three bands and at £2.50 a ticket you couldn't go wrong.

On the first night of the tour, Juliet De Vie became the band's manager, she'd been involved with organising the tour and Neol Davies felt it was right to ask her. She was also a change from the norm in those days as she was a woman in charge of a majority male band, a welcome change. Despite being only 20 years old and a woman in a very male dominated industry, she held her own.

The tour continued to be popular all over the country and the nation were given a taste of how much 2 Tone was taking over when they tuned into *Top of the Pops* on November 8th and saw The Specials, Madness and The Selecter all on the same show. The Selecter were performing *On My Radio* with the single at No.21 and it peaked at No.8 two weeks later. Not bad for a band that'd played their first gig in July!

After the success of their first single as a proper band, The Selecter were back in the studio working on their debut album. They released their second single, *Three Minute Hero* on February 20th 1980, where they were backed by Joe Reynolds, a saxophonist from Coventry who was friends with Neol Davies and Desmond Brown. Reynolds speaks fondly of his involvement; "I knew all the guys from The Selecter and The Specials through various bands I had played and recorded with, in particular Neol Davies and Roddy Byers were old friends". Reynolds wasn't the first saxophonist to play on the track however; "My friend and one-time mentor, Jim Laing recorded the track first but Neol telephoned me because he thought the sound was too smooth and jazzy. Originally I was supposed to lend the Madness sax player (Lee Thompson) my horn as his was being serviced.

It was a weird situation because I don't remember ever being asked to play, it just happened". The obligatory *Top of the Pops* appearance followed and they were joined by Reynolds; "I remember going on *Top of the Pops* and they made us re-record the track, as was normal back then, I played my bit and there were loads of mistakes! They stopped recording and said it would be fine, I told them that we couldn't put it out as I'd make mistakes on the solo, they said 'oh don't worry, we'll just switch the tapes' and I got a fee for the session! Playing with The Selecter on *TOTP* was one of the highlights of my career".

It's interesting to note that The Selecter differed from The Specials as they were very much a guitar driven band, whereas The Specials relied on a horn section of Rico and Dick Cuthell for their authenticity. The Selecter, in their original form, surprisingly never had a recognised horn section.

The single was followed by the album *Too Much Pressure,* released just three days later on February 23rd. The album was 2 Tone's second and it showed the public that The Selecter weren't just hanging on the coattails of The Specials.

It was a great first effort, containing a re-recorded *Too Much Pressure,* a faster and more musical version than the 'B' side on the single. It wasn't a Neol Davies dominated album neither, he'd provided *Three Minute Hero, Missing Words, Street Feeling, Too Much Pressure, Out On The Streets* but Pauline Black chipped in with *Black and Blue* and *They Make Me Mad* (co-written with Desmond Brown) and some covers, *Time Hard, Murder, Carry Go Bring Come, James Bond* and *My Collie (Not A Dog)* which was a rearranged tune borrowed from *My Boy Lollipop* (adapted by Charley Anderson), this was topped off with *Danger,* credited to The Selecter. Dick Cuthell and Rico were borrowed from The Specials to play trumpet and trombone respectively, they both appeared on *Carry Go Bring Come* and Rico also played on *Black and Blue.*

Despite being a decent album, some of the band were ultimately unhappy with the finished product with Pauline Black criticising the producer Errol Ross in her book; "In my opinion, he single-handedly ruined the sound of our first album, *Too Much Pressure,* although fortunately not the songs. They were too good and couldn't be harmed, but his production skills were minor at best and majorly ruinous at worst"[3].

It was recorded at Horizon Studios, Coventry and was a fraught process, with the band being asked to do long hours of guide vocals and day after day of recording basic instruments. They perhaps missed the production skills of Roger Lomas and he probably wouldn't have charged the record company for the use of his shoe leather for walking a few hundred yards from the tube station to the Chrysalis office for meetings!

Ross wasn't popular with the band and he had no further involvement with them after the album was finished. As of 2020, Neol Davies is currently working with the record company to remaster the album with the intention of making it sound how it should have done back in 1980.

To coincide with the release, the band began their Too Much Pressure Tour in the same month, supported by The Bodysnatchers and Holly & The Italians.

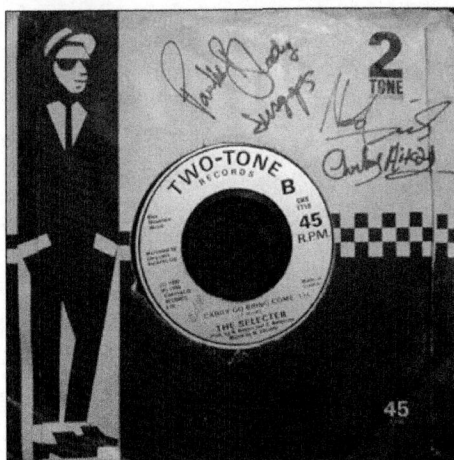

Missing Words single signed by Neol Davies, Pauline Black, Gaps Hendrickson and Aitch Bembridge

Sadly, the tour was marred with violence, something which was becoming an increasing occurrence at 2 Tone gigs in general, and Holly & The Italians quit the tour shortly after it began after they were abused and some of their fans were attacked. They were replaced by fellow Coventry outfit, Swinging Cats who contained Steve Wynne on bass, Wynne had played with Neol Davies, Pauline Black and Desmond Brown in various bands before The Selecter.Despite the violence, the tour was a success and shortly afterwards they released another single from the album. *Missing Words* was put out in March but only reached No.23, a reasonable placing but nowhere near the success they'd experienced with their first couple of singles. The single also saw a welcome return for producer Roger Lomas, who had remixed the track. The band then set off to North America in April on a mammoth two month tour of the US and Canada which concluded in June with a week of sellout shows in Los Angeles.

Around the first anniversary of the inception of 2 Tone in July 1980, The Selecter began to kick up a fuss about the direction they believed the label was heading and suggested to Jerry Dammers that they shut it down while it was at the top of it's game. However, after a meeting, Dammers disagreed and The Selecter left to sign to Chrysalis. They issued the following statement upon their departure; "2 Tone was intended to be an alternative to the music industry, a label that took risks and, we hope, injected some energy into what had become a stale music scene. The time has come when we want to take risks again". Neol Davies has since said about this period; "2 Tone ceased to be something The Selecter, as a band, felt increasingly unable to contribute to. So we put our energy into ourselves and tried to survive the changes"[2].

The Selecter had also been blighted throughout its short life with divisions, and a band whose members were from a variety of different backgrounds, it was probably inevitable.

With Davies being the sole white member of the band, the accusations that he was receiving all the credit or that it was his band only because he was white were often brought up in the heat of an argument. This led to issues with perceived racism within the band, with some of the black members sensitive to any perceived white favouritism. It seemed that whenever there were disagreements, race found its way into the argument. At one point, Desmond Brown had to be dragged off Pauline Black when he attacked her on the tour bus. The race issue had also previously led to Roger Lomas being fired as producer in 1979 and replaced by black producer Errol Ross. The band suffered from problems that would also be experienced by The Specials as they were both bands that had been put together with each member hand-picked rather than a bunch of friends coming together and forming a band. Another spanner in the works occurred when Juliet De Vie began a relationship with tour manager, Malcolm Rigby.

With Chrysalis, The Selecter were offered a similar deal to The Specials, they would have their own label. Although it remained nameless it did have its own logo designed by Jane Davies. This coincided with a change in direction, seeing them move from their ska and reggae roots to a more new wave sound. They were soon back in the studio at Horizon to record a non-album single. There were all sorts of politics blighting the band at the time, Charley Anderson wanted the band to stay true to their roots and follow a more reggae sound whereas Neol Davies was aiming for a rockier sound. From these sessions, *The Whisper* was released in August and the change of direction was there for all to see. Jane Davies also influenced a change in style. Pauline Black's trilby, Fred Perrys and dark suits were ditched and it was suggested that she had a frizzy afro and wore a jumpsuit. The idea was for Black to feminise herself to appeal to a wider audience and the other members also changed their style, with Neol Davies sporting pointed Midge Ure style sideburns and even a perm!

The contrast between the band that had burst onto the scene with *On My Radio* and the one that released *The Whisper* was startling. Despite this, the single performed respectably, reaching No.36, leading to an appearance on *Top of the Pops* at the end of August. This appearance had been preceded by the exits of Desmond Brown and Charley Anderson. Brown decided to leave the band and just 48 hours later was followed out the door by Anderson, who was asked to leave. This plunged the sessions into chaos and by the time they appeared on *Top of the Pops*, there were only five members present. Compton Amanor had to play bass and Gaps Hedrickson had to play the keyboards during the performance.

The band were now without a keyboard or bass player as the recording of the new album was about to begin. While Anderson's replacement was sourced, producer Roger Lomas filled in on bass before Norman Watt-Roy joined the band briefly.

Ian Dury & The Blockheads had appeared on the same edition of *TOTP* and noticed The Selecter were light on numbers. After bumping into each other in a lift, Dury suggested that The Blockheads bass player play on some of the tracks until they found a replacement. The band were delighted to borrow him and he played on *Celebrate The Bullet* and *Washed Up And Left For Dead*.

Pauline Black was full of praise in her book; "Norman Watt-Roy was the quintessential New Wave bassist. Immediately Norman started playing on the two tracks, it was obvious that he understood the sparing subtlety required to match the evocative vocal lines and poignant guitar melodies". She goes on; "The precision of his playing, tinged with an indefinable melancholy, remains unsurpassed and makes both of these tracks classics of that Selecter period"[3].

Brown and Anderson were replaced by James Mackie and Adam Williams respectively, two musicians from the Lancashire band, The Pharaohs.

Pauline Black has since described this period as the beginning of the end of The Selecter and remarked that it was never the same after the departure of Charley Anderson and Desmond Brown [4]. Neol Davies has since commented that when Desmond Brown left the band, it was never the same and they should have called it a day there and then. Davies is always complimentary about Brown in interviews and has said; "Desmond was one of the finest musicians I've ever known".

During this period, the band parted company with manager Juliet De Vie and opted to manage themselves. It was far from ideal and they did plan to recruit a new manager eventually but wanted it to be a better controlled situation, feeling that any future relationship with a manager would be better controlled as they now had experience in management.

The new lineup played some shows, with the first one at Birmingham Polytechnic where James Mackie and Adam Williams were learning the material right up until soundcheck! This show was recorded and has since been broadcast on BBC Radio, despite only learning the material in the days leading up to it, the new recruits seem to be in fine form as are the rest of the band. A number of the new songs were previewed including; *Selling Out Your Future, Cool Blue Lady, Washed Up And Left For Dead, Red Reflections* and *Tell Me What's Wrong*. They didn't leave without playing the hits either, with *Out On The Streets, Danger, Missing Words, Street Feeling* and *On My Radio* all being played.

They also recorded another Peel session in November, their second, recording versions of *Selling Out Your Future, Deep Water, Tell Me What's Wrong* and *Washed Up And Left For Dead*. The session was broadcast in December and later repeated on New Year's Day 1981.

Except for the odd gig, this was the first opportunity for the listening public and Selecter fans to hear the new material.

The sessions continued and *Celebrate The Bullet* was the first single to be released in February 1981 though it failed to chart and had the misfortune of being released just two months after John Lennon's assassination in December 1980. Mike Read, ever the purveyor of good taste, decided to ban the record on Radio One as he, wrongly, assumed the band were trying to make light of Lennon's assasination. Read had actually been in the audience at the Birmingham Poly a few months previously and didn't realise the song had been recorded months before Lennon's murder and was actually both anti-violence and anti-war.

Meanwhile, the band appeared on *Dance Craze* in February 1981. Neol Davies doesn't look back fondly on the film and even refused the silver disc as he was unhappy with the finished product where The Selecter were concerned. The film contained live performances of *On My Radio, Missing Words, Three Minute Hero* and *Too Much Pressure*, these were also included on the accompanying LP with the exception of *On My Radio*. All the performances are live but some of the guitar parts were overdubbed later on in the studio. As the footage had been filmed in 1980, the band was unrecognisable to the current band, with two different members and a completely different image. It did however, feature the mock fight scene that was a highlight of The Selecter's early shows where they would pretend to have a brawl on stage during the set to show the audience how stupid they looked when they decided to fight.

The bad fortune with their new material continued, despite rushing out the album in an attempt to show the single in more context, just a month after it was released at the end of February, John Hinckley Jr. shot US President Ronald Reagan in Washington DC. The album was a marked difference from their first offering the year before, it seemed more true to the roots of the original *The Selecter* track than anything that had appeared on *Too Much Pressure*.

It wasn't too far removed from the ska-sounding first album but it was almost like a distant cousin, the songs weren't any less political, just less danceable and rather moody. The album saw the welcome return of producer Roger Lomas with Barry Jones also returning, he'd played trombone on the original *The Selecter* track back in 1977. It wasn't so much a complete change in direction from their first album, more a development. Neol Davies has explained this change; "I felt it made a connection back to my original *The Selecter* instrumental, the guitar and drums especially. It was more musically ambitious than some of the early tracks and that was intentional"[2]. The band organised a two and a half week tour to coincide with the release.

Despite the title, the album is anti-violence and *Celebrate The Bullet* is an ironic title, the song itself is anti-gun. How can these lyrics be anything other than anti-gun?

> *Celebrate the bullet*
> *Put your finger on the trigger*
> *But you don't have to pull it*
> *Cause you know it won't bring them*
> *Back to you, back to you.*

Due to the Lennon and Reagan incidents, the album was finished and quickly sunk without trace although John Peel played a number of the album tracks between February and March. The Selecter limped on for just a while longer before Pauline Black decided she'd had enough and left the band to go solo. The Selecter tried to carry on, auditioning replacement singers, including Stan Campbell, but they were eventually dropped by Chrysalis and by the start of 1982, the band had gone their separate ways and it was over. Davies has since said; "The single was released, received top reviews and then no airplay at all. The band could not recover from this because of the huge effort making the album, the line-up changing the day before we were booked in the studio and touring. And then no sales to keep things moving. Pauline left to a solo deal at the label, who then dropped our contract. The end"[2].

Reunions

After ten years away, The Selecter reformed in 1991 with Neol Davies and Pauline Black teaming up with Martin Stewart, Nick Welsh. Perry Melius of Bad Manners. Davies and Black guested at some Buster's All Stars shows throughout 1990 and were surprised there was still love for the music. They agreed to reform the band when Martin Stewart managed to book a seven date UK tour and three weeks in the US.

These shows went down well and when they returned to the UK, they decided to continue on a full-time basis, with Welsh, Stewart and Melius leaving Bad Manners for good. Following the tour, Stewart secured a one-off deal with Pagan Records, owned by Andy Cowan-Martin and Russell Bell, who also became the band's management.

The band were soon in the studio and re-recorded *On My Radio* and *The Selecter* which was re-packaged and released as *On My Radio 91* on vinyl and CD. It didn't replicate the original release's success but then again, why would it? None of the band members have ever spoken fondly of the release and although it has appeared on certain compilations, it doesn't hold a candle to the original.

This didn't curb the band's enthusiasm though as they embarked on the Out On The Streets Again Tour in 1991 where they toured Europe. This was marked with the release of the live album *Out on the Streets* in 1992. This was quickly followed by another tour, Pressure 92, which was the biggest yet and saw the band performing 36 shows in 40 days. They then embarked on a tour of Japan with The Skatalites and Prince Buster, who asked The Selecter if he could perform with them for one of their two Tokyo shows. The band agreed and he performed *Madness, Al Capone, Orange Street* and *Rough Rider*. The latter is perhaps the most famous as it has appeared on ska compilations over the years and was sampled by Mint Royale on their 2002 song *The Sexiest Man in Jamaica*.

Shortly after appearing with The Selecter at a show in London, Prince Buster recorded some tracks with them which were released as an EP in 1994. Another American tour followed in 1992 and the band's year ended at a Belgium festival where they supported Steve Harley & Cockney Rebel.

By 1993, Neol Davies had left the band to pursue his own solo project and with Davies gone, Nick Welsh and Pauline Black started working on new material. They were soon joined by Gaps Hendrickson, who returned in 1994. The Selecter went into the studio to record a new album and *The Happy Album* was the result of this. The album was released in July 1994 on Demon Records and featured the regular line-up of Pauline Black, Martin Stewart and Nick Welsh (who'd also had a hand in producing the album), and Gaps Hendrickson.

The replacement for Davies came in the shape of Paul Seacroft and the album even included a guest appearance from Rico on trombone, reminiscent of his involvement on the original band's first LP. The band toured to promote the release and took in the UK, Ireland and Canada, later touring with The Skatalites in early 1995. Despite the relentless touring, the album failed to make an impact on the charts.

After another American tour, the band were soon back in the studio to record the second album of the reformation and the fans were treated to a preview when the *Hairspray EP* was released in the summer of 1995, containing two new tracks as well as two live recordings of old hits.

The EP was followed by the album *Pucker!* in August, the second album to feature the lineup of Black, Hendrickson, Welsh and Stewart and the second to be produced by Welsh, although he feels his production was lacking. The band toured to promote the album and although it failed to chart, the tour led to the recording of a live album, *Live at Roskilde Festival*. The band also released the *Too Much Pressure '96* EP with re-recorded versions of *Too Much Pressure, Three Minute Hero, Missing Words* and *On My Radio*.

This was released shortly before the *Selecterized* album which contained all the best songs from 1991 onwards as well as numerous re-recordings of hits from their heyday. Gaps Hendrickson departed the band again in 1996, after a disagreement with the tour manager, leaving Pauline Black as the sole original member.

By 1997, New Labour were in full force and the term "Cool Britannia" had been coined to go with it. Tony Blair was the most popular man in the country and had been elected with a 179 seat majority, the biggest landslide in the party's history. Pauline Black had written her own take on "Cool Britannia" with *Cruel Britannia* and it was on this basis the band started to work on their next album.

Dave Barker was invited into the fold by Nick Welsh and he shared the vocals with Pauline Black on some of the songs. The album was released in 1998, *Cruel Britannia* was a critical success and the political nature of the lyrics were praised, although it ultimately failed to chart. The usual tour that comes with a new album came and went but it did nothing to help the sales of the album, leaving the band disappointed.

Following Barker's involvement with *Cruel Britannia*, Nick Welsh was invited to produce his next solo project, *Kingston Affair*, but after some deliberation with who the record would be credited to, the record company wanted it to be released under the moniker of Dave Barker & The Selecter.

It was eventually released under that name, much to the displeasure of Welsh, but not until the year 2000.

The next project for The Selecter was to record some Trojan covers with Roger Lomas. The offer came from Trojan Records to record three albums worth of covers. These three albums were packaged as *The Trojan Songbook* and released in volumes, the first coming out in 1999, the second in 2000 and the third in 2001.

While the band took a sabbatical in 2001, Nick Welsh decided to play some solo acoustic gigs but was convinced by Pauline Black to do it as a duo. This culminated in some Selecter Acoustic gigs in 2002 and this arrangement continued occasionally until 2006. The first tour of shows saw the release of *Unplugged for the Rude Boy Generation* credited to Selecter Acoustic and was recorded at The Sonic Bunker, London and produced by Welsh. This acoustic effort was followed by the release of *Reel to Real* in 2003. The Selecter continued to tour all over the world until 2006 when they went their separate ways after 15 years together.

By the time 2009 had come around there was renewed interest in the original line-up of The Selecter and there were some discussions as to whether the band would reunite for the 30th anniversary of 2 Tone. Pauline Black, Neol Davies and Aitch Bembridge had already performed a short acoustic set in Coventry at the Stand Up To Hatred walk in January 2009 in aid of Holocaust Memorial Day.

Charley Anderson then managed to reunite Neol Davies, Aitch Bembridge and Gaps Hendrickson to perform at his Charley Anderson & Friends show in April in Coventry.

Neol Davies released a new song, *Return of The Selecter*, in July as a free download to celebrate the 30th anniversary.

Ultimately the attempts to reunite The Selecter failed but in 2010, fans were treated to two versions of the band. Pauline Black and Gaps Hendrickson teamed up to perform as The Selecter in 2010, initially for a one-off show but then decided to reform the band on a full-time basis.

Pauline Black's version of The Selecter

This line-up consisted of; Pauline Black (vocals), Gaps Hendrickson (vocals), John Thompson (bass), Anthony Harty (guitar), Neil Pyzer (saxophone), Orlando Larose (saxophone), Greg Coutson (organ) and Winston Marche (drums).

Meanwhile, Neol Davies began to perform as Neol Davies a.k.a The Selecter, launching his version of the band at the Hoxton Bar & Grill, London in July 2010. The lineup consisted of; Neol Davies (guitar/vocals), John Gibbons (lead vocals), Daniel Crosby (drums), Dean Ross (keyboards), Andre Bayuni (bass), Tim Cansfield (guitar), Victor Travino (percussion), Ellie Smith (horns), Hannah Taylor (horns) and Faye Treacy (horns). Davies had wanted to create a new version of The Selecter to bring it up to date and showcase a number of new songs he'd written and felt belonged in The Selecter era.

The following year, Pauline Black's Selecter released the single, Big in the Body, Small in the Mind in May 2011 and just two months later it was revealed that Black had registered The Selecter as a trademark, giving her the right to tour and record as The Selecter.

The band wasted no time in releasing more music as just two weeks later, they released another single Back to Black, a cover of the Amy Winehouse song. Winehouse tragically died shortly after the release and her untimely death led to the single being deleted shortly afterwards. Meanwhile, Neol Davies a.k.a The Selecter released a single of his own Dolla Fe Dolla in April 2012 but he ceased playing later that year and hasn't performed as The Selecter since.

The Selecter, in its current form, are perhaps the only 2 Tone band that have stayed true to their roots. The new music they release is reminiscent of the original band. This is also true of Neol Davies, when he was performing with his version of The Selecter, as his original songs such as Dolla Fe Dolla and Return of the Selecter were reminiscent of the classic Selecter sound.

It's interesting that both Davies and Black's versions boasted brass sections whereas the original band never had a permanent one, although Joe Reynolds, Dick Cuthell, Rico and Barry Jones guested at various times.

The Selecter performing in 2019 with special guest Rhoda Dakar

Pauline Black and Gaps Hendrickson have continued to tour and have released three albums; String Theory (2013), Subculture (2015) and Daylight (2017). The final two spent one week each in the charts, peaking at No.54 and No.66 respectively. The band performed a co-headline tour with The Beat between 2017 and 2018 before Ranking Roger's death brought this to an end. In 2019, they toured for the 40th anniversary of 2 Tone and it was announced in April 2020 that they would support From The Jam on their autumn tour of 2020. They were also due to support Toots & The Maytals on selected dates of their final UK tour in 2021 which was originally arranged for May 2020 but postponed due to Covid-19. However, Toots Hibbert sadly passed away in September 2020. The Selecter now consists of; Pauline Black (vocals), Gaps Hendrickson (vocals), John Robertson (guitar), Andrew Pearson (bass), Lee Horsley (keyboards), Winston Marche (drums) and Neil Pyzer (saxophone).

Releases on 2 Tone:

On My Radio (1979) - Single

Three Minute Hero (1980) - Single

Missing Words (1980) - Single

Too Much Pressure (1980) - Album

Neol Davies
Guitar, Vocals 1977-1982, 1991-1993

Davies was the founding member of The Selecter, having recorded the track *The Selecter* in 1977. After the breakup in 1981, he began to teach guitar and has continued with this throughout the years. He later teamed up with Pauline Black to guest with Buster's All Stars and appeared on their 1990 release *The Sound of Ska*. This led to the reformation of The Selecter in 1991 and Davies remained in the band for two years before his departure in 1993, when he left to pursue other projects.

He formed Selecter Instrumental in 1995 and then founded his own label, VoMatic Records, which came in handy when he formed the band Box of Blues with Horace Panter in 1998 and the album *Box of Blues* was released later that year. Davies later guested with the Mk.2 Specials in 2000 on their albums *Conquering Ruler* and *Skinhead Girl* and went on to sing backing vocals on the Bob The Builder album, released in 2001. He was working in the studio next door when he was asked to pop in and provide some vocals on the album. Annoyingly, he's credited as Noel Davis! A year later, he released *Future Swamp*, his first solo album. Davies re-emerged in 2009 for the 30th anniversary of 2 Tone celebrations and formed his own version of The Selecter in 2010, Neol Davies a.k.a. The Selecter and released some new music. However, he ceased to perform with his version in 2012 and has only since guested with other musicians, such as Aitch Bembridge's band Ruder Than U in 2014 on their song *Sent To Coventry*. He is a regular at the 2 Tone Village and is still living in Coventry. Davies appeared with Neville Staple on numerous occasions in 2019 for 40th Anniversary of 2 Tone and also launched John Coles' photo exhibition at the Village in August 2019.

Pauline Black performing with Gaps Hendrickson

Some new music is expected to be released in 2020 and he helped remaster the *Too Much Pressure* album due for re-release in 2020 for the 40th anniversary of it's original release.

Pauline Black
Vocals, 1979-1982, 1991-2006, 2009-present

(Pic. Miles Gehm)

Black had been working as a radiographer before she was asked to join the band in 1979. She became synonymous with The Selecter sound and, as one of the only women involved with the movement, became something of a pin-up. She was in the band until 1982, when she left to pursue a solo career, a venture which was rather short-lived but resulted in the release of the singles, *Shoo-Rah, Shoo-Rah* (1982) and *Threw It Away* (1983). Black then worked on the one-off single *Pirates on the Airwaves* with Neville Staple and Lynval Golding in 1984 and later found work as an actress, appearing in *The Bill, The Return of Shelley, Shrinks, The Vice* and *Doctors*, having already presented the TV programme *Hold Tight* with Bob Carolgees and Spit The Dog in 1982 and *Black On Black*.

She also appeared in a number of stage productions including playing Millie Small, before she reunited with Neol Davies to reform The Selecter in 1991. In 2001, she formed 3 Men + Black, a group that featured Jake Burns, JJ Burnel and Nick Welsh. The lineup continued to alternate through the years and included Bruce Foxton, Roddy Radiation and Dave Wakeling. She also performed some dates with the 2 Tone Collective throughout the 2000s. The Selecter continued in various guises until it disbanded in 2006. After this, Black concentrated on writing her autobiography which was released in 2011, *Black By Design* was critically acclaimed. She then reformed The Selecter in 2010 and continues to tour the world with Gaps Hendrickson. Since 2015, Black and Hendrickson have performed as special guests with Jools Holland and his Rhythm & Blues Orchestra. Black currently lives in Coventry with her husband, Terry.

Charley Anderson
Bass, 1979-1980
Anderson had played with members of The Selecter before and was well known on the music scene around Coventry. He left in 1980 after musical differences and formed The People with Desmond Brown (who had also left the band), releasing the single *Musical Man* in 1981 before they disbanded in 1982. Anderson has since led an adventurous life, playing with the Century Steel Band, working as an entertainments manager at a hotel in Kenya, living and working in Rome, forming The Skalatones in Sweden in 1995 and recording two albums before their breakup in 2001, living in Cambodia in the late 2000s and also tried to get The Selecter back together in 2009. He was back in Coventry for the 30th anniversary of 2 Tone celebrations and was a frequent face at many of the events, including his own show Charley Anderson & Friends where he managed to reunite Neol Davies, Aitch Bembridge and Gaps Hendrickson. As well as The Skalatones, Anderson has played with Charley & The Vikings. He continues to work on his own music from his base in Jamaica and occasionally returns to Coventry.

Charley 'Aitch' Bembridge
Drums, 1979-1982

Bembridge was the original drummer in The Selecter and had been playing in Hard Top 22 beforehand. When The Selecter broke up in 1982, he became a social worker in Coventry and when The Specials reunited in 1993, he joined the band on drums in place of John Bradbury. Bembridge appeared on all their releases throughout the decade and also toured the world with the band until 1998. He later moved to New Mexico where he set up his own concrete staining business and also played drums for Native Roots, a local reggae band. Bembridge has since returned to England and in 2014 starred in the musical, Three Minute Heroes, inspired by the music of The Selecter, The Specials and the rest of the 2 Tone bands. The original run had occurred in the year 2000 and when the musical returned, Bembridge was part of the live backing band. When the show came to an end, the cast decided to carry on and formed Ruder Than U. They continue to play with Bembridge on the drums, he also plays in UB40 tribute band UB42 and up until recently was playing in The AC30's and still deputises for them occasionally.

Aitch Bembridge after a gig in 2020

Arthur 'Gaps' Hendrickson
Vocals, 1979-1982

Gaps Hendrickson with stage invader

Hendrickson joined the band in 1979 as a vocalist and remained until the breakup in 1982. Following this, he returned to his native West Indies but later returned to Coventry and took a media studies course. He later worked caring for the elderly but rejoined the reformed Selecter in 1994, remaining for two years before departing in 1996. He has been playing with Pauline Black in her version of The Selecter since 2010 and has guested with Black as part of Jools Holland's Orchestra over the years.

Desmond Brown
Hammond Organ, 1979-1982

Brown had been playing in Transposed Men and in a band with Pauline Black before he joined The Selecter in 1979. His keyboard playing is memorable on some of The Selecter's biggest hits including *On My Radio* and *Too Much Pressure*. Brown later left the band unexpectedly in 1980 and formed The People with Charley Anderson before leaving music completely in 1982 and is now living the quiet life in Coventry after a period of ill health. Brown was referenced in the 1998 Mk.2. Specials song, *Tears Come Falling Down My Face*.

David 'Compton' Amanor
Guitar, 1979-1982

Amanor had been in Hard Top 22 with Charley Anderson and Aitch Bembridge before he joined The Selecter. He remained in the band until the breakup in 1982 and later left the music business. Amanor worked exporting lenses and optics supplies and went on to study a degree in Communications at Goldsmiths, the University of London, graduating in 1998. He joined the BBC World Service soon after as a presenter and producer and continues to work for them, having worked on a number of documentaries and radio shows.

Adam Williams
Bass, 1980-1982

Williams was in The Pharaohs before he joined the band in 1980 to replace Charley Anderson, playing bass on the band's second album. After the band split up in 1982, Williams later worked with The Eurythmics and produced one of their albums. By 1986, he was working full time in production and was the engineer on Bronski Beat's album *Truthdare Doubledare*, as well as playing bass. Williams is currently living in London with his family and has continued to work in music production.

James Mackie
Keyboards and Saxophone, 1980-1982

When Desmond Brown left the band, he was quickly replaced with James Mackie. Mackie had been playing with The Pharaohs, before he joined the band after a successful audition. He played keyboards and saxophone on *Celebrate The Bullet* before the band went their separate ways in 1982. Mackie later played with Madness on a live tour in 1984, replacing recently departed Mike Barson, before he became a creative designer. For 15 years, he ran his own business, Mackies of Lancaster, before the shop closed in 2015. He lives in the city with his wife, Christine, who is an actress. Musically, Mackie has been playing keyboards in his own band, Get Carter since 2004 and they play regularly in Lancaster and beyond.

Guest Musicians

Barry Jones
Trombone, 1977 & 1980

Barry Jones was a friend of Neol Davies and played trombone on *The Selecter* in 1977, Jones owned a sweet shop in Coventry at the time. When The Selecter began to add brass to their songs, Jones returned in 1980 and featured on the *Celebrate The Bullet* album. He later moved to Devon in the mid 1980s to become a newsagent and married John Bradbury's sister, Ann. Jones is now retired and living in Plymouth and still has his silver disc from The Selecter on his living room wall.

Joe Reynolds
Saxophone, 1979

Joe Reynolds in 2020

Reynolds guested with the band in 1979 on *Three Minute Hero*, playing the saxophone and subsequently appeared on the first LP, *Too Much Pressure*. He was friends with some of the band, particularly Neol Davies and was asked to play the part. After his short time with The Selecter, Reynolds carried on playing in various bands around Coventry until 1984 when he left music to do a degree. This led to him working in Formula 1 racing as a manufacturing engineer and operations director before retirement in 2018. He still plays for fun and recently took the ABRSM grade 8 and is involved in racing triathlon, writes his own poetry, dotes on his grandchildren and travels a lot with his wife, including to the opera.

Norman Watt-Roy
Bass, 1980

(Pic. Don Wright)

Norman Watt-Roy was the bass player with Ian Dury & The Blockheads and worked with The Selecter for a short period after Charley Anderson's exit. This came after The Selecter were on the same edition as Ian Dury & the Blockheads and Dury noticed that the band were short of members and suggested that Watt-Roy play on the album until they replaced Anderson. Watt-Roy played on two tracks on *Celebrate The Bullet* before Adam Williams joined later in 1980. Away from The Blockheads, Watt-Roy has worked with a number of musicians over the years, including Roger Daltrey, Wilko Johnson and even played on The Clash's *Sandinista!* and *Cut The Crap* albums. He also guested with Madness during Mark Bedford's absences during the 1990s and early 2000s. Watt-Roy continues to play with The Blockheads and Wilko Johnson, having been part of his live band since 1985, and is currently living in Fulham.

Roger Lomas
Producer, Bass 1977-1981
Lomas deserves a mention thanks to his involvement with The Selecter, The Bodysnatchers and Bad Manners. He produced the original *The Selecter* track in his garden shed in 1977 and was asked to produce The Selecter when they became a band, producing *On My Radio* but was not invited to produce the first album. He later produced both singles by The Bodysnatchers and also the first four albums by Bad Manners.

He was invited back to work with The Selecter in 1980 on *Celebrate The Bullet* and due to the departure of Charley Anderson, filled in on bass until a replacement was found, playing on *Deep Water*. After 2 Tone, Lomas went on to have a wide and varied career in production, working with Lee 'Scratch' Perry, Ozzy Osbourne, The Bluetones, The Bangles and Uriah Heep amongst others. He even won a Grammy for Lee 'Scratch' Perry's 2002 album *Jamaican ET*. Lomas went on to work with The Specials and The Selecter during their reformations during the 1990s and is a regular visitor to the 2 Tone Village in Coventry, where he still lives.

Madness

The Invaders were formed in 1976 by Mike Barson (keyboards), Lee Thompson (saxophone) and Chris Foreman (guitar).

They began by practicing in Barso's bedroom and he was the musical anchor in the band being the only member able to play an instrument! Chrissy Boy went out and bought a guitar whereas Thompson went out and stole a saxophone from Dingwalls! They soon recruited John Hasler (drums) and Dikron Tulaine (vocals) and the early days saw a number of disagreements between Barson and Thompson, usually leading to the latter quitting. They drew on their influences of rock 'n' roll, reggae and r'n'b and were heavily influenced by the music they'd grown up with such as Ian Dury and The Kinks but also ska artists such as Prince Buster. The Invaders were usually confined to rehearsals, reluctant to play any live gigs until they were certain they could actually play. Their first gig was at a party in June 1977 though Dikron Tulaine decided midway through the set that he didn't want to do it so the rest of the performance saw the band playing instrumentals. Importantly, two young lads by the names of Cathal Smyth and Graham "Suggs" McPherson were at the party.

The band were in need of a singer after Tulaine's departure and Suggs went along to audition, getting the job after no one else turned up, singing *See Ya Later Alligator*! Smyth also joined on bass, despite not being able to play it, having to place stickers on the guitar so he knew which notes to play! This arrangement didn't last long, Smyth was soon replaced by Gavin Rodgers. Lee Thompson had another one of those arguments and stormed out to be replaced by Lucinda Garland, though she only lasted for one gig before Thompson returned. After another gig in April 1978, Rodgers decided he'd had enough and left the band, closely followed by Lee Thompson and Suggs, the latter was sacked for choosing to watch his beloved Chelsea rather than attend rehearsals! He was replaced by John Hasler, who was replaced on drums by Garry Dovey, Mark "Bedders" Bedford also joined on bass. These constant changes are hard to keep up with as Lee Thompson rejoined...again, though this led to Dovey's departure after Thompson decided to punch him at a rehearsal! Dovey was replaced by Bedford's friend Daniel "Woody" Woodgate and Suggs later rejoined, replacing John Hasler who became the band's manager.

After a short time as Morris and the Minors, the band changed their name to Madness in early 1979 in tribute to Prince Buster, one of their heroes, after Chrissy Boy had suggested it. Madness were big fans of the ska legend and had been playing covers of some of his other hits such as *One Step Beyond* and *Madness*.

Cathal Smyth, now known as Chas Smash, had become involved with the band again, jumping on stage and dancing during their sets although he wasn't recognised as an official member.

Madness had started to build up a loyal following in London with the Dublin Castle being one of their regular haunts. Madness were playing ska music and unbeknown to them, another band were playing a similar style, The Special AKA who hailed from Coventry.

Eventually their paths crossed when Jerry Dammers became aware of the band after spotting some graffiti on a toilet door in London. The Special AKA played a gig at the Hope & Anchor, Camden in May and as this was Madness's local, they attended. The Madness lads were impressed by the band and after hearing a similar style of music to what they were playing they felt that they were heading in the right direction, feeling vindicated.

Suggs got talking to Dammers that night and comically, The General had nowhere to sleep so ended up kipping on the settee at Suggs' mother's house! They got chatting and it was here Dammers told him about his idea for setting up the 2 Tone label. Suggs played him a demo tape they'd produced and although he felt they needed a lot of work, Dammers was impressed with *My Girl*. He asked them to support The Special AKA in June at the Nashville, which they agreed to despite already having a gig booked for the same night at the Dublin Castle. A disaster was averted as they just played both gigs on the night!

By June, Madness were in the studio, with a £300 budget, and under the supervision of Alan Winstanley and Clive Langer, they recorded *The Prince, Madness* and *My Girl*. *The Prince* and *Madness* made it onto the single, which was released in August. *The Prince* was a Lee Thompson composition written in tribute to Prince Buster and it was backed by their cover of Prince Buster's *Madness*. The saxophone solo on the 'A' side was pinched from *Texas Hold-Up*, a 1967 tune from the Prince.

Just days after the release, they recorded their only Peel session where they performed versions of *Bed & Breakfast Man, The Prince, Stepping Into Line* and *Land of Hope & Glory*. The session was aired in August and by September, they'd hit the charts for the first time, entering at No.74. As the weeks progressed, the single climbed the charts, leading to their first *Top of the Pops* appearance on September 6th 1979. After a few more weeks of climbing, it peaked at No.16 in early October. This was great news for 2 Tone, the label now had three bands on it who'd all released successful singles and Madness were included on the 2 Tone Tour, organised for October.

Copy of The Prince, the band's only 2 Tone single, signed by Suggs and Bedders

As the 2 Tone deal was just for one single, Madness were free to look for their own deal and were quickly inundated with numerous offers from labels offering them vast amounts of money. Jerry Dammers actively encouraged them to go out and

2 TONE | MADNESS

get the best possible deal and unlike other labels, 2 Tone wanted to give bands a leg up and were happy when they went on to better things. Madness eventually signed to Stiff Records after playing Dave Robinson's wedding in August. Robinson had founded Stiff back in 1976 and wanted to sign the band but due to conflicting schedules he decided to ask them to play at his wedding! Robinson was impressed although he got the cold shoulder from his new wife as he was paying more attention to the band than to her!

Madness were soon in the studio and began working on their debut album and this led to the release of One Step Beyond… in October. The album contained a number of originals as well as covers and they also re-recorded The Prince and Madness (which appeared as a secret track). The band were still a six-piece as Chas Smash was not recognised as an official member, he didn't appear on the front cover but there were numerous photos on the back of the cover depicting him dancing.

The album was followed by the first single One Step Beyond, the title track of the album and originally by Prince Buster. It wasn't even going to be on the LP, it was merely played by the band at the beginning of shows and lasted barely a minute. However, Dave Robinson was insistent that they record it and put it on the album, though the band were sceptical. The finished song was actually a rough mix which had been looped, as the original recording was only around a minute long. The track featured an introduction from Chas Smash; "Don't watch that, watch this, this is the heavy heavy monster sound…one step beyond!".

The album version contained a longer introduction, which in itself was a nod to the old Blue Beat records which would occasionally contain a "I am the magnificent" introduction, such as on Dave & Ansell Collins' 1970 hit Double Barrel. Amusingly, Lee Thompson's saxophone was actually out of tune on the album, only learning later that he'd been tuning his sax

all wrong due to being self taught! The single eventually peaked at No.7 and led to an amusing Top of the Pops appearance where the lads abandoned the stage and did the Nutty Dance through the audience!

After a week of rehearsals at the Roundhouse, Chalk Farm, Madness (along with The Specials and The Selecter) embarked on the 2 Tone Tour on the same day that the album was released, playing at Top Rank, Brighton on the first night. The band were second on the bill, with The Specials at the top and The Selecter at the bottom. It was agreed beforehand that Madness would be on the tour until the 15th of November, after which they would be embarking on their own tour.

Meanwhile, on the tour they were going down well, and as 2 Tone had started to sweep the nation by then, the venues were packed out wanting to see all three of the bands and at £3 a ticket, who could blame them?

Despite the success, some of the gigs on the tour were marred with violence but thankfully these incidents were few and far between with the worst occurring at Hatfield Poly where some unsavoury people broke in and slashed some of the audience. The band weren't helped in this regard by their skinhead reputation and the unsavoury characters that supported the band, although thankfully these were in a minority.

As agreed, Madness left the tour halfway through to begin their own tour of America. Madness left the tour while The Specials were on stage with all seven members of the band walking across the stage, with their luggage, waving goodbye!

They were replaced on the tour by Dexy's Midnight Runners. It has been rumoured that Madness were forced to leave the tour because of the growing reports about their skinhead fanbase and the accusations of racism. However, this is not true and the agreement had always been that they would play half of the tour before leaving.

Before they left, Madness played three shows at the Electric Ballroom, London supported by Red Beans & Rice and Bad Manners. Sadly some neo-Nazis got into one of the gigs and were sieg heiling at the lead singer of Red Beans & Rice as she was black. This nasty incident led to Suggs coming on to the stage to plead with the audience to pack it in, and after Chas Smash also asked them to stop, the support band came back on to finish their set. These incidents were on the increase at gigs and the band's reputation for sharing these views was also increasing.

The reason for heading to the States was simple, they wanted to crack America before The Specials did and began the tour with four sell out dates in New York. Just days into the tour, an unfortunate article appeared in the *NME* with the headline "Madness - Nice band, shame about the fans". This stemmed from comments by Chas Smash who was quoted as saying; "We don't care if the crowd are in the NF, or BM or whatever, so long as they're behaving themselves, having a good time, and not fighting.

They're just kids"[1]. There had been some rumours at the time that Madness were racists. Whilst it was true that a large chunk of their support at the time were skinheads, their first single had been a tribute to Prince Buster and the 'B' side had covered one of his old hits, *Madness*, the song from which they had borrowed their name. And the original skinheads had originated in Jamaica and weren't racists, although this had become twisted by the late 1970s and many skinheads were racists that were associated with the National Front and other racist organisations. The fact they were the only 2 Tone band not to feature a black member didn't do them any favours either. This incident led to Smash writing *Don't Quote Me On That* which was released on the *Work Rest and Play EP*. The band were caught in the middle as they clearly weren't racists but the majority of their supporters were skinheads, a number of them with disgraceful views. Anyone that listened to Madness and saw their musical influences knew that they weren't racist. Another interview appeared on the same day in *Sounds* where they tried to distance themselves from the allegations.

Madness at the Lyceum Ballroom, December 1983. Mike Barson's last gig with the original band
(Pic by Michael Baxter)

Suggs categorically stated that he hated "all this BM business, but a lot of kids get taken in by it" and also acknowledged; "They're just ordinary kids being like their mates, and the BM thing gives them a sense of identity. It don't mean a lot to most of them outside of that. The way I see it if they're all dancing to black music that means more than shouting at 'em or slicing 'em up. Personally I'm more worried about violence at our gigs". Chas Smash also stated; "If they fuck around at our gigs we don't wanna know. They're out"[2]. These allegations would continue to plague the band until a change in musical direction a couple of years later.

Madness saw out 1979 with a performance on the BBC's *Old Grey Whistle Test* and a short UK tour. The tour coincided with the release of the third and final single from the album. *My Girl* had been recorded during the 2 Tone sessions but re-recorded for the new LP and released days before Christmas. Written by Mike Barson, it told a story of someone in a relationship that was dominated with arguments and endless hours of talking on the telephone. The single entered the charts at No.54 and peaked at No.3 at the end of January. Once again the band headed to *Top of the Pops* to perform the song and it became the first to be played on the show in 1980.

They embarked on a tour of Europe in early 1980 before returning to the UK in February to perform a couple of shows before a second US tour commenced after the release of *One Step Beyond...* in the States.

Chas Smash finally became an official member around this time, shortly before the release of the *Work Rest & Play EP* which featured a Smash original *Don't Quote Me On That* alongside *Night Boat to Cairo, Deceives the Eye* and *The Young and the Old*. The release came about when Dave Robinson wanted to release a fourth single from *One Step Beyond...* but the band disagreed, feeling they'd exhausted the output on the album and preferred to look to the future.

They decided to release an EP with one of the songs from the album and three new ones. The EP was popular, reaching No.6 and Chas Smash was finally able to quash the rumours that he agreed with the small racist faction that tagged along to Madness gigs with *Don't Quote Me On That.*

"But as far as I'm concerned, as as far as I'm concerned

You don't have to be black, white, Chinese or anything really

Just enjoy. Shut up, listen and dance...".

The EP was followed by the band's second album *Absolutely,* recorded in July and released in September. The album was a resounding success, peaking at No.2 and remaining in the charts for 47 weeks.

The single *Baggy Trousers* was released a few weeks prior, going on to spend four months in the charts, peaking at No.4 and was followed by *Embarrassment,* released in November. *Embarrassment* is one of their most well known songs and was written by Lee Thompson. He wrote it about his sister, who had had the audacity to fall pregnant to a black man. Unfortunately, society wasn't so accepting of mixed race couples in 1980. The song lyrics are based on conversations and things that were said by various members of Thompson's family at the time, as he was away on tour and only aware of the unfolding events through letters and phone calls. The story does have a happy ending though, Thompson has since said that the family soon accepted the baby once she was born and all the hostility evaporated.

The single reached No.4 and spent 12 weeks in the charts. Parts of *Absolutely* remained true to the band's roots and the ska influence was still evident in the music though some of the other tracks revealed an experimentation with a more commercial sound. This was confirmed with the album's third single release, *The Return of Los Palmos 7,* which was far removed from anything they'd previously released.

The band were competent musicians by now, rather than just a group of friends learning their trade and playing for enjoyment. Chas Smash had also become more involved musically, aside from providing his usual backing vocals, he also played trumpet on *Embarrassment* and wrote the song *Solid Gone,* which he also sang lead vocals on. Smash wanted to prove his credentials as a musician, rather than just providing the dancing and backing vocals, so purposely learnt the trumpet.

Footage of the band appeared on the 1981 film *Dance Craze* as well as the LP release, although they didn't appear on the US release due to legal constraints with the record company. The filmmaker Joe Massot had originally planned to release a film of live Madness performances but decided to capture all the 2 Tone bands at that time to document the 2 Tone explosion that was in full swing by 1980. Madness appeared in the film playing *The Prince, Swan Lake, Razor Blade Alley, Madness, Night Boat to Cairo* and *One Step Beyond.* The LP included *Razor Blade Alley, One Step Beyond* and *Night Boat to Cairo.* Incidentally, Chris Foreman and Mark Bedford have recently given a print of the film to the BFI, Foreman had spotted it on eBay and bought it with Bedders. The film has taken on cult status among the 2 Tone faithful and the *Dance Craze* songs have appeared on occasional Madness compilations or Deluxe albums.

Madness continued to move towards a more commercial sound and the sound was almost unrecognisable as 1981 progressed. *Grey Day* was released in April, although it was written during the early days, the sound is far removed from their early 2 Tone days representing the ever changing sound of the band, who were evolving as time went on. They recognised that ska wasn't going to last forever so they adapted. The single performed well, peaking at No.4 and remaining in the charts for 10 weeks.

A five week Far East tour of Australia, New Zealand, Malaysia and Japan followed and

Suggs later described it as "the tour where we nearly split up under five weeks of intensive hell. It was probably the closest we ever got, with people at each other's throats"[3].

They continued to record the next album, with the sessions taking place in Nassau, Bahamas as the band decided to record abroad for tax reasons. Their accountant had informed them that if an album was recorded abroad, they'd only be taxed on the first 25% of profit!

Aside from the usual TV promotional appearances, the band managed to fit in another trip to Japan to film a television commercial for Honda! The song *In The City* had been written by Bill Crutchfield, Chas Smash, Chris Foreman, Daisuke Inoue, Mike Barson and Suggs and was recorded specifically for the advert. This was immediately followed by the release of *Shut Up* in September in the UK which was another resounding success, reaching No.7.

The band's third album, *7,* was released in October and went on to reach No.5, spending 28 weeks in the charts. This album saw them continue to change and adapt their sound and cement their status as a pop group. The biting social commentary was still evident, just wrapped in bubblegum! Madness had an almost unique talent of taking a serious song and making it sound fun.

They also released a film, *Take It or Leave It,* which saw the band playing themselves in a re-creation of the early days. It's very much a cult film but there are some funny moments in it, it had a budget of £400,000 with Stiff providing £250,000 and the seven members putting up the rest.

The success continued in November with the release of *It Must Be Love,* a non-album single which saw the band cover the Labi Siffre song, originally released in 1971. It had become a staple of their live set and would always go down well so they decided to record it. The song is one of the band's best known releases and reached No.4 in the charts.

Despite being preceded by a non-album single, the band released another single from the album, *Cardiac Arrest*, in February 1982, a Chas Smash song about a workaholic who suffers a heart attack on his way to work! The band played it on *Top of the Pops* but it was soon banned by Radio 1 and sales suffered, with the single peaking at just No.14, their lowest chart placing since *The Prince*. The story goes that one of the Radio 1 DJs' family members had recently died from a heart attack so it was banned.

Despite the continuing success, the greatest hits compilation *Complete Madness* was released in April - not bad going for a band who'd been in the charts for barely more than two years! It sold well and went straight into the charts at No.2, later reaching No.1. It was Dave Robinson's idea and he also suggested they add a new recording to the album alongside the old hits. The new song was *House of Fun* and the single was released just days after the LP and reached No.1 in amongst the 9 weeks it spent in the charts. Surprisingly, this is the only Madness single to ever hit the No.1 spot in the UK. There was an accompanying VHS thrown in for good measure which contained all the band's music videos and there was an extensive advertising campaign on British television, something that wasn't too common back in 1982.

Suggs on the Mad Not Mad Tour, Sheffield 1985
(Pic by Karl Overend)

Aside from performing the new single on *Top of the Pops,* they also played it on the popular comedy show *The Young Ones,* when they appeared in the third episode, recorded in August and aired on November 23rd.

The album led to a promotional tour of Japan throughout May. They also recorded more television commercials for Japanese television and another single surfaced in July, *Driving In My Car,* written by Mike Barson. It was very much a novelty song, a far cry from their superb back catalogue up until this point and frankly a complete letdown. Despite the novelty and muted response from the music press, the single reached No.4 and is one of their most famous songs and a regular feature of their live sets. Annoyingly, it was later covered by Maureen Rees in 1997, Rees had become famous for appearing on *Driving School* where she'd been attempting to learn to drive. Her version of the single was even worse but this didn't stop it from reaching No.50 in the charts!

The sessions for the new album concluded in early October and *The Rise & Fall* was released in November, later reaching No.10. The original idea for the album was for it to be a concept album with Chas Smash suggesting they write songs about their own childhood memories and then link them together. Eventually, the idea was scrapped though some songs did remain such as *Our House*, which was released as the first single just a week later.

Our House was the band's biggest hit in America, reaching No.7 on the Billboard 100 and also No.5 in the UK, the music video is also memorable and the success of the single led to Chas Smash and Chris Foreman receiving an Ivor Novello award for Best Pop Song in 1983. The Nutty Boys saw out the year with some gigs in Belgium, Holland and Germany and an appearance of *Top of the Pops* performing *House of Fun*. The final single from the album, *Tomorrow's (Just Another Day)* was released in February 1983 and later peaked at a respectable No.8.

A UK tour followed across February and March before they went to Germany to perform on *Musikladen*. This is an important event as Mike Barson didn't turn up for the show, suggesting for the first time that problems were afoot. This went further in June when, during rehearsals for the new album, he disappeared to go on a camping holiday with his wife and dog, leaving the rest of the band to rehearse without him.

At some point, Madness had gone into the studio to record *Wings of a Dove*, a Chas Smash and Suggs composition that featured the talents of The Inspirational Choir of the Pentecostal First Born Church of the Living God, a gospel choir that had appeared on a TV programme that Smash had been watching. The song also featured steel drums played by Creighton Steel Sounds. It was released in August as a standalone single and performed well, spending five weeks in the charts, peaking at No.2. It was denied the top spot by the horrendous *Red Red Wine* by UB40, but did reach No.1 in the Irish Singles Charts.

Work soon began on the next album as well as discussions about a television series with the comedy writers Ben Elton and Richard Curtis. In fact, two 10 minute pilots were filmed with the plot focusing on Suggs running the country having been voted in as Prime Minister after Margaret Thatcher had been exposed as an alien and returned to Mars! The idea was thrown out by the BBC, although it wouldn't have really mattered as by October, Mike Barson decided he'd had enough and informed his bandmates that he was leaving to spend more time with his wife.

While the band was imploding, their next single *The Sun and the Rain* was released at the end of October, another non-album single. It peaked at No.5 and even made waves on the US Billboard Hot 100, reaching No.72.

In the meantime, Barson agreed to remain until the album was finished and his final appearance on stage came in December at the Lyceum Ballroom, London.

Madness were on the bill alongside Ian Dury and Neil from *The Young Ones*! *Michael Caine* became the first single release in January and it featured a guest appearance from Caine himself. The famous line "My name is Michael Caine" is uttered throughout the song and when the band approached him to lend his voice to the track he turned them down as he didn't know who they were! When his daughter found out she made him change his mind as she was a big fan! Despite being called *Michael Caine*, the song is about an informer during the Troubles that'd been relocated under a witness protection scheme. The single performed well and peaked at No.11 and was followed by the album, *Keep Moving* in February.

The album was a commercial success and performed well, peaking at No.6. The second single, *One Better Day*, was released in May but only peaked at No.17, their lowest chart placing at the time. Barson briefly returned to film the music videos for *Michael Caine* and *One Better Day* before officially leaving in June. He was replaced by various keyboard players for live performances including Paul Carrack, James Mackie, Seamus Beaghen and Terry Disley. Suggs has since said; "That moment when Mike left was the moment when the band finished really and that should have been that and we just stumbled on blindly, down different alleys looking for a reason to stay together"[5]. Also in June, they appeared in the second series of *The Young Ones*, with their appearance coming in Episode 5, playing *Our House* during a street riot! Madness are the only band to appear on the show twice.

For the first time since their formation, Madness were without the leadership and direction of Mike Barson and they also parted company with Stiff in May after relations had soured. Without a record deal for the first time since they'd met Jerry Dammers back in 1979, they struck a deal with Virgin Records, who were willing to give them their own label. By August, they'd set up Zarjazz, named after the fanzine for the comic 2000AD, the name having been chosen by Chas Smash, despite asking the members of the Madness Fan Club for suggestions!

The first release on Zarjazz was Feargal Sharkey's, *Listen to Your Father,* which had been written by Chas Smash and the band had attempted to record in the past but it just hadn't happened. The association with Sharkey came after a chance encounter between him and Chrissy Boy on the set of *Top of the Pops* in the autumn of 1983.

The single featured Madness as Sharkey's backing band, although Suggs was not involved with the session. The single was eventually released in October, despite being recorded back in March, and reached a respectable No.23 before they appeared on *Top of the Pops*. The single launched Sharkey's solo career, after he'd left The Undertones the previous year, but after the success he signed for Virgin as the Madness boys hadn't actually got him to sign a contract! *Listen To Your Father* was followed by a release credited to the Fink Brothers, which was Suggs and Chas Smash with the single *Mutants in Mega-City One,* based on the 2000AD comic and actually endorsed by the comic. The single peaked at No.50 and resulted in an appearance on the *Oxford Road Show.*

The band were involved with the Starvation project in late 1984, similar to the Band Aid project that occurred in December 1984 where a group of musicians got together to record a charity single for famine relief. *Starvation* was a song by The Pioneers and it was considered an appropriate song to record for the single.

The idea had come from a young Madness fan who'd approached some of the band in their Zarjazz office and the idea went from there. The band's Liquidator Studios was used for the recording and it featured a number of respected musicians from 2 Tone circles and beyond including Jerry Dammers, Lynval Golding, Dick Cuthell, Ranking Roger and Dave Wakeling alongside Bedders and Woody. Dammers combined his keyboard playing with the production and *Starvation/Tam Tam Pour*

L'Ethiopie was finally released in March 1985 and despite having the idea before Band Aid, it had taken months to record, mix and master and the moment had effectively been stolen by Bob Geldof and co. Despite this, it was still a good gesture and all profits from the single were donated to Oxfam, War On Want and Medecins Sans Frontieres. The single itself peaked at No.33 in the charts.

After signing to Virgin, Madness were paid a huge advance to get to work on their next album. This would be the first one to not feature Mike Barson, and as the musical anchor and creative force of the band his absence left a gaping hole. They went into AIR Studios in March 1985 to begin the recording though the process was fraught and saw band relations breaking down. There were also a large number of session musicians involved in the recording, which was a first for Madness. The previous albums had featured guest musicians or the odd backing vocalist but nothing on this scale. Jerry Dammers was briefly involved, playing keyboards on *All I Knew,* the eventual 'B' side to *Yesterday's Men.*

Madness were asked to play Live Aid in July but turned down the opportunity and August saw the release of the first single from the album, *Yesterday's Men* was released but only managed to reach No.18. Time was moving on and Madness were no longer the force they had been, with this being the lowest placed single up to now.

The album *Mad Not Mad* was released in September and compared to previous releases it was a much slicker affair, containing drum machines and synthesisers. Mike Barson was replaced by Steve Nieve from Elvis Costello & The Attractions and Afrodiziak also provided backing vocals. The second single was released in October, but *Uncle Sam* only reached No.21. The album wasn't as successful as previous efforts but still reached No.16.

Madness then promoted the album on the Mad Not Mad Tour commencing in late October and ran for a total of 28 dates.

The Friday Club, then on 2 Tone, were the support act on the tour. The band saw out a troubled year with a live appearance on *The Old Grey Whistle Test* on New Year's Eve.

New year, new start? Not quite, as the trouble that'd been brewing throughout 1985 continued and they were no longer enjoying themselves. They continued to perform however, joining the Red Wedge Tour in January. The tour also coincided with the release of *Sweetest Girl* in February, a non-album single that reached a lowly No.35. By April, another tour was being planned but they were struggling financially due to the high costs of running the studio and offices at Zarjazz.

Eventually, the office was closed, people were laid off and the band went on tour with some dates in Europe before six weeks in Australia. They later played Glastonbury in June and announced their intentions to begin recording a new LP in August. The sessions began but were virtually impossible, the relations in the band had started to deteriorate although a number of demos were recorded.

They were still running Zarjazz, which was hemorrhaging money and they were heading for financial meltdown, something had to give. It did, as Madness released a statement on September 1st 1986 announcing they were breaking up and also mentioned the possibility of a farewell single and concert. The final single to be released was *(Waiting For) The Ghost Train* in October, which spent 9 weeks in the charts, peaking at No.18. The song had seen a welcome return for Mike Barson though he didn't appear in the subsequent video.

The band did the TV circuit, promoting the single on *The Tube* and *Top of the Pops* where Bedders and Chrissy Boy held up their guitars spelling "The End". The band then released *Utter Madness,* their second greatest hits compilation and after an almost seven year dominance of the charts, their time had come to an end.

Reunions

Suggs, Chas Smash, Lee Thompson and Chrissy Boy decided to continue working together in early 1987, working on some of the songs that'd been written for the aborted last album. They soon decided on the very imaginative name of The Madness and went into the studio in early 1988 to record an album. The sessions saw the involvement of a plethora of session musicians including Elvis Costello, Steve Nieve, Jerry Dammers, Bruce Thomas, Dick Cuthell and Earl Falconer.

The Madness was released in May 1988 but bombed, reaching No.66. The reviews weren't kind and they had parted ways by the end of 1988. Suggs has since said that they shouldn't have carried on as The Madness, acknowledging that they should have ended it completely in 1986, perhaps even when Mike Barson left in 1984.

Woody commented in the 2000 *Young Guns* documentary that the decision to continue as The Madness was a "complete copout" and "they should've told him and Bedders that they didn't want to work with them".

Meanwhile, Lee Thompson and Chris Foreman formed the duo The Nutty Boys in 1990 and released the album, *Crunch!* The pair had originally intended for the album to be called *The Nutty Boys* and the band to be called Crunch! but the names were reversed in a mixup and the name was kept. Thompson and Chrissy Boy occasionally played live shows, including a French tour. They also released the single, *It's OK I'm A Policeman* in 1992 but it failed to chart. They later changed the name to Crunch! and continued to play occasionally throughout the rest of the 1990s.

By 1991, Virgin wanted to issue a *Best Of* CD and VHS and were in touch with Chas Smash, who was keen to be involved with the project. Along with releasing the compilation, he wanted to get the band back together and they soon met up, the first time they'd all been in a room together since the split.

By February 1992, the reunion was gathering pace and when Virgin re-released *It Must Be Love* as a single it reached No.6 in the charts.

This was followed by the release of *Divine Madness*, the greatest hits compilation which had been mooted in 1991. The album was backed by a massive media campaign and topped the charts for three weeks, later spending a total of 96 weeks in the charts, becoming the best-selling album of 1992!

The success of the two releases boosted the band's confidence as they previously hadn't realised the love that the public had for them and this was when serious discussions began to take place about reforming. As the rumours gathered pace, numerous offers began to come in and as the band toyed with the idea of doing an arena tour, it was suggested they do a one-off concert in London. They played a secret show at the end of March at the Notre Dame Church Hall, London, although they only played four songs for an invited audience.

This was filmed for a TV pilot called *Spunk,* which never saw the light of day.

House of Fun was re-released in April and followed by a statement in May announcing that they would be playing a reunion concert in August at Finsbury Park. The reaction was extraordinary, with 36,000 tickets selling out in days and leading to a second show being announced. The shows were billed under the *Madstock!* banner. This was quickly followed by a *Top of the Pops* appearance playing *My Girl*, which was re-released complete with a new cover. This contained updated photographs of each member, except for Mike Barson who refused to be photographed!

The *Madstock!* shows were a resounding success and the first night saw them cause an earthquake which measured 4.5 on the Richter Scale! After the audience hadn't taken too kindly to Morrissey (one of the support acts), he was bottled off the stage but Madness stormed it and despite it being their first gig in six years, it was as if they'd never been away.

Suggs during the early 2000s - Pic by Joe Kerrigan

The band played all the classics and even threw in some early favourites such as *Swan Lake, Rockin in A Flat* and *Land of Hope and Glory*. The second night was just as successful and even featured a guest appearance from Prince Buster! He was guesting with The Selecter in a nearby pub and the band approached him to ask if he would guest with them on *Madness*, he said he would but wanted £2500 to appear! The band just agreed to it as it would be a momentous occasion to have him on stage at their homecoming, especially after he was one of their heroes and a major influence.

The shows spawned a live album, *Madstock!* and a new single, a live version of Jimmy Cliff's *The Harder They Come*, both released in November. They later appeared on *Top of the Pops* to promote the single, performing it live from Red Square, Moscow! The band were genuinely surprised by the warm reaction they'd received and decided to reunite for a short Christmas tour later that year and subsequent *Madstock!* festivals took place in 1994, 1996 and 1998 as well as the odd tour in between. Bedders left the band between 1994 and 1996, being replaced by Norman Watt-Roy for live shows.

After numerous rumours were swirling around and worries about becoming a cabaret act, the band got back together full time to rehearse and record a new album in early 1999. They were reunited with producers Clive Langer and Alan Winstanley and the first single emerged in July. *Lovestruck* was a Chas Smash composition and chosen as the first release, a decision that was justified as it hit No.10, not bad for the band's first studio offering in 13 years! Predictably, the success of the single led to appearances on *Top of the Pops* and *TFI Friday,* the public were now aware that Madness were back. Dr. Martens even jumped on the bandwagon by creating a special Madness boot, in honour of the Nutty Boys. Weeks before the album's release, a second single *Johnny The Horse* was released but was ultimately a damp squib, failing to reach the Top 40. The new album, *Wonderful* was released on November 1st and despite the anticipation, it fell short and reached No.17. The album went down relatively well and the reviews were mainly positive so it was disappointing it wasn't reflected in the sales, the band had been expecting it to perform much better and the eventual chart placing was ultimately a disappointment.

Chas Smash plays the trumpet at a 2008 gig - Pic by livepict.com

The album was notable for including a collaboration with Ian Dury, *Drip Fed Fred* being the final song he recorded before his death in March 2000. The song itself was released as a single in January but only reached No.55. Dury's final performance before his death saw him perform the song with Madness in October 1999 on *Later... with Jools Holland*. The band felt they were repaying a debt to Dury as he'd been one of their main influences, sadly Dury was dying from cancer but he still managed to pluck up the strength to take part in the accompanying video. Although he looks very ill, he looks to be enjoying himself.

Despite the disappointment with the album sales, the opportunity was seized to release more greatest hits compilations including *The Lot*, which contained all the previous album releases. After the attention had died down, the members got stuck into other projects and Madness remained dormant throughout the rest of the year 2000 except for one solitary live show. The band played at Ian Dury's memorial concert which took place in June at Brixton Academy and later recorded *My Old Man* for inclusion on a Dury tribute album in 2001.

By 2002, the wheels were set in motion for a musical set around Madness songs and by June, it'd been announced that *Our House* would open on the West End in October and had the band's full support. The original idea had come from Chas Smash and Suggs after they'd decided they wanted to write a musical and after spending time working on songs for it, Smash's wife suggested they use the band's songs instead. In 2003, the musical won the Olivier Award for Best New Musical and even saw Suggs join the cast in April.

Madness had played the odd show since *Wonderful* but decided in 2004 to mark the 25th anniversary with some shows at the Dublin Castle as their alter egos, The Dangermen, playing covers of ska and reggae tunes. This resulted in the release of *The Dangermen Sessions Vol. 1* in August 2005, the sessions didn't go by without some drama though as Chrissy Boy left the band due to "the petty, time consuming bollocks that goes on in the band". The album reached a respectable No.11 but the two singles *Shame & Scandal* and *Girl Why Don't You?* performed poorly, the latter failed to chart completely. The change in direction failed to hit the spot and it's a strange and confusing part of the band's story. The Dangermen had been left behind by 2006 and the band started to work on a new album, with Chris Foreman rejoining.

The band were quick to leave V2 Records after The Dangermen period and formed their own label Lucky 7, releasing the single *Sorry* in March 2007. They have since released three more albums *The Liberty of Norton Folgate* (2009), *Qui Qui Si Si Ja Ja Da Da* (2012) and *Can't Touch Us Now* (2016), all on Lucky 7, as well as performing umpteen tours and live performances.

Madness albums still perform well in the charts, with the last three releases all reaching the Top 10, the related singles don't usually fare as well but some releases have managed to hit the Top 50 but they haven't reached the Top 100 since 2013 when they reached No.88 with *Never Knew Your Name*. The band's last single to date was *The Bullingdon Days*, an attack on the Prime Minister Boris Johnson and the fact that 19 of the 54 Prime Ministers have been educated at Eton, and 40 years on showing that they are still willing to make a social comment with their music.

These days, Madness are a far cry from their 2 Tone days, but it's quite telling that they are the only band still around in their original form. If they hadn't adapted and progressed as a band they would have probably gone the same way as their counterparts. They have adapted and changed their sound throughout the years with continued success, although they have seen several members leave at different times, Bedders left during the 1990s and in 2009 before returning in 2012, Chrissy Boy left for a short time in 2005 before returning in 2006 and the band are now without Chas Smash, who decided to leave in 2014 to pursue a solo career.

Madness seem to be aware that you can come back but you can't come back all the way, their new material does remain faithful to the old days but you are under no illusion that it is completely new stuff. They've never fallen into the trap of trying to force their new material down people's throats or completely abandoning the music that made them famous. Granted, the band have never reached the heights of their 1979-1984 heyday but have become something of a national treasure in the last few years, which led to them playing the closing of the 2012 Olympics and also playing on top of Buckingham Palace for Queen Elizabeth's Jubilee in the same year.

They still have their hardcore support from the rudeboys but there's an awful lot of people that support them who aren't and never were rudeboys, it really is an eclectic mix and they are the only 2 Tone band that's still touring and recording regularly in its (almost) original form.

Madness continue to tour the world when schedules allow and in the last few years have been known to play racecourses and big stadiums but marked their 40th Anniversary with three intimate nights at Camden Roundhouse in December 2019,

a year which had also seen the release of a book credited to the band, *Before We Were We*. It was intended for the release of the paperback version of the book to be marked with an intimate Q&A and signing session at The Dublin Castle, London in April 2020 but this was cancelled due to the coronavirus pandemic.

Releases on 2 Tone:

The Prince (1979).

Where are they now?

Graham McPherson (Suggs)
Vocals, 1977, 1978-1986, 1992-present
After Madness split in 1986, Suggs, Lee Thompson, Chas Smash and Chris Foreman carried on as The Madness and released a solitary album in 1988. He later rejoined the band in 1992 for the reunion and has remained ever since. Away from Madness, Suggs has enjoyed a wide and varied career. After leaving Madness, he tried his hand at stand-up comedy and became the manager of The Farm, helping to produce their 1991 album *Spartacus*, which later went to No.1. Suggs has also ventured into television, working as a TV

Madness playing Camden Roundhouse in December 2019

Suggs - Pic by Tracey Salford

presenter, presenting a variety of shows including; *Night Fever, Salvage Squad, Disappearing London Inside Out* and *WW2 Treasure Hunters*. He also appeared on *A Question of Pop*, as one of the team captains between 2000 and 2001. He's also tried acting, featuring in a number of films including *The Tall Guy, Don't Go Breaking My Heart* and in 2001 he starred in *Comedy Club: I Think I've Got A Problem*, a radio play about Tom, a guy who couldn't stop singing at inappropriate times.

Suggs played Tom and Bob Monkhouse played his rhyming psychiatrist! He later starred in another radio play *Deep Down and Dirty Rock 'n' Roll* in 2011 as an ageing rock star that was heavily in debt and narrated his own life story, *My Mad Life Crisis* which was adapted for radio in 2013. Suggs was also surprised by Michael Aspel in 2000 for an edition of *This is Your Life*.

Suggs also enjoyed a moderately successful solo career in the 1990s, starting with the album *The Lone Ranger* in 1995, which hit No.14 in the charts. Two of the singles from the album, *I'm Only Sleeping* and *Camden Town* reached No.14 and No.7 respectively. He later released *The Christmas E.P.* in

December 1995 and a third single from *The Lone Ranger, Cecilia* reached No.4 in the charts, spawning a *Top of the Pops* appearance in 1996. *Cecilia* is perhaps his best known solo record. He later recorded *Blue Day* in 1997, the official FA Cup song for Chelsea as they reached the 1997 FA Cup Final. Suggs released his second album, *The Three Pyramids Club* in 1998 but hasn't released any further solo stuff since. He also released his autobiography *That Close* in 2013 and has toured a one man show since 2011. Suggs currently lives in London with his wife Anne, also known as Bette Bright, and has two grown-up daughters, Scarlett and Viva.

Cathal Smyth (Chas Smash)
Vocals, Various Shouts & Fancy Footwork, Trumpet,1979-1986, 1992-2014

Chas Smash was not an official member of the band when *One Step Beyond* was released but became an official member in 1980. He is often wrongly dismissed as a dancer or a Bez type figure in the band. However, as time progressed, Smash proved his worth as a musician and a songwriter. He learned the trumpet in order to prove he could be a musician and tried his hand at songwriting, the first being *Don't Quote Me On That*. He later co-wrote *Our House* which became an international hit. He remained in the band when they continued as The Madness but they disbanded in 1988 and in 1990 he became a record executive for Go Discs! He also collaborated with Morrissey on his version of The Jam's *That's Entertainment* in 1991 and turned down the opportunity to be his manager. Morrissey later dedicated his song *This One's For You Fatty* to Smash.

Smash was the main player in the 1992 reunion and he became involved on the management side. He also wrote the song *Green Eyes* for Suggs' album *The Long Ranger* in 1995 and performed backing vocals on the album.

Away from Madness, Smash formed his own folk band The Velvet Ghost in 1999 and founded his own record label, Rolled Gold Records, in 2002, releasing his debut single *We're Coming Over*. He was also involved in charity work with his work as an ambassador for The Prince's Trust and he also tried his hand at writing a musical although it never made it to production. He left Madness in 2014 to pursue his own solo projects which culminated in the release of his first solo album, *A Comfortable Man*, in 2015 which was followed by some live performances in London.

Although he is no longer a member of the band, Smash contributed to the book *Madness: Before We Were We* in 2019 and was present at the unveiling of a slab for Madness on Camden's Music Walk of Fame in March 2020. Smash is now living the quiet life and residing in Ibiza, having moved there in 2008 and has three grown up children, Caspar, Milo and Eloise with his former partner.

Lee Thompson (Kix)
Saxophone, 1976-1977, 1978-1986, 1992-present

(Pic. Tracey Salford)

Thompson was a founder member and remained until the breakup in 1986. During his time in Madness, Thompson moonlighted with The Specials on *More Specials,* playing saxophone on *Hey Little Rich Girl.* After the split, Thompson, Chris Foreman, Suggs and Chas Smash continued as The Madness, releasing the self-titled album in 1988. The band fizzled out soon afterwards but Thompson continued to work with Foreman and they released the album *Crunch!* in 1990, credited to The Nutty Boys. The names were later reversed, with the duo becoming Crunch! They released the EP, *It's OK, I'm a Policeman* in 1992, shortly before Madness reunited for the *Madstock* concerts.

Away from music, Thompson ran a mountain bike shop and even worked as a binman after he hit financial difficulties. Away from Madness, Thompson has since led his own bands, The Dance Brigade, formed in 2007 with Jennie Mathias, and The Lee Thompson Ska Orchestra was formed in 2011. TLTSO released the album *The Benevolence of Sister Mary Ignatius* in 2013 and later released the single *Bangarang* in 2014. Thompson also made his own film, One Man's Madness which was released in 2018 to critical acclaim and his autobiography in 2021. During the coronavirus pandemic in 2020, Thompson recorded a number of saxophone tutorials on Facebook for his fans. Thompson still performs with Madness, lives in Barnet with his wife, Debbie, and has three children, Daley, Tuesday and Kai.

Mike Barson (Monsieur Barzo)
Keyboards, 1979-1983, 1992-present
Barson was a founding member of the band back in 1976, playing the keyboards. He became the band's de-facto musical director with most of the band's songs revolving around his brilliant piano and keyboard playing. He has penned a number of the band's hits including; *My Girl, Baggy Trousers, Night Boat to Cairo, House of Fun* and *Bed and Breakfast Man.* Barson remained with The Nutty Boys until 1983, leaving the band to spend more time with his wife in their new home of Amsterdam.

Mike Barson (Pic. Ian James)

Dan Woodgate (Woody)
Drums, 1978-1986, 1992-present
Dan 'Woody' Woodgate joined in 1978, replacing John Hasler, and remained with the band until 1986. He later joined Voice of the Beehive (with Bedders) and didn't work with any of the other Madness members until the reformation in 1992. Woodgate also formed his own band Fat in 1992, releasing a single with them, *Downtime* in 1995, shortly before his departure.

His last appearance with the band was at the Lyceum Ballroom in December 1983. Barson did return for a short while to film the music videos for a couple of songs before leaving for good in 1984. He returned briefly in 1986 to play on the band's final single, *(Waiting For The) Ghost Train* but didn't appear in the video. After living the quiet life in Amsterdam, Barson rejoined the band in 1992 for the *Madstock!* reunion concerts and continued to join the rest of the band for reunions in 1994, 1996 and 1998 and has appeared on all releases since. Away from Madness, he has made the occasional guest appearance with other bands such as Audio Bullys on their 2005 song *This Road* and then again in 2010 on their song *Twist Me Up*. He also produced some of the tracks on Suggs' 1995 album *The Long Ranger*.

He moved into production, producing some tracks for King Prawn on their 1998 album *Fried in London*. Woodgate reunited with his former bandmates once again in 1999 when Madness reformed and later worked for a pest control company in 2000 before he formed his own company Woody's Floors, where he worked as a floor sander.

He then moved into teaching, where he worked at a school in Kent teaching music technology and media arts between 2004 and 2007. He later teamed up with his brother, Nick in 2013 to form the duo Magic Brothers later releasing the album *The Magic Line*. Woodgate then collaborated with Dan Shears to release the album *In Your Mind*. He also watches Chelsea FC, lives with his girlfriend in the English countryside and continues to play in Madness.

Woody on the drum kit

Mark Bedford (Bedders)
Bass, 1978-1986, 1992-2009, 2012-present

Became the bass player in 1978 after talking to a member at an early gig. He remained in the band until the initial split in 1986 but didn't work with his old bandmates when some of them reformed as The Madness shortly afterwards. He has worked on advertisements as well as guesting with a number of other musicians including Voice of the Beehive (with Woody), playing with Terry Edwards as the duo Butterfield 8 recording a self-titled album in 1988, and with Morrissey on his 1991 album *Kill Uncle*. Bedford later re-trained at the London College of Printing and founded his own design studio Mar Mar Co. Some of the clients Mar Mar Co have worked for include The Imperial War Museum, The Cuban Honey Company and Dr Martens as well as designing for both Madness and Near Jazz Experience. He later reunited with his old bandmates in 1992 for the *Madstock!* concerts and remains in the band, although he has left on occasion in the past. Away from Madness, Bedford has since played in Lee Thompson's Ska Orchestra and also plays with Terry Edwards and Simon Charteton in Near Jazz Experience, a three piece band that was formed in 2017. They play regular shows in St. Leonards and across the country, and have released an album and an EP, the latest being *The NJE* released in 2019.

Chris Foreman (Chrissy Boy)
Guitar, 1976-1986, 1992-2005, 2006-present

(Pic. Simon Bennett)

Foreman was a co-founder of the band with Mike Barson and Lee Thompson and wrote a number of the songs in the early days. After the breakup in 1986, he teamed up with Lee Thompson, Chas Smash and Suggs to form The Madness. When this came to an end in 1988, Foreman and Lee Thompson formed the duo The Nutty Boys in 1990, releasing *Crunch!*. Foreman rejoined Madness for the *Madstock* festival in 1992 and remained until 2005. He rejoined just in time for the band's Christmas 2006 tour and has remained ever since. Away from Madness, Foreman has guested with other artists over the years. Foreman currently lives in Brighton with his wife Melissa and has three children, Matthew, Felix and Frankie.

John Hasler
Minder, 1979
John Hasler was the original drummer but when Suggs was fired from the band, Hasler took his place on vocals as they'd already decided they needed a better drummer. When Suggs returned, he became the band's manager and was no longer in the band by the time they recorded their first album *One Step Beyond...* but was listed on the album as Minder. He also wrote the song *Believe Me* and was the inspiration for the song *Bed and Breakfast Man*. Hasler appeared as himself in the 1982 film *Take It Or Leave It*. He is now playing in his own band, Crabs!

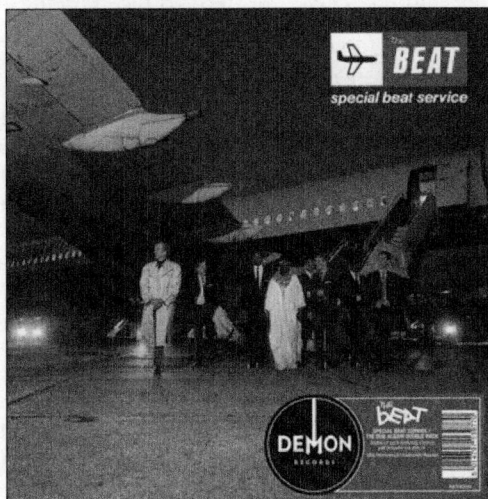

The Beat

Dave Wakeling and Andy Cox first met at a further education college in Birmingham and after becoming friends they moved to the Isle of Wight in November 1977 to build solar panels for Cox's brother-in-law.

Here they began to write their own songs and after being complimented on them, they decided to try and form their own band.

Cox and Wakeling ended up joining a local band after seeing an advert in the paper, unaware it was a Thin Lizzy tribute band until the audition. The association didn't last long and after they were unable to play their own songs, the pair left due to musical differences! By the start of 1978, Dave Wakeling had placed an advert in the local paper seeking a bass player and received only one reply, from David Steele, who wanted to know their musical tastes before agreeing to join them.

Cox began reeling off the names of The Clash, The Buzzcocks and Siouxsie and the Banshees. Luckily, Steele was a punk and was impressed so arranged to meet them in town. While they were waiting for him that afternoon, Wakeling thought he'd spotted Joe Strummer on the island when he saw a man striding towards him in a pair of bright green trousers but it turned out to be Steele! He soon joined and the trio began playing together and rehearsing some songs including *Best Friend, Two Swords* and one of Steele's songs, *Twist and Crawl*, which he'd written with his friend Dick Bradsel.

It was going well but they realised that their potential was limited on the island so took the decision to move back to Birmingham in September. Steele began working as a mental nurse at All Saints Mental Hospital, after discovering he could do his training in the city.

The band continued to work hard perfecting their sound but needed a drummer. Steele had been talking to a colleague who mentioned that she knew a drummer who was at a loose end after his band had broken up. The drummer was Everett Morton and Steele rang him, inviting him to Andy Cox's flat to rehearse at the weekend.

Morton turned up as arranged and brought a pal of his with a portable studio in tow.

The band recorded versions of *Two Swords, Twist and Crawl* and *Click Click,* with Wakeling and Cox playing acoustic guitars and Steele on bass. Upon hearing the playback, Morton and his pal were impressed and so were the band but decided that they needed some electric guitars and a proper rehearsal space. They enquired at The Yorkshire Grey and would practice there for £3 on a Tuesday night. Morton joined, having liked what he'd heard during the first meeting. The rehearsals began the following Tuesday though the session was a complete disaster, owing mainly to the lads not having any reggae songs to play. Morton, who was a few years older than the rest, had been drumming in reggae bands for years and wasn't a punk drummer. After a few frustrating hours, they decided to reconvene at the same time next week.

Meanwhile, Steele had decided they needed a better rehearsal space and found the perfect place...at work! The band dragged all their equipment into the Main Hall at the hospital and practiced there. Steele hadn't expected the sound to travel but discovered the following day that it had been echoing through the long and lonely corridors of the hospital and the patients had complained! He was undeterred and they rehearsed there again a week later, however, this time he received a severe bollocking from his bosses! The band had to rehearse elsewhere in future and found refuge in Wakeling's house, rehearsing in his back room. He was sharing a house with Dave Crook at the time, a prominent reggae DJ in the city and it was from here where the band's eventual sound was born.

Crook would DJ at discos and house parties, playing a mix of punk and reggae records. Cox and Wakeling would watch him at work and whenever he played punk singles they noticed that everyone would go mad but would be knackered after a few songs so the atmosphere would go flat!

Alternatively, if he played all the reggae records together, the atmosphere would be chilled and boring! So he would play punk and reggae records one after the other and the dancefloor would always be full. This planted a seed and they wondered about the possibility of mixing punk and reggae, later deciding that this would be the direction that they'd take.

The band continued to rehearse and by early 1979 were becoming competent musicians, capable of actually making music, rather than just producing noise! David Steele, who was now known as "Shuffle" thanks to Everett Morton's mum noting the bizarre shuffling motion he would do with his feet while playing, had been trying to convince the band to play some gigs. The others were sceptical but were swayed when Steele came out with the words; "One gig is worth a thousand rehearsals". They managed to secure a support slot with local band, the Dum Dum Boyz, at the Matador. There was just one snag...the band didn't have a name! As folklore goes, Dave Wakeling grabbed a thesaurus and looked up "harmony" and an alternative word to that was "beat". The thesaurus also mentioned that the opposite of "beat" was "clash" and "discordant". They eventually decided on The Beat, as The Automo-beat didn't sound right! The lads were now ready for the gig and it went well, the crowd cheered, danced and wanted more. Not bad for the first gig!

After the reception at that gig, it was decided they needed a manager, or at least someone to secure gigs. Steele found Bruce Melbourne, a brother of a colleague who already had experience managing local band, Mosiah. Melbourne, and his friend Jayne, ran 20/21 Management and the band sent them a demo tape. The tape contained; *Noise in This World, Click Click, Perfect Setting (For a Third World War)* and *Jackpot.* Melbourne's friend listened to the tape and felt that the first three songs were far too punky, whereas Melbourne took a shine to *Jackpot* and agreed to get them some gigs through John Mostyn, a booker on the Birmingham scene.

The band secured their second gig, supporting Mosiah at the Bournebrook, Selly Oak. The gig didn't go as planned, Wakeling was pissed, the PA was constantly feeding back and the audience soon lost interest, with the queue for the bar bigger than the audience! Despite this disappointment, The Beat secured a residency at the Mercat Cross every Tuesday. The band played the recognisable tunes of *Click Click, Two Swords, Jackpot* (an old Pioneers song), *Twist and Crawl, Noise in This World, Mirror in the Bathroom* and a cover of Smokey Robinson's *Tears of a Clown.*

Similar to what was happening with The Special AKA in Coventry and Madness in London, the band were learning their craft and gaining experience in front of a familiar audience. It was around this time that Roger Charlery, a 16 year old black punk, began to hang around with the band. He was a drinking pal of Dave Wakeling, who'd told him to come along to the Mercat to see them play. Charlery had been at The Beat's first gig, he was the drummer in The Dum Dum Boyz. Impressed with what he'd seen, he started to attend gigs, bringing his punk friends along with him to boost the crowd numbers. It wasn't long before Charlery, or Ranking Roger as he was known, was jumping on stage to toast over the songs and it had become popular.

Amusingly, the band only had one microphone, which they'd stolen from Generation X when they'd played Barberella's in Birmingham, and Roger would take the microphone and toast over the songs when Wakeling wasn't looking! It became a regular fixture of The Beat's live set, usually during the reggae numbers.

Roger had first come to prominence in Birmingham at a Damned gig that had been interrupted by some National Front fools, where he took the DJ's mic and began toasting "Fuck off, fuck off de National Front" and managed to get the whole crowd chanting it. He also sported bright orange hair at this time so was rather notable and instantly recognisable.

The residency came to an end after a few months though Roger remained with the band and eventually joined officially when he was invited to a band meeting and everyone assumed he was in the band anyway!

Although the band were really coming into their own, they almost packed it all in when Andy Cox was reading a copy of *Melody Maker* and read about The Special AKA who were doing a similar thing, though were blending punk and ska rather than punk and reggae. They considered giving up but after some deliberating, decided to carry on and continued to gig around Birmingham, building up a loyal following.

The Special AKA and Madness had already hit the charts and were receiving regular airplay on the radio. Shortly afterwards, in June, The Beat played a show at Aston University, supporting John Peel, which has since gone down in folklore. The Beat played their set first and Peel was so impressed with them, he spun a few records and made them play the set all over again! It is said that he swapped the cheques around at the end of the night although the amounts have changed over the years from anywhere between £40 and £400 and £80 and £800. The band took Peel out for a curry afterwards but whilst they were in the restaurant, someone smashed into their van!

By August, 2 Tone were aware of The Beat and Jerry Dammers had invited them to a Selecter gig in Blackpool. At the end of the gig, he offered them a support slot at the Hope & Anchor, London, supporting The Selecter. This would be their first gig out of the Midlands and it proved to be a great success, leading to the offer of more dates with The Selecter. Dammers was even spotted in the audience dancing with Lynval Golding, Pauline Black and Neol Davies at one gig! He was impressed with what he'd seen and heard on the demo tape that they'd sent to 2 Tone. It contained early versions of *Mirror in the Bathroom, Ranking Full Stop* and *Tears of a Clown.*

The General wanted them to play some London shows, with some support slots with The Selecter coming up. Neol Davies told them they could have any support slots they wanted as they liked them and the other support bands previously hadn't cut the mustard. Though Davies was at pains to tell them that he could only give them petrol money but The Beat agreed to play some dates with them in the Midlands.

After a gig at London's Electric Ballroom, Dammers and the rest of The Special AKA asked The Beat if they'd like to record a single on 2 Tone. Ever since the second time they'd seen them, they wanted to offer them the deal but Dammers wanted to wait until they proved themselves in London, rather than just the familiar surroundings of the Midlands. Ironically, The Beat had been planning on raising money to record their own single and distributing it similar to what The Special AKA had done. Dammers wanted them to get it done quickly so it could be released in the run-up to Christmas.

Shortly before the recording, in October, John Peel, by now a firm fan and champion of The Beat, booked them in for a Peel session and under the supervision of producer Bob Sargeant, they recorded *Tears of a Clown, Mirror in the Bathroom, Ranking Full Stop, Click Click* and *Big Shot*. This was broadcast in November and Peel regularly talked them up on his show, once saying they were "the best band in the world after The Undertones".

Days before the 2 Tone recording was due to start, the band recruited a sixth member. Saxa was a 49 year old Jamaican saxophone player that Everett Morton knew, he'd played with The Skatalites and even claimed he'd played a late night party with The Beatles during the 1960s. By now he was playing his saxophone at The Crompton, Handsworth and The Beat felt they were missing the brass that was prominent on the other 2 Tone releases and Saxa joined them for a warm-up gig at the Bournebook, Selly Oak.

Famously, Shuffle Steele asked Saxa if he wanted to know which key the songs were in to which he responded; "You just play and me'll blow, me'll blow!". Saxa was the missing piece of the jigsaw and was just in time for the 2 Tone recording.

The original plan was to record the single at Horizon Studios, Coventry with Roger Lomas. However, they took umbrage to the studio and after experiencing numerous technical problems, and decided to use their own producer. They approached Bob Sargeant, who'd produced their Peel session, and ended up recording at Sound Suite Studios, London.

For the first single, Jerry Dammers wanted to release *Mirror in the Bathroom* but also mentioned that Chrysalis would have the rights to the single for five years, preventing it from being included on any forthcoming album. It was the subject of a number of discussions between the label and the band before they decided to record another number from their live sets when Chrysalis wouldn't budge. The Beat recorded a cover of Smokey Robinson's *Tears of a Clown* and backed it up with an original tune, *Ranking Full Stop* which exposed Ranking Roger's excellent toasting to the public for the first time.

Tears of a Clown was eventually released in December and after scraping into the charts it peaked at No.6, leading to their first *Top of the Pops* just weeks later. It was 2 Tone's fifth consecutive Top 20 hit and The Beat later performed on the show for a second time in January 1980.

By the end of 1979, just like Coventry, Birmingham was booming musically and had become a hotbed for new talent with The Beat being joined by Dexy's Midnight Runners, UB40 and the Au Pairs.

Labels were now clamouring for the band's signature, offering vast amounts of money to sign them. The Beat had decided they wanted a similar deal that The Specials had with Chrysalis.

Tarquin Gotch, head of A&R at Arista approached them after a gig at the Underworld Club, Birmingham and conceded he couldn't offer them millions but would allow them the freedom they wanted.

Arista offered The Beat a deal where they could set up their own label to release their own music and also allow for six releases a year by other bands. They did just that and Go Feet Records was launched, licensed to Arista.

The band also pushed for a clause in the contract known as the "keyman clause", which would give them the right to leave the label if the rep who'd signed them ever left the company.

Go Feet was very much their own version of 2 Tone with the same ideals, they wanted to be able to release their own music as well as the music of other upcoming bands. They felt that they should try and help bands in the same way that The Specials had helped them. Dave Wakeling said; "The more we looked at it, the more sensible it seemed. So we decided that if anyone offered us a deal, we'd go for the same sort of thing as 2 Tone. 2 Tone did us a lot of good, so it would be nice to pass it on and do the same for other bands"[1].

The first non-Beat release was *Heart of The Congos*, a re-issue of the 1977 album, and was released as the band were big fans of The Congos. They had found it difficult to pick up copies of the album so decided to reissue the LP on their label and also released an accompanying single *Fisherman*. The Congos were led by Cedric Myton and the reissue had sparked some new interest in the band, with Myton recording a new album on the label. This culminated in the release of *Face The Music* in 1981, later spawning the single *Can't Take it Away* in September 1981. Due to the renewed interest and their willingness to release his music, Cedric Myton relocated to Birmingham for a while and returned the favour by singing backing vocals on *Doors of My Heart* on The Beat's second album.

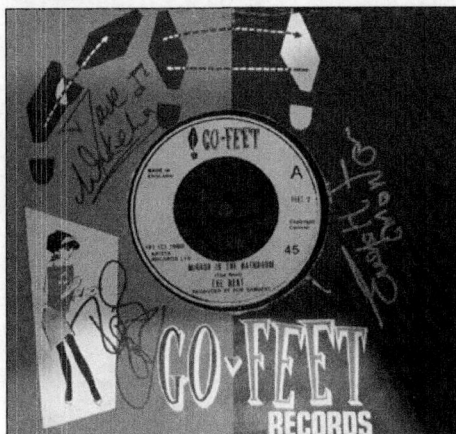

Go Feet sleeve signed by Dave Wakeling, Ranking Roger and Everett Morton

The band threw themselves into establishing Go Feet and the label soon had its own logo, designed by Hunt Emerson.

Emerson also designed the "Beat girl", which was the band's logo. Dave Wakeling had come up with the idea after violence was on the rise at their gigs, as well as other 2 Tone bands' gigs. Wakeling pointed out that Walt Jabsco (the 2 Tone man) had no one to show off to. Once the Beat girl was designed, lots of girls started to attend the gigs and the skinheads were trying to impress them rather than fighting, this cut the violence down and after a few months, the violence seldom happened at Beat gigs.

The first single on the label was *Hands Off She's Mine/Twist and Crawl*, released as a double 'A' side in February 1980. The reason for the double 'A' side was because they'd decided on *Hands Off She's Mine* but Andy Cox felt that *Twist and Crawl* would be a stronger choice and eventually a compromise was reached.

The single reached No.6 and there's since been discussion about *Hands Off She's Mine* and its sexist connotations. Wakeling denied it was sexist and said it was parody. There's also been some confusion over Ranking Roger's toast; "Get your hands off me darta", which has often been mistaken for "Get your hands off me daughter".

With "darta" being Jamaican slang for "girlfriend". The band did the obligatory *TOTP* appearance, notable for the first appearance of Saxa's son, Lionel Martin, on saxophone alongside his father.

The Beat were soon back in the studio to work on their first LP, they were originally recording at Ridge Farm Studio, Surrey but after two weeks, the equipment in the studio was replaced and the band relocated to Roundhouse Studios, London.

The first single to emerge was *Mirror in the Bathroom*, released in April and is perhaps their most famous song, reaching No.4. The single was backed by *Jackpot*, a cover of The Pioneers' song, and the song on the demo that'd convinced Bruce Melbourne that they were worth booking just a year before.

The accompanying music video was filmed in the Rum Runner, a nightclub in Birmingham. They were soon on the road, embarking on their first European tour in 1980, although it was thrown into chaos when the tour manager quit unexpectedly just before they were due to set off! Luckily a replacement was found, local character Clint Norton. Just weeks after the success of *Mirror in the Bathroom*, they released their first LP, *I Just Can't Stop It*, in May.

The LP has the distinction of being the country's first digitally recorded album and was warmly received, going straight in at No.3, eventually spending 32 weeks in the charts. The Beat toured the UK and also flew out to Holland and then Germany to perform on television. The album's success led to them being noticed among their peers and The Police offered them the support slot for their tour of France, which they accepted, leading to a friendship with The Police, and Sting, in particular.

Back in the UK, one more single was released from the album in August, *Best Friend*, backed by a dub version of *Stand Down Margaret*. It reached a respectable No.22, leading to another *Top of the Pops* appearance. The 'B' side is a dub version of a song from the album and the title speaks for itself, aimed at Margaret Thatcher and

it politely asks her to stand down as Prime Minister. To avoid being called hypocrites for profiting from a protest song, The Beat donated the proceeds of the single to the Campaign for Nuclear Disarmament (CND) and the Anti-Nuclear Campaign (ANC).

In September, another Peel session followed where they recorded four songs; *Too Nice To Talk To, Walk Away, Monkey Murders* and *New Psychedelic Rockers*, which were broadcast later that month.

Shortly after the session, the band embarked on their first American tour where they supported The Pretenders and Talking Heads. The lighting guy, Dave 'Blockhead' Wright joined the band as an official member having fallen into it by accident, after Saxa pulled out of a performance, Blockhead mentioned he could play all of Saxa's notes on the organ....provided they found one in time for the gig! Luckily, an organ was sourced and Blockhead hit every note perfectly on the night and it went down well, from then on he was included for live performances.

The tour went well and they impressed the audiences, especially when they supported The Pretenders. They were starting to get noticed in America although they were billed as The English Beat due to another band called The Beat.

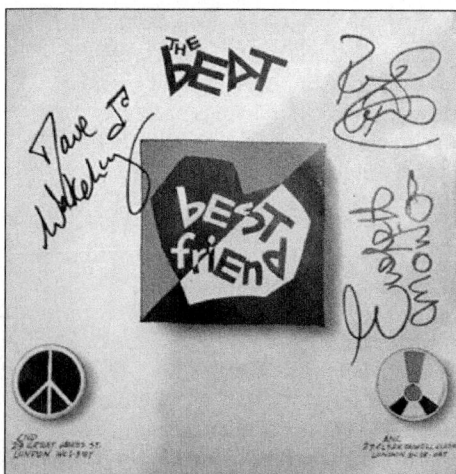

Best Friend single signed by Dave Wakeling, Ranking Roger and Everett Morton

They thought they'd ruined everything when they failed to show up for their first gig with Talking Heads, being stuck in traffic on their way back from Disneyland! Luckily, David Byrne thought it was hilarious and they made sure they were on time for the next gig! Thankfully, the rest of the tour passed without incident. Unlike The Specials, who showed their disdain for touring America, The Beat embraced it and were probably the most popular 2 Tone band to tour there.

The Beat released a non-album single in December, *Too Nice To Talk To*. It'd been written in the States and spent 11 weeks in the charts, peaking at No.7, leading to yet another *Top of the Pops* appearance. The Beat and The Specials were both on the same edition and the bass players swapped places. Horace Panter played bass with The Beat whereas David Steele played bass with The Specials on *Do Nothing*.

The second appearance, in January 1981, saw Chas Smash, Chris Foreman and Mark Bedford from Madness jump on stage for a dance! February saw the release of the 2 Tone film *Dance Craze*, featuring all the bands including The Beat.

Whilst they were in the States, Joe Massott filmed a gig in New Jersey and chose to show The Beat playing *Ranking Full Stop, Big Shot, Rough Rider, Twist and Crawl* and *Mirror in the Bathroom*. *Big Shot, Mirror in the Bathroom* and *Ranking Full Stop* appeared on the accompanying LP release. During the same month, the band were back in the studio working on their next album, with the first single being released in April. The double 'A' side *Drowning/All Out To Get You* peaked at No.22. Interestingly, amongst all the other instruments on *All Out To Get You*, Andy Cox played the garden shears!

The single was soon followed by the album *Wha'ppen* in June, which went straight in at No.5, peaking at No.3 a week later. It saw a change in musical direction, the first album had been fast and maintained a punk edge but the second was more relaxed and drew on their influences of reggae.

Similar to what The Specials had done with *More Specials*, they recognised the need to progress musically. *Wha'ppen* saw the band transform from rookies on the first album, Saxa aside, to fully fledged professional musicians by the second. The recording had taken around three weeks and cost half as much as the first one as they were far more efficient and competent now. *Wha'ppen* also contains more instruments than the first and they experimented with steel drums, a trumpet and a marimba (played by producer Bob Sargeant).

Blockhead also made his first appearance on a Beat album, having played with them since early 1980. The album was followed by the single *Doors of Your Heart*, released weeks later although it only reached No.33, their lowest chart placing at the time.

The Beat toured to promote the release and their ranks were expanded to include trumpet player Eddie Saltin and backing singer Cedric Myton who'd both appeared on the album, Myton was one of the band's heroes and had performed backing vocals on *Doors of Your Heart*.

They were supported by numerous bands across the tour, having advertised for bands to send tapes in. The Au Pairs, The Belle Stars and Musical Youth supported on various dates. Another band to support the band was The Mood Elevators, who went on to sign to Go Feet and released the single *Annapurna* in April 1981, though it failed to chart. David Steele and Andy Cox produced it under the guise of The Punjab Brothers.

The UK tour was quickly followed by a European one, taking in Germany, France and Holland and they did the usual TV circuit too, including a memorable performance on the kids TV show *Get Set For Summer*. They were booked to play three tunes, but played *Stand Down Margaret* at the end of their set, which included a choreographed moment where the band members took off their jackets to reveal t-shirts with "Stand Down Margaret" emblazoned on them!

To add to the shock, Buster Bloodvessel appeared wearing a white dress and a Beat t-shirt! After exhausting the album's content, a non-album single surfaced in November with *Hit It*, a lovely song about masturbation! The decision was Arista's but it was a commercial failure, reaching a low No.70. Ranking Roger considered it one of their worst singles.

By the end of 1981, 2 Tone was on its knees, The Specials and The Selecter had broken up and Madness were unrecognisable. The Beat's popularity in the UK was also fading, leading to a change in direction. Feeling that they'd exhausted their political messages in the songs, they went for a more pop and love song approach realising that commercial music had its plus points. This change was also designed to help them to try and crack America, where they'd been popular since their first release and the popularity was continuing to grow.

Unfortunately, Saxa retired from touring soon afterwards though he would remain active on the band's recorded output. He was replaced by Wesley MacGoogan for live performances and it was here that the dynamic of the band, in particular live performances, changed somewhat.

Everett Morton has since commented that MacGoogan found it difficult to step into Saxa's shoes; "Wesley had a hard road to travel to follow Saxa because they were different types of players".

Ranking Roger had a similar view and commented that he was a much quieter person than Saxa and had a totally different style of playing. However, both were complimentary about him, with Roger continuing; "He did a great job in having to do the stuff that Saxa did and having to keep up with someone of that calibre"[2].

Appearance on Top of the Pops

In March, The Beat recorded their third Peel session and recorded six songs; *Spar Wid Me, Till The End of the Party, She's Going She's Gone, Save It For Later, Sole Salvation Army* and *Pato and Roger A Go Talk*, with the session airing on March 29th 1982. They also appeared on *OTT*, a late night version of *Tiswas*, where they performed *Save It For Later* and *Stand Down Margaret*. Meanwhile, the sessions for the third album took place at Roundhouse Studios with Bob Sargeant overseeing production.

The first single to emerge was *Save It For Later*, released in April. Wakeling had written the song years before but each time he'd tried to get the band to record it, he was knocked back. Eventually they agreed and it has become one of their best known songs, particularly in the States. However, the band's grip on the charts was loosening and the single only reached No.47, music was changing and the New Romantics scene had taken over.

The Beat began to focus on America, where they were making lots of progress, and the single hit No.58 on the Billboard Dance/Disco chart. In June, they joined The Clash on a short tour of the States, with Ranking Roger in particular becoming friendly with them. He would join them on stage to toast over *Armagideon Time* and also ended up recording a toasted version of *Rock The Casbah* although it was never released. The Beat were popular on the tour and had gone down well and as the 2 Tone flame had gone out in the UK they decided to try and crack America, feeling that they'd already made significant progress.

In the early days, Dave Wakeling was the main songwriter but now all the members were contributing their own lyrics and songwriting was much more of a collective effort. The Beat were a socialist outfit, splitting the royalties equally between the members, with each member receiving a songwriting credit on all original songs. However, this was causing problems for Wakeling, who kept trying to convince Ranking Roger to leave with him to form a new band.

The album *Special Beat Service* was released in September, signalling another change in direction, the reggae roots were still there but they had moved towards a pop sound. The album also saw a number of session musicians play on some of the tracks as well as Bob Sargeant playing the telephone! It was followed by the release of *Jeanette*, the second single from the album. The disappointing chart run continued and it only hit No.45. The album performed slightly better but still only peaked at No.21, with their previous two albums hitting No.3, this showed that the UK had moved on, though America was listening perfectly. The album became the first to chart in the Top 40 of the Billboard 200 in the States, reaching No.39. The release coincided with the band's appearance at the US Festival in September with Everett Morton since describing it as his best moment with the band.

The final single to be released from the album was *I Confess*, a song based around a tune Blockhead had been playing on the piano whilst Dave Wakeling was in the studio. Wakeling was impressed and went away and wrote a song about pin up magazines and the emotional vibe of them. Despite the important message, the single was once again a disappointment, reaching just No.54, though it did reach No.34 on the US Dance Chart.

The music video saw the band taking the piss out of the New Romantic movement, which was now in full flow, and saw Wakeling sporting some rather glamorous makeup and eyeliner!

It is ironic that some of the band's most popular songs placed so lowly on the charts. Some of this is down to the popularity of 2 Tone being on the floor by 1982, with the label itself focused on funk groups such as The Apollinaires and The Higsons.

The Beat were now focused on America as their songs were achieving decent chart placings there. This was partly due to their music videos getting significant airplay on the new MTV channel.

The Beat are probably the only 2 Tone band that had a proper shot at cracking America, but ironically broke up just as they were breaking through.

The Beat were quiet during the opening months of 1983 but went on the second leg of the Special Beat Service Tour of the States at the end of February through to the end of April. April had also seen the release of a single, *I Can't Get Used To Losing You*, which originally appeared on the first album but had been remixed for release as a single. The single shot up the charts and eventually peaked at No.3, leading to two *Top of the Pops* performances. The band returned to the States in May and played some more shows, most notably the 1983 US Festival. They also released *What Is Beat?* in May, a compilation of greatest hits, which performed well, reaching No.10 as well as No.87 on the US Billboard 200. June saw The Beat play Glastonbury and also the release of their final single, *Ackee 1-2-3*. Unfortunately, the single was not a success, reaching just No.54, a far cry from their previous release.

Despite the release of a greatest hits compilation, the band intended to carry on and record new material. Ranking Roger has since revealed that they had plans to release a fourth album and in his words; "The fourth album we were going to do would have been the one that was gonna absolutely smash America to bits"[2], he also revealed that three quarters of the album had already been written.

In July, The Beat supported David Bowie for two nights at the Milton Keynes National Bowl on his Serious Moonlight Tour. On the first night, Saxa mistook David Bowie for a waiter! Bowie had popped his head into the dressing room to see if everyone was okay and he mentioned to Saxa that he played the saxophone but not as well as he could. Saxa stood up and took Bowie to the fridge and mentioned there was no Red Stripe. Bowie disappeared for a few minutes before he returned with 12 cans of Red Stripe, much to Saxa's delight, Bowie took it in good

humour and when Saxa asked the rest of the band who it was and he couldn't believe it was Bowie, as he'd been dressed as The Thin White Duke.

Both of the gigs went well and Bowie came into the dressing room on the second night and asked them to support him on his next tour. However, there had been growing tensions in the band after spending almost four years endlessly touring and recording. David Steele in particular wanted a couple of years off from their tireless schedule, he was only 22 years old at the time and wanted to experience a bit of normality away from The Beat.

Dave Wakeling and Ranking Roger had recently started families and both have since acknowledged that they left the band to make more money. Due to the band's socialist ideals, all the money was split equally between the six members of the band but Wakeling and Roger figured that if their band only contained them two, they would be making more money for themselves. Shortly after the Bowie gigs they decided to leave The Beat to form a new band, General Public. They revealed their intentions by posting a letter to the record label, the rest of the band had no idea. After considerable chart success spanning almost four years, Wakeling and Roger were gone, leaving the rest of the members in the lurch and out of a job.

Reunions

Everett Morton and Saxa teamed up with Tony Beet to form The International Beat in 1990 after Beet had been talking to the pair in a Birmingham pub. The band consisted of; Tony Beet (vocals & guitar), Neil Deathridge (guitar), Kent Peters (bass), Everett Morton (drums), Mickey Billingham (keyboards) and Saxa (saxophone). The International Beat would also see occasional guest appearances from Ranking Roger and Dave Wakeling. They later released an album of original material, *The Hitting Line* in 1991, featuring a guest appearance from Roger on backing vocals and he also helped produce the album.

Ranking Roger, Everett Morton and Saxa formed Twist & Crawl in 2001 where they would perform Beat songs. Dave Wakeling also started to perform as The English Beat in California during the same year. He'd initially attempted to distance himself from The Beat, performing under the name Bang. However, most promoters would bill him as The English Beat so he gave in.

By 2003, 20 years since the breakup, MOJO contacted Wakeling to see if he was interested in reforming the band. He contacted Ranking Roger, who'd been playing gigs with Everett Morton and Saxa, and asked if he was interested. He was, and he also had Morton and Saxa on board and also managed to convince keyboard player Blockhead to return, although efforts to convince Andy Cox and David Steele to return proved fruitless, though Cox was involved in early rehearsals.

The reunion gig took place at the Royal Festival Hall, Birmingham and was a sell-out, it also saw Ranking Roger's son Ranking Junior join the band on stage for a couple of numbers. The show was filmed and later released as a DVD in 2005. Ranking Roger, Dave Wakeling, Everett

Morton, Saxa and Blockhead continued to play as The Beat after the reunion but after a bust-up between Roger and Wakeling, the latter ceased to be involved.

Just a year later, in 2004, VH1 attempted to get the band together for their show Bands Reunited and the viewers were treated to an hour of watching the rather annoying Aamer Haleem referring to the band as The English Beat and staking out both Andy Cox and David Steele's houses. Despite this, the programme managed to reunite Dave Wakeling, Ranking Roger, Everett Morton and Saxa, but were unable to convince Cox and Steele, the constant banging on their doors by Haleem and a specially recorded message from Saxa did nothing to persuade them. Viewers were treated to clips of Wakeling playing with Ranking Roger's Beat in Birmingham before he flew home.

Ranking Roger and Dave Wakeling continued to run their own versions of The Beat, with the former based in Birmingham and the latter in California. In the early days, they rarely stepped on each other's toes but as time went on they would tour in each other's backyards.

Ranking Roger and Ranking Junior perform as The Beat - Pic by Joe Kerrigan

Ranking Junior joined his father's band in 2003 and at one point this version boasted original members Everett Morton and Saxa alongside keyboard player Blockhead. Morton remained in the band until 2010 when he was sacked by Roger, leading to a war of words in a local Birmingham newspaper.

By now, Roger's Beat had been including new songs and after the success of the *Live in London* album in 2013, they recorded a new album which was released in 2016. *Bounce* was credited to The Beat Feat. Ranking Roger and hit No.49 in the charts. The album was accompanied by the release of a single, *Walking on the Wrong Side.*

They continued to tour the world and after years of headlining their own tours, they teamed up with The Selecter for a co-headline tour in 2017 and another one in 2018. Sadly, Ranking Roger suffered a stroke in August 2018 and the band was effectively finished when he passed away seven months later in March 2019.

The band's second LP was released in January 2019, *Public Confidential*. The band's lineup in their final days consisted of; Ranking Roger (vocals), Ranking Junior (vocals), Andy Pearson (bass), Fuzz Townsend (drums), Andy Perriss (guitar), Bobby Bird (guitar) and Chiko Hamilton (saxophone).

After years of performing the greatest hits Dave Wakeling announced in 2014 that he'd be recording a new album of original material entitled *Here We Go Love!* and a PledgeMusic appeal was set up allowing fans to donate to the band to fund the recording.

Other goodies were also on sale, such as the opportunity to join the band on tour, backstage passes, handwritten lyric sheets and even the chance to have a phone call with Wakeling himself!

The release of the album became a bit farcical, with the band not receiving the funds on time and the release of the album being continually delayed. Although Wakeling was quick to offer his apologies and was constantly seen offering to put disgruntled fans on the guestlist of various shows in order to compensate for the delay.

The album was eventually released in May 2018 to moderate reviews and featured guest appearances from Everett Morton and Andy Cox. Bob Sargeant also served as the executive producer. In 2017, shortly after Saxa's death, The English Beat performed a show which saw Cox guest on guitar. Wakeling's band's lineup currently consists of; Dave Wakeling (vocals & guitar), Antonee First Class (toaster), Chuck Elder (bass & vocals), Kevin Lum (keyboards & vocals), Minh Quan (keyboards & vocals), Brian Cantrell (drums), Matt Morrish (saxophone & vocals). The English Beat were due to perform a 40th anniversary tour of the UK in 2020 but was rearranged for 2021 due to the coronavirus pandemic.

Dave Wakeling's version of The Beat - Pic by Darin Barry

Everett Morton's band Beat Goes Bang

Everett Morton has been performing with his own band Beat Goes Bang since 2014 and although they haven't released any new material, they released a version of *Can't Get Used To Losing You* in 2018. BGB have played infrequently since their formation but shows have become more frequent since 2019 when they toured to commemorate the 40th Anniversary of 2 Tone and continued to play in 2020, with a new singer. The current Beat Goes Bang lineup consists of; Everett Morton (drums), DemenNus (vocals), Mickey Billingham (keyboards), Neil Deathridge (guitar), Theo Hockley (bass) and Sean Williams (saxophone).

Releases on 2 Tone

Tears of a Clown (1979).

Where are they now?

Dave Wakeling
Vocals and Guitar, 1978-1983

Dave Wakeling was co-founder of the band and the one who eventually wielded the axe in 1983, departing with Ranking Roger to form General Public. They released the album *All The Rage* in 1984, which was a minor success. General Public were more successful in the States and released one more album in 1987 before breaking up. Wakeling later guested with The International Beat on occasion and went on to release a solo record. Whilst in California, he fell in love with the place and moved there permanently. The album, *No Warning*, was released in 1991 before he started to work for Greenpeace as Special Projects Director.

Wakeling also performed numerous benefits for them before he was convinced to return to full-time performing after Elvis Costello told him that his place was on the stage and that he should consider returning to it. Wakeling heeded the advice and started to play up and down California and was soon asked if he'd be interested in recording a tune for the soundtrack for the upcoming film *Threesome*. He was interested and decided to reform General Public to do it, convincing Ranking Roger to record *I'll Take You There*. They officially reformed in 1994 to record it and when the film was released, the song took off, reaching No.1 in the Billboard Dance charts. The success led to a new album and a tour to accompany it. However, the success died down pretty quickly and they broke up in 1995. Wakeling now tours the world with his version of The Beat, The English Beat and has done since 2001. He plays extensively in California but often tours the UK and released an album in 2018 of original material which he claims to be the 4th Beat album. Wakeling remains in California with his family.

Andy Cox
Guitar, 1978-1983
Cox was the co-founder of the band, with Dave Wakeling, and remained with the group throughout it's life. After the breakup, he teamed up with David Steele to form a new band and were inundated with tapes from potential singers. They decided on Roland Gift, a young singer from Hull, after they'd seen him on television and set about tracking him down. The song *Johnny Come Home* soon surfaced, credited to Fine Young Cannibals, although they struggled to get a record deal. Once the music video was shown on *The Tube,* the offers came flooding in and the band were signed to I.R.S. and soon released the debut album *Fine Young Cannibals* in 1985. Throughout the 1980s, the band achieved considerable chart success before breaking up in 1992. While FYC were on hiatus in 1987, Steele and Cox released a house single, *Tired of Getting Pushed Around* which was credited to Two Men, a Drum Machine and a Trumpet.

Away from FYC, Cox played with Alison Moyet on her 1991 tune *Back Where I Belong* as well as producing the song with David Steele. After FYC disbanded in 1992, Cox played on and produced much of Al Green's 1993 album *Don't Look Back*. More work with Alison Moyet, Al Green and Gabrielle followed before Fine Young Cannibals reunited in 1996 to promote the release of their Greatest Hits album, *The Finest* which included new single, *The Flame*. Since his work with the FYC, Cox has continued to work in music and formed the duo Cribabi with Japanese artist Yukari Fujiu in 2001, later releasing the album *Volume*. The guitarist is currently living in London and surprisingly played a gig with Dave Wakeling's English Beat in 2017 as a tribute to Saxa, who'd recently passed away and also featured on the album *Here We Go Love* in 2018.

David Steele
Bass, 1978-1983
David "Shuffle" Steele was living on the Isle of Wight before he joined The Beat in 1978 and before the band turned professional he was working as a mental nurse in Birmingham. When The Beat broke up in 1983, Steele and Andy Cox formed the Fine Young Cannibals with vocalist Roland Gift. They achieved a number of hit singles before breaking up in 1992, briefly reforming in 1996 to release a single to coincide with the release of the Greatest Hits compilation *The Finest*. Away from FYC, Steele and Cox teamed up to release a house single, *Tired of Getting Pushed Around* which was credited to Two Men, a Drum Machine and a Trumpet. Steele and Cox both played on and produced a good chunk of Al Green's 1993 album *Don't Look Back*. More work with Alison Moyet, Al Green and Gabrielle followed before Fine Young Cannibals reunited in 1996 to promote their Greatest Hits album, *The Finest* and this included returning to the studio to record the single, *The Flame*. The band didn't continue beyond 1996 and Steele continued to work in production, producing for Europop band Madasun in 2000 and the Australian artist Friendly in 2001.

Steele then teamed up with American singer, Jonte Short, to form the duo Fried in 2004, releasing a self-titled album in the same year. It was later re-released as *Things Change* in 2007 with some new tracks on it. 'Shuffle' has since lived a quiet life and is living in London.

Everett Morton
Drums, 1978-1983

Everett Morton is originally from St. Kitts but moved to the UK in the 1960s and settled in Birmingham, he'd played in a number of reggae and soul bands and worked during the day in a kettle spinning factory before he joined The Beat. When the band broke up in 1983, Morton was left in the lurch and later played with The Supernaturals before he formed The International Beat with Saxa in 1990. They played for a number of years before eventually disbanding.

He later became a landlord, running The Crusader and The Swan & Mitre in Birmingham before joining Ranking Roger's Beat in 2003, remaining until 2010 when Roger sacked him after Morton had some time off with an injury. They fell out over this and the dispute saw Morton form his own Beat, but they reconciled shortly before Roger's death in 2019. Morton is now playing with Beat Goes Bang who have been playing live since 2014.

Ranking Roger
Vocals, 1979-1983

'Ranking' Roger Charlery was the youngest person involved in the whole 2 Tone movement, he was only 16 when he joined The Beat in 1979. He left to form General Public in 1983 with Dave Wakeling and remained until 1987. After General Public disbanded, Roger released a solo album and toured with Special Beat until 1993. Later reformed General Public in 1994 with Wakeling but after their new album *Rub It Better* flopped in 1995, they disbanded once again. A year later, Charlery teamed up with Pato Banton to record *The Bed's Too Big Without You* and then joined Big Audio Dynamite and appeared on their final album, *Entering A New Ride,* in 1997. The same year, he recorded a version of *Black & White* with Jimmy Nail, perhaps one of the most bizarre duets in musical history! At the turn of the century, Charlery began to record his second solo album, *Inside My Head,* released in 2001. Outside of music, Roger worked as a roller skate instructor and could often be seen skating in the local skateparks. Between 2017 and 2018, The Beat had been touring with The Selecter on a co-headline tour before the tour came to an abrupt end in August 2018 when Roger suffered a stroke.

Although it appeared he was getting back to full health, he was diagnosed with lung cancer and a number of brain tumours in early 2019 and passed away in March 2019. Ranking Roger's autobiography, *I Just Can't Stop It: My Life in The Beat* was posthumously released just a few months after his death, in June 2019.

Saxa
Saxophone, 1979-1983

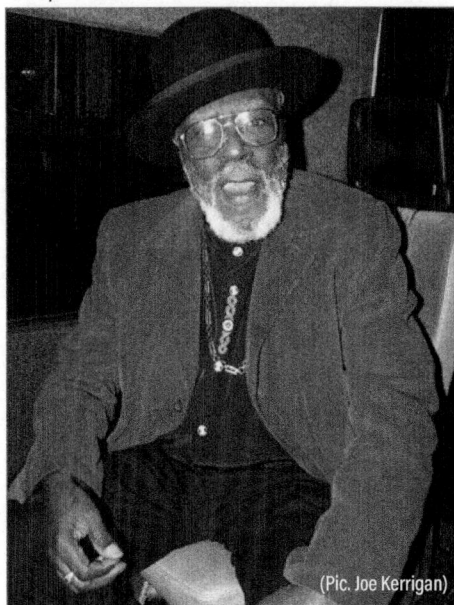

(Pic. Joe Kerrigan)

Saxa, real name Lionel Martin, was already a veteran when he joined The Beat. He originated from Jamaica but moved to the UK in 1960, originally living in London but later settling in Birmingham. He was known for playing his saxophone in the pubs of Birmingham and was asked to join before they recorded the first single in 1979 after the band had seen him playing in The Crompton, Handsworth. Saxa had played with a number of Jamaican ska artists over the years. He retired from touring in 1981 but continued to record with the band. Saxa later formed The International Beat with Everett Morton in the late 1980s, played with General Public in the 1990s and also with Ranking Roger's version of The Beat in the 2000s. He remained in Birmingham for the rest of his life and sadly passed away in 2017 aged 89.

David 'Blockhead' Wright
Keyboards, 1980-1983

'Blockhead', a former geography teacher and social worker, had been the lighting guy for the band and first started to work with them on the first tour in 1979. He later became the tour manager until he was drafted in on keyboards when Saxa became ill before one of the shows. Blockhead told the band that he would be able to replicate all of Saxa's notes on the keyboards as long as they could find him one! After that show, Blockhead remained in the band, originally just playing the live shows before he played on the album *W'happen* but merely as a session musician, later being upgraded to a full time member shortly after the album's release. When The Beat broke up, Blockhead formed Two Nations, releasing an album and five singles in 1986 and 1987, with *Living in Two Nations* being the most memorable. He later played keyboards in Ranking Roger's Beat in 2003 for a few years before eventually leaving. Blockhead is still based in the Midlands living in retirement and watches his beloved West Bromwich Albion regularly.

Wesley Magoogan
Saxophone, 1981-1983

After Saxa decided to retire from touring in 1981, he needed to be replaced. The band approached Magoogan to replace him for live performances. He'd previously worked with Hazel O'Connor playing the saxophone solo on her hit *Will You*. He became a full time member of the band and as well as the sax, he played clarinet, lyricon and the sax FX unit on the final Beat album, *Special Beat Service* in 1982. When The Beat broke up in 1983, Magoogan worked with Joan Armatrading, playing saxophone on her song *Persona Grata* and on three tracks on her album *Sleight of Hand*. He also played with Billy Ocean, Magnum and Crazy House but is now no longer involved in the music business. His saxophone playing sadly came to an end when he lost his fingers in a freak accident with a circular saw. Magoogan now focuses on his son Lester who suffers from Down's Syndrome, running a website showcasing Lester's many talents.

Elvis Costello & The Attractions

The career of Declan Patrick MacManus, OBE, better known as Elvis Costello, began in the early 1970s and he formed the band Flip City in 1975.

Flip City attracted interest from Dave Robinson, later of Stiff Records, and a release was planned but then pulled by Robinson. Flip City later broke up and Costello decided to go solo, performing under the name of DP Costello.

Eventually, he recorded some of his own music and managed to get a tape played on BBC Radio London. By 1976 Dave Robinson had founded Stiff and Costello sent a demo tape to them, which impressed the label. A recording session was organised and produced by Nick Lowe and shortly afterwards, Costello was signed to the label though took a day job as a computer operator.

He soon got to work in the studio and a single was released in March 1977, *Less Than Zero*. The song itself was a song about Oswald Mosley, a famous British fascist. This was soon followed by an album, *My Aim Is True*, in August. The album was moderately successful and reached No.14 in the charts. However, the single failed to chart, as did the following two; *Alison* and *(The Angels Wanna Wear My) Red Shoes*. Costello was backed by Clover on the album but set about recruiting his own permanent backing band before the album's release.

Auditions were held and adverts posted in the music press leading to Steve Nason and Bruce Thomas auditioning on keyboards and bass respectively. Nason later became Steve Nieve, a deliberate misspelling of naive. Meanwhile, Pete Thomas (no relation to Bruce) was a drummer who'd been working in California with John Stewart but returned in the summer of 1977. He was added to the lineup and Steve Nieve (keyboards), Bruce Thomas (bass) and Pete Thomas (drums) made up The Attractions.

Rehearsals began and Costello & The Attractions began to play live in July, their first performance coming in Penzance supporting Wayne County and the Electric Chairs.

They were soon in the studio to re-record *Less Than Zero,* with the intention of replacing the original recording on any future re-pressings, though this ultimately never happened. The first appearance of The Attractions on record came in October with the release of *Watching The Detectives,* they appeared on the 'B' side which featured live versions of *Blame it on Cain* and *Mystery Dance.*

The single was Costello's first to chart, hitting No.15 and he embarked on the A Bunch Of Stiffs tour with The Attractions. The tour saw a rotating line-up of Stiff artists including Costello & The Attractions, Wreckless Eric, Ian Dury and The Blockheads and Nick Lowe's Last Chicken In The Shop.

November also saw Costello & The Attractions make their first appearance on *Top of the Pops,* performing the single. Costello had previously appeared in September performing *Red Shoes.*

Days after the performance, their first tour of the US commenced on November 11th and they played some moderately successful shows alongside Tom Petty and Talking Heads. It was during their time in the States, in December, where they made their most famous appearance on American TV. The Sex Pistols had been booked to play on *Saturday Night Live* but were unable to get into the country due to problems with obtaining visas. Costello & The Attractions agreed to step in, with Costello wanting to play *Radio Radio,* but the record label told him to play *Less Than Zero.* Costello felt that a song about a British fascist would be lost on an American audience and decided to halt the band a few bars into the song and began to play *Radio Radio* instead. This incident led to Costello being banned from the show until 1989!

The sessions for the first Costello & The Attractions album began at Eden Studios, London towards the end of 1977 and were completed by January when they went back to the US for their second tour at the end of the month.

The first single credited to the group was released in March and *(I Don't Want To Go To) Chelsea* peaked at No.16. The song had been written by Costello in the office when he worked as a computer programmer and after everyone had gone home, he sat alone with his guitar and wrote it.

The single was followed by their first album, *This Year's Model,* a great blend of pop music and punk venom which soared to No.4. The album is still considered to be one of Costello's best, it was No.3 in the *NME's* Album of the Year 1978 and was included in Robert Dimery's *1001 Albums You Must Hear Before You Die* in 2005. The next single *Pump It Up,* was released in April and again successful, reaching No.24. It has since become a classic and the music video for the single is best remembered for Costello's dancing where he dances on the sides of his feet and risks a sprained ankle at any moment! The 'B' side featured Mick Jones on guitar, he'd been approached to play on the 'A' side but it failed to materialise. The final single to be released was *Radio Radio* in October, which reached No.29. It was a cynical dig at the commercialisation of British radio and saw Costello & The Attractions at their best.

Following the US tour, Costello & The Attractions toured the UK in March and April to promote the album. The tour saw Nick Lowe become an Attraction for the last few shows, stepping in on bass after Bruce Thomas damaged his hand in a juggling accident! They headed back to the US for another tour between April and early June. With Bruce Thomas still out of action, he was replaced on the first few dates by Johnny Ciambotti, from Costello's old backing band Clover before Thomas returned later.

They were busy boys during this period as the US Tour was followed by a European one in June and July. After a short rest, they were back at Eden Studios to record the next LP. The 2nd day of recording saw a BBC film crew ejected from the studio! This had followed a dispute with the management over working conditions.

The album was soon recorded and in the run-up to its release, Costello & The Attractions appeared at Rock Against Racism in September, appearing on the same bill as Sham 69 and Aswad. This was followed by a tour of Canada in November before they toured Japan, Australia and then the UK, which came to an end in January 1979. The Australian tour courted some controversy after they played the Regent Theatre, Sydney. The audience rioted after the band refused to perform an encore after only playing a 35 minute set. The audience didn't take too kindly to this and ripped seats out of the auditorium and hurled them at the empty stage.

The release of *Armed Forces*, overlapped with the tour when it was released and became their highest charting album, reaching No.2. This release saw Costello maintain his raw anger from the first two releases though some of the album wasn't as vitriolic, it's still a great listen and shows Costello at his best and perhaps marks the end of the angry records that he had become known for as he became more ambitious and willing to develop his sound on his future releases.

The first single to be released was *Oliver's Army* in February, written by Costello about The Troubles after he'd been in Belfast and was shocked to see British soldiers walking around with machine guns. It also covers the end of the British Empire with Oliver referring to Oliver Cromwell. The use of "white nigger", a derogatory term used to describe an Irishman, caused some uproar. Costello no longer sings it, having rewritten the whole verse in the 2010s. The single became their highest charting single when it hit No.2, being denied the top spot by The Bee Gees' *Tragedy* and then Gloria Gaynor's *I Will Survive*!

The success was followed by a mammoth two and a half month tour of the US, with the Armed Funk Tour commencing in early February.

The album also performed well in the US, reaching No.10 in their charts.

During the tour, an unsavoury incident occurred, where a drunk Costello caused a brawl with some racist comments. It had begun in a Holiday Inn in Ohio where Costello & The Attractions had bumped into some of the Stephen Stills Band, and an already drunk Costello was attempting to goad them with disparaging remarks about America.

He continued this and referred to James Brown as a "jive arsed nigger" and Ray Charles as a "blind ignorant nigger" before he was punched by Bonnie Bramlett. Costello faced accusations of racism, leading to death threats and the boycott of his music. A hastily arranged press conference saw Costello explain what had happened, blaming it on drunkenness and weariness from touring, though he didn't apologise.

The backlash eventually calmed down and back home, the second single from *Armed Forces* was released in May. *Accidents Will Happen* didn't reach the heights of the previous few singles, but it did reach a respectable No.28.

Costello & The Attractions played Pinkpop in the summer, but more notably, Costello worked on the production of the first album from The Specials. By the summer of 1979, The Specials had exploded onto the scene with *Gangsters* and every record company with any sense wanted to sign them. They'd eventually agreed to sign with Chrysalis and with this deal they got their own label, 2 Tone. Costello was a fan of the band and had attended a number of gigs before he approached them to produce their debut album. The recording took place in the summer and *Specials* was released in October to critical acclaim. As will soon become clear, this wasn't the last involvement with 2 Tone.

In the autumn, Costello & The Attractions played some Scandanavian and European dates before they went into Eden, to record their third album together. The sessions were soon finished and they went on to play the Concert For Kampuchea in December.

One of the songs on the upcoming album was *I Can't Stand Up For Falling Down*, a cover of a Sam and Dave song. Bruce Thomas was sceptical; "I recall when Elvis suggested recording *I Can't Stand Up*, I said I couldn't see the point and I recall saying I thought it was Sam and Dave's 16th best song, so what was the point? Of course, their version was a slow ballad. But I pushed to rearrange it - which we did and turned it into the uptempo track you are all familiar with". *I Can't Stand Up For Falling Down* was pressed on 2 Tone in January 1980 and released though the stories differ depending on who you speak to.

Costello had worked with The Specials on their album and was no stranger to 2 Tone or Jerry Dammers. He had also just parted company with his label Radar and was a free agent. The single was discussed in the *NME* on January 12th; "Initially, *I Can't Stand Up* was going to be a 2 Tone single, until such time as Off-Beat was operational, but as 2 Tone is a co-operative, the release date of January 11 clashed with a live Specials EP and the new Selecter single.

This meant the Costello single would be delayed almost a month which didn't coincide with Costello tour dates"[1]. Off-Beat, the new label, later became F-Beat after being shortened from Fuck Beat! The single was pressed but subject to an injunction from WEA, preventing many of the 13,000 copies from hitting the shops.

An alternative version of events appeared in *Record Collector* in 1987; "Costello had been signed to Radar in 1978, via a licensing deal from Riviera Global Productions. Radar collapsed towards the end of 1979, and so Elvis's manager Jake Riviera alighted upon The Specials' 2 Tone label as an ideal venue for a holding operation - a one-off single - until Elvis sorted out a deal for the *Get Happy* album. WEA, who had distributed Radar, were not happy: they felt they had a stake in Costello's career by virtue of the success of the records they had distributed for him, and so they obtained a court injunction to stop the 2 Tone single being sold"[2].

Jerry Dammers spoke with the same magazine in 2009 but disagreed with this account; "Jake Riviera cheekily printed up a few thousand Elvis Costello singles on the 2 Tone label, obviously thinking that I would be delighted to have such a major star on the label, but I was having none of it, 2 Tone being strictly ska at that time. So Elvis was forced to give these singles away free at his gigs"[3].

One more version appeared in Franklin Bruno's book on *Armed Forces*; "Roughly 13,000 copies were pressed with the label's distinctive logo, and a few found their way into shops in January 1980. The rest fell afoul of WEA, which demanded that the pressing be withdrawn, arguing that Elvis Costello was still signed to the parent label despite the demise of Radar; the bulk of the pressing was given away or sold at concerts in 1980-1981"[4].

Bruce Thomas and Pete Thomas have no idea of how the record ended up on 2 Tone with Bruce commenting; "I never took much interest in the machinations of the business, just counted the royalties". Pete was also nonplussed simply saying; "I'm sorry to say but I haven't got a clue about what happened". Bruce was seemingly unaware of the impact of 2 Tone at all; "Was it a one-off or a failed project that didn't last very long? There's your answer! I Googled the label and was shocked to see that it lasted till 1985. Yet my only memory of the label is our brief involvement with it. Maybe we allied with them briefly to give them a bit of a PR kick start?". What we do know is, the original pressings of the single were handed out at a gig at the Rainbow Theatre and these were marked with a 2 Tone catalogue number of TT-7. However, more singles were pressed months later to be given out at gigs in both London and America and contained the catalogue number for the F-Beat single.

After the trouble with 2 Tone, *I Can't Stand Up For Falling Down* was released on F-Beat in February and it was a success, reaching No.4 in the charts.

The next album, *Get Happy!!*, was released just a month later. The album was successful but considerably different from the first two that'd been recorded with The Attractions. They'd been very much punk influenced whereas *Get Happy!!* had been influenced by ska, soul and R&B. They had originally played a number of the songs in their "normal" style, but once they were in the studio the songs sounded like new-wave. They didn't want to sound new-wave so decided to play some of the songs in a slower, more soulful way.

The sessions saw some tension between the band, with Costello deciding this would be their last album, pondering the possibility of going solo. They toured to promote the release in the UK in February and March and then released *High Fidelity* in April, which reached No.30. The next single, *New Amsterdam*, was released in June though credited to Costello. It didn't fare too well, only reaching No.36, and Costello left The Attractions for a short while.

They ended up releasing an album of their own, with *Mad About The Wrong Boy* arriving in August. It failed to make an impact on the charts but it's a pleasant enough affair, seemingly led by Steve Nieve, who contributed most of the lyrics, under the pseudonym Norman Brain! It also spawned two singles, *Single Girl* which had been released a month before the album in July and *Arms Race* in December although neither troubled the charts.

After the success of the previous album, Costello teamed up with The Attractions once again and they were soon back in the studio. They attempted to move on from their previous album, with Costello refusing to be pigeon-holed into one genre.

The recording took place at DJM, London but this didn't last long and they soon moved to Eden. Drug taking going on between the various members hampered progress and they didn't get any more sober despite the shift in studios. Costello was happier with the sessions once they'd moved studios and they were completed in November.

The first single was released in December, *Clubland* was ultimately a disappointment, reaching No.60.

The album, *Trust*, followed in January 1981 and performed well in the UK, reaching No.9, but failed to spawn any successful singles with the second, *From A Whisper To A Scream* failing to chart completely.

The single was notable for featuring guest vocals from Glenn Tilbrook from Squeeze, this was due to Costello losing his voice during the sessions and Tilbrook offered to put down a guide vocal for the rest of the band. Costello was impressed and decided to do the song as a duet. Squeeze had already supported Costello & The Attractions in 1980 and Costello later produced their album *East Side Story*, released in May.

Trust is perhaps the most underrated album from Costello & The Attractions, an album that refuses to be put into one box and features a diverse number of influences.

After completing the A Tour To Trust tour in March, Costello & The Attractions headed to Nashville in May to record another LP. Costello had always taken an interest in country & western music and was heavily into it at the time of recording.

He was becoming bored of singing his own tunes and decided to change tact, by recording an album of country covers in an attempt to get his fanbase to listen to music they wouldn't have listened to voluntarily. He'd originally planned to record an album of ballads, including covering Frank Sinatra, but it ultimately didn't happen.

The recording took eight days to complete and the album, *Almost Blue*, was released in October. Despite being far removed from any of the material they'd previously released and being described by Trouser Press as "a dud", it performed well in the UK, peaking at No.7, an improvement on the previous album.

In true Costello fashion, the cover featured a warning label which stated; "This album contains country & western music and may cause offence to narrow minded listeners". It shows that Costello was willing to try fresh challenges and explore a completely alien genre, he also knew that some of his fanbase wouldn't be on board and also the critics, hence the rather witty message on the cover.

Almost Blue spawned the No.6 single *Good Year For The Roses*, which was released prior to the album in September. A further single, *Sweet Dreams*, appeared in December but barely troubled the charts, peaking at No.60.

In between the recording and the release of the album, Costello & The Attractions performed a short tour of Sweden in July and in December, they saw out the year on the Almost '82 Tour which came to an end in Dublin in January 1982.

The decision to record *Almost Blue* had been a brave one, but commercially it floundered. It was time for the next album and they headed to AIR Studios for a twelve week session.

It was needed, as much of the material hadn't been written. They also spent a week in Devon rehearsing and emerged with an album's worth of songs. These were then recorded, although some were re-written and restructured in the studio.

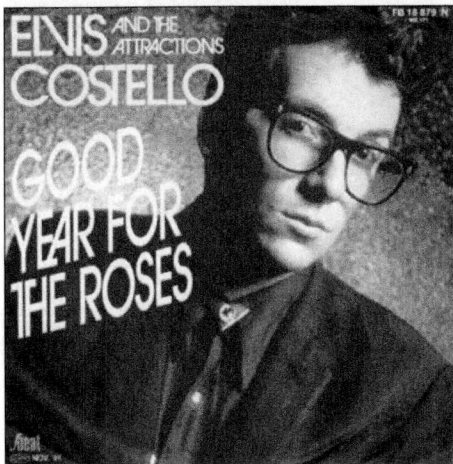

The recording engineer and co-producer for the sessions was Geoff Emerick, he'd worked with The Beatles and was producing Paul McCartney's *Tug of War* at the same time. The first single, *You Little Fool*, was released in June but failed to get any higher than No.52.

The finished album, *Imperial Bedroom*, was released in July and was an eclectic mix of different styles. It was a critical success, reaching No.6, and praised heavily by the critics, even being included in *NME*'s Top 10 Albums of the Year at the end of 1982.

The album was followed by another single, *Man Out Of Time*, which performed even worse than the last, reaching No.58.

The band were soon out on the road promoting the album and completed a massive three month tour of America and Canada before heading back to the UK in September for the Bedrooms of Britain Tour. This coincided with the release of the single *From Head To Toe*, which reached No.43. They ended the year with two nights at the Royal Albert Hall.

Although their albums were relatively successful, the singles were faring less well and the hits had dried up by 1983, the last Top 10 hit had been *A Good Year For The Roses* in 1981.

Costello decided the next album would be produced by Clive Langer and Alan Winstanley, who had been producing Madness. He also released his own single, as 'The Imposter', with *Pills and Soap* being released in May, reaching No.16.

A short UK tour beckoned in June, where they played Belfast, Dublin, Loughborough, Norwich, Liverpool, Canterbury and London before the next single, *Everyday I Write The Book*, was released in July and quickly followed by the album *Punch The Clock* in early August. Prior to the release, they headed to the US for the month long Clocking In Across America Tour before returning to the UK in October to play the Clocking In Across the UK Tour!

The tour came to an end in Bradford in November and they played on *The Tube* before they jetted off to Brussels to begin the Clocking In Across Europe Tour which saw them take in Utrecht, Paris, Zurich, Vienna, Berlin, Copenhagen, Stockholm, Lund, Gothenburg, Oslo and Hamburg before returning to the UK at the end of November. In and amongst the relentless touring, the album performed well and peaked at No.3, the highest placing since *Get Happy!!* hit No.2 in 1980. The album was later listed at No.1 in the *NME*'s Albums of the Year for 1983 and featured a number of guest musicians such as the TKO Horns and Afrodiziak.

By 1984, tensions were plaguing the band, mostly between Costello and Bruce Thomas but not exclusively. They headed into Sarm West Studios, London in February with Langer and Winstanley. The finished result was *Goodbye Cruel World*, released in June. The album was a complete failure and the bubble had been well and truly burst.

Although it did reach No.10 in the charts, it took a hammering from the critics. Costello has since acknowledged that he knew the album was going to be a failure but was forced to release it as he would have taken a big financial hit had he not done so.

The album was far removed from anything they'd released up to this point, relying on electronics and was far too polished. It can be argued that Costello's best music was the uncomplicated stuff, something that is lacking on this album. One amusing note is the credits section where Steve Nieve is credited under his alias of Maurice Worm providing "random racket"!

June also saw the release of the single *I Wanna Be Loved* which performed well and hit No.25. Following the recording of the album, Costello ditched The Attractions and embarked on a solo tour across America, his first solo tour since 1977. He returned and toured with The Attractions across Australia, New Zealand and the UK before seeing the year out with a solo European tour.

Costello & The Attractions were relatively quiet in 1985, playing just one gig, a miner's benefit in London. Costello however continued to be busy and most notably appeared at Live Aid singing a cover of *All You Need Is Love* by The Beatles.

The Attractions weren't invited and this caused tension between them and Costello, annoyed that he'd played the show without them.

Costello then threw himself into recording a solo album which would be credited to The Costello Show. It was intended for The Attractions to play on half the album but due to conflict between them, only one track was completed and the sessions involving them were disastrous. Steve Nieve additionally played piano on another track.

The album, *King of America*, was released in February and reached No.11. Relations were strained due to Costello's willingness to work with other musicians and the band were beginning to fall apart. They'd worked together almost non-stop for a decade and it had taken its toll, Costello had also been venturing into solo work as early as 1984, perhaps a sign that it was all coming to an end.

The sessions for the new album were a particularly fraught affair with the tension between Costello and the rest of the band being ratcheted up a few notches throughout the recording. Despite this, it saw Nick Lowe come back to work as producer, his first involvement since 1980. *Blood & Chocolate* was released in September and reached No.16 in the charts.

It was a welcome return to the raw and intense albums that'd gone beforehand. In October, the band headed to the US for one final tour before heading to Europe in November where they played in Sweden, France, Holland and Italy before arriving in London for six back-to-back gigs at the Royalty Theatre, London. Gigs in Dublin and Edinburgh followed before they played two back-to-back nights at the Royal Court Theatre, Liverpool in December.

They played three more shows in January 1987 at the Royal Albert Hall before appearing at Glastonbury in June. Costello was the headline act and began the gig playing solo before the curtain dropped to reveal The Attractions who played until the end of the set. Sadly, this would be their last show together.

Reunion

After three years as a solo artist, in 1990, Costello wanted to record a new album with The Attractions but it came to nothing, with contractual negotiations breaking down before anything was recorded.

Two years later, Costello was in the studio working on some new songs and had already planned to have Pete Thomas to drum on the tracks, he'd worked with Thomas after parting company with The Attractions and Nick Lowe was recruited to play bass. Then, after a chance meeting with Steve Nieve, Costello invited him to the sessions to play keyboards.

Songs were recorded although Lowe declined to play on some of them. Mitchell Froom was producing the album and his wife Suzanne Vega was working with Bruce Thomas. Costello and Thomas had not spoken for a number of years but Costello invited him along to play bass on the songs Lowe had declined. These sessions led to the album *Brutal Youth* and was recorded over the course of 14 months, beginning in December 1992 and finally ending in February 1994. Steve Nieve and Pete Thomas played on every track, while Bruce Thomas played on five tracks (Nick Lowe played bass on the other seven).

Despite not being planned as a reunion, the label were keen to push the album as a Costello & The Attractions release. The eventual album didn't mention The Attractions but the collaboration paved the way for a full reunion in 1994 and they embarked on a tour of the US & Canada in May, including appearances on the *Late Show with David Letterman* and *The Larry Sanders Show*.

They played Glastonbury in June and shows in France, Germany and Denmark before the UK tour began in July with three back-to-back shows at the Royal Albert Hall. Shows in Liverpool, Newcastle and Glasgow followed before they toured Europe at the end of July and then Japan in September.

Costello & The Attractions were quiet in 1995 and only performed occasional shows. including a gig at Shepherd's Bush Empire in May, a festival in Denmark in July and then five back-to-back shows at the Beacon Theatre, New York in August. They also appeared on *Later...Live with Jools Holland* and *Late Show with David Letterman* and spent some time in the studio working on the album *All This Useless Beauty*, which was released in 1996, the final release credited to Elvis Costello & The Attractions.

Costello played some intimate gigs with Steve Nieve on the piano without involvement from either Thomas. The group then went on tour, first in Europe, before fitting in a number of UK gigs before heading to the US for the final time in August. They then performed a short tour of Japan culminating in the final Costello & The Attractions gig on September 15th 1996 in Nagoya, Japan. Although Steve Nieve and Pete Thomas have consistently worked with Costello since, this marked the last time Costello and Bruce Thomas played together.

Finally, there was a reunion in 2003 when they were inducted into the Rock 'n' Roll Hall of Fame.

Thomas took to the stage for the induction but stormed off when he picked up his award. Costello played a short set with Steve Nieve and Pete Thomas but Bruce was not involved. Costello had commented in an article with *Rolling Stone* when asked if Bruce Thomas would be playing on stage with the rest of The Attractions; "I only work with professional musicians. As far as I know he isn't a professional musician, so I don't imagine so"[5].

Releases on 2 Tone:

I Can't Stand Up For Falling Down (1979).

Where are they now?

Elvis Costello
Guitar and Vocals, 1977-1987

Away from The Attractions, Costello has enjoyed a wide and varied career and has had much success. He continues to tour and record to this day. He has worked with Paul McCartney, Nick Lowe, Madness, The Brodsky Quartet, The Pogues and Diana Krall. He also became an occasional TV presenter, filling in for David Letterman on *Late Show with David Letterman* in 2003 and presenting his own series *Spectacle: Elvis Costello With...* in 2008 and 2009. Costello also published his memoirs *Unfaithful Music & Disappearing Ink* in 2015. He now tours with his new band The Imposters, which includes Steve Nieve and Pete Thomas. Aside from the countless awards he has received for his music, Costello accepted an OBE for services to music when he was nominated in the 2019 Birthday Honours list. He currently resides in Vancouver, Canada with his wife.

Steve Nieve
Keyboards, 1977-1987

Nieve wasn't too worried when The Attractions broke up as he was in demand as a session musician. His CV can boast of work with David Bowie, Squeeze, Kirsty MacColl and Madness. He replaced Mike Barson when he left Madness in 1984 and remained with the band for two years before they broke up in 1986.

He also played piano in JB's Allstars, featuring on their 2 Tone single, *The Alphabet Army*. Away from his session work, Nieve featured on Jonathan Ross's show *The Last Resort with Jonathan Ross* leading the house band, known as Steve Nieve and The Playboys.

Now living in France with his wife Muriel and still tours with Elvis Costello as part of The Imposters. He ran his own *Daily Improvisation* show on Facebook Live during the coronavirus pandemic in 2020 playing the piano, a couple of the editions featured special guest appearances from Elvis Costello!

Bruce Thomas

Bass, 1977-1987, 1994-1996

After The Attractions split up, Thomas went on to work with Billy Bragg and Suzanne Vega before he began a writing career, releasing *The Big Wheel* in 1990. This caused a rift between him and Costello as the book was a memoir that although the key characters were all recognisable, they were never actually named, and one unsavoury character was said to be based on Costello. Despite this, Thomas did reunite with Costello and the rest of The Attractions between 1994 and 1996 but the rift continued and Thomas has not played with Costello since. Although he did join them on stage in 2003 when they were inducted into the Rock 'n' Roll Hall of Fame, he didn't join the rest of The Attractions for the live performance that followed. Thomas is now a best-selling author and has released a number of publications since 1990, including three on Bruce Lee, *Fighting Spirit, Beyond The Limits* and *The Tao of Bruce Lee* and also released his autobiography *Rough Notes* in 2015.

Pete Thomas

Drums, 1977-1987, 1994-1996

When The Attractions broke up in 1986, Thomas continued to work with Elvis Costello, drumming on the albums *Spike* (1989), *Mighty Like A Rose* (1991) and *Kojak* (1995).

He also toured with Costello's live band The Rude 5 between 1989 and 1991. He reunited with the rest of The Attractions in 1994, touring and recording with them until 1996. Thomas reunited with Costello once more in 2001 to record the album *When I Was Cruel* and although credited to Elvis Costello, his new band was now known as The Imposters. Thomas continues to tour with The Imposters. Away from Costello, Thomas has been a successful session musician, working with Graham Parker, Suzanne Vega, Neil Finn, Sheryl Crow, Wild Colonials, Tasmin Archer amongst others and became a member of Squeeze in 1993. He played on their album *Some Fantastic Place* and also joined them for their tour in support of the album. He is now living in Los Angeles with his wife Judy and plays local gigs in LA with Davey Faragher and Val McCallum as the band Jackshit when he's not touring with Costello.

Pete Thomas

(Pic. Gillian Flanagan-Jones)

The Bodysnatchers

Nicky Summers worked on a London market and was a regular on the music scene. She had joined a punk band but they'd never managed to play a gig.

Her musical tastes began to stray towards reggae and ska and she wanted to form her own all-girl band. Summers had become friendly with Jane Summers (no relation), who'd travelled to London from Portsmouth with the intention of joining a band and was sleeping on Nicky's bedroom floor. Jane was a drummer and had brought her drum kit with her from Portsmouth.

In order to put her band together, Nicky placed adverts in the music press asking for "rude girls", and after wading through the dirty phone calls, she'd recruited her members by September 1979. Jane Summers was in, Sarah-Jane Owen and Stella Barker had seen the ad and joined, Penny Leyton had spotted it on a notice board at college and Miranda Joyce was still at school when she joined.

Summers' conditions for being in the band were simple; turn up regularly for rehearsals. The line-up consisted of; Nicky Summers (bass), Penny Leyton (keyboards), Sarah-Jane Owen (lead guitar), Jane Summers (drums), Miranda Joyce (saxophone) and Stella Barker (rhythm guitar).

The rehearsals were going well but the band were missing a singer and Summers struck gold when she went to watch a band called Sta-Prest at the Greyhound, Fulham one night. Also at the gig was a young civil servant called Rhoda Dakar and she had been talking to Shane MacGowan, a friend of Summers and a regular on the London music scene. MacGowan introduced Dakar to Summers, who asked her if she'd like to join a band.

Summers later said; "Rhoda was the last to join, I just saw her image and everything and thought God! I've never seen anything like it. I just went up to her and just asked her if she could sing. She said "yeah" and came down to the next rehearsal and that was that"[1].

The rehearsals intensified and three nights a week they could be found in rehearsal rooms on Royal College Street, London learning their instruments. This continued for around seven weeks and they emerged playing their own modern version of rocksteady.

It was time to play a show and Nicky Summers spoke to Shane MacGowan, who said they could support his band The Nips at the Windsor Castle, Maida Vale. However, they needed a name and after rejecting Nicky Summers' initial suggestion of Pussy Galore, decided on The Bodysnatchers, which was simply the name they all hated the least! The band logo was designed by Sarah Jane Owen and Penny Leyton, both of them were art graduates.

The first gig took place in November 1979 and the audience contained Jerry Dammers, Pauline Black, Juliet De Vie and Richard Branson! The gig wasn't bad for a first attempt though they seemed to fall apart towards the end of their set. They impressed the audience though as Richard Branson expressed an interest in signing them and Dammers felt they were suited to 2 Tone.

Before their next gig, they practised hard and by the time the gig came around, they were much more competent and confident. Following this gig, they were offered a support slot on The Selecter's upcoming Too Much Pressure Tour which was due to begin in February 1980.

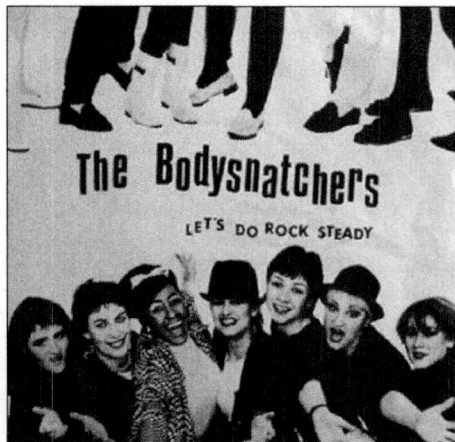

The Bodysnatchers
LET'S DO ROCK STEADY

Gaz Mayall was a friend of Nicky Summers and he suggested that she wrote an anthem so she went away and wrote *Ruder Than You*. Another song that was written around this time was *The Boiler*, a daring number about rape which began as a monologue by Rhoda Dakar while the band jammed with their instruments.

They continued to gig around the capital and were becoming popular, a lot of this was down to their apparent association with 2 Tone. Their early setlist contained mostly covers of old Trojan and ska favourites such as *Double Barrel, Let's Do The Rocksteady, 007 (Shanty Town)* and *Monkey Spanner*. They were nowhere near ready but were enjoying themselves. The Bodysnatchers were in the unique position of learning their instruments on the job and it seemed that the mistakes they made on stage added to their appeal. As Nicky Summers commented in an interview; "Even if a band is lousy, or just not very competent like us, you'll still get more out of seeing someone like us because you'll be dancing".[1]

Towards the end of 1979, the band's popularity went through the roof, they appeared in a December edition of *Sounds* and a deal on 2 Tone was becoming inevitable. 2 Tone was now the biggest thing in the country and at the height of its powers, the rumours that they wanted to sign The Bodysnatchers just wouldn't go away. Horace Panter spoke about this in *Record Mirror*; "I'm not sure if it's too early for some of the groups. Sometimes I get a bit worried. Like if we sign The Bodysnatchers, what are we letting them in for?"[2].

Eventually, Jerry Dammers informed them that he was offering them a two-single deal on the label. However, it wasn't a simple case of accepting, there were other offers on the table. EMI were interested and Richard Branson offered them an album deal with the opportunity of recording in Memphis! The majority voted against it as they did with the EMI deal. Eventually, five of the seven members voted to sign with 2 Tone.

Summers was one of the two, feeling that 2 Tone was a safe and predictable option.

The rise had been incredible, though they were thrown in at the deep end and found themselves in a business they hardly knew a thing about. They didn't even have a manager and any business decisions would be taken by the seven of them as a collective. As part of the deal with 2 Tone, they went into the studio to lay down the tracks for their first single. Roger Lomas would be on hand to produce, having already produced The Selecter by now.

Chrysalis wanted The Bodysnatchers to release a cover of Dandy Livingstone's *(People Get Ready) Let's Do The Rocksteady* as the first single but some of the band wanted to release *The Boiler*. It was soon decided that it would be commercial suicide to release it as their debut single. *Let's Do Rock Steady* was a part of their live set and considered a safe option, it sounded good and wasn't controversial. *Ruder Than You* was chosen as the flip side. The reasons for recording *Let's Do Rock Steady* were discussed by Jane Summers in *Smash Hits*; "We didn't set out to record a cover version because many of the other 2 Tone bands had found success that way. We found that none of our other material was strong enough at that point, and that *Rock Steady*, which has a catchy tune and simple words, had always gone down particularly well with audiences" [3].

Around this time, Frank Murray, who had been on tour with The Specials in America, became the manager of The Bodysnatchers on the suggestion of Rick Rogers. However, this arrangement only lasted two months before he left the post. Murray wasn't replaced throughout the band's life. The Bodysnatchers was a democracy, with all seven members having an equal vote. This probably went against them as this was the time they needed managerial guidance the most. They were still relatively new in the business and unaware of their surroundings, they needed someone who was able to look after that side of the band, but it never came.

The Bodysnatchers joined the Too Much Pressure Tour in February and were initially bottom of the bill. A bit of good fortune came their way when Holly & The Italians quit the tour just a few dates in. They were getting lots of abuse from the crowd and they weren't a good fit for the bill, they weren't remotely 2 Tone or ska and it was an odd fit. Jane Summers later reflected on this and how it benefited the band; "Though I was sorry to see Holly go, I found things so much better when we were the second band on. The first band has the job of really warming the audience up, most of whom are still arriving and also it means that you are very rushed". They were replaced by Swinging Cats and this saw The Bodysnatchers move up the bill. The single was released in March to coincide with the tour and entered the charts at No.44. It went on to peak at No.22 and The Bodysnatchers were thrust into the public consciousness for the first time when they appeared on *Top of the Pops*. Their appearance came on March 20th 1980. They appeared once again on April 10th and this appearance saw a hilarious moment where Jane Summers threw her drumsticks in the air and decided to dance around the rest of the band!

Stella Barker (Pic. Gillian Flanagan-Jones)

95

By April, The Bodysnatchers became the fifth 2 Tone band to record a Peel session and this saw them record versions of; *What's This?, Happy Time Tune, The Boiler* and *The Ghosts of the Vox Continental*. Some of The Bodysnatchers appeared on *Tiswas* in April and were soaked with water while locked in a cage with some of The Specials, The Beat and John Peel!

They were receiving a lot of attention in the music press by now, they had become pin-ups mostly due to the fact that they were an all-girl band. It would be stupid to expect the press to understand that they were much more than that. Miranda Joyce felt that being an all-girl band definitely helped them, commenting in May 1980's *Smash Hits*; "Being all girls helped us a lot, merely because it's still a novelty to find seven females in one band - because music is still very much a male dominated field".

Joyce laughed off the idea of having men in the band; "I don't think I would have joined a group if there had been men involved. Boys usually start learning an instrument at about 14 or 15 and as we were all joining to learn as we went along, it would have made us look ridiculous"[3].

The Peel session had allowed the public to listen to *The Boiler*, which had been a staple in their live set for months. The term "boiler" is a derogatory term to describe women that are perceived as ugly and a song was born. Anyone who has listened to the song will agree that it is a challenging piece of music and rather disturbing. However, that is the whole point and shows that the band weren't scared of tackling tough subjects that needed to be spoken about. It's a shame that no one was daring enough to release it as a single during the band's life though Jerry Dammers would later adapt the song and release it with The Special AKA. John Peel once described it as a "thoroughly chilling piece" on his radio show. The song would get a muted response from the audiences, mostly due to the subject and because it was a standout song in the set, the only one you couldn't really dance to.

Nicky Summers has since said; "The audience reaction was generally stunned silence. They didn't used to even clap hardly after we played it, but they were definitely transfixed by the song"[4].

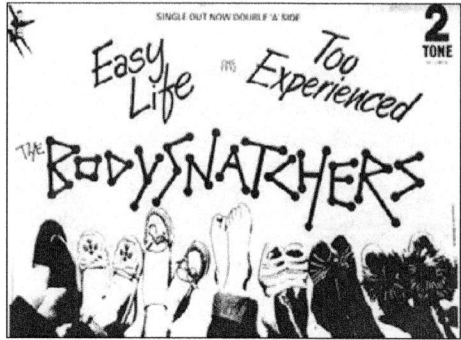

Advert for the release of Easy Life/Too Experienced.

The Bodysnatchers headlined their own tour in May, playing 18 dates which culminated in a Camden Town show. Then, they were back in the studio to record the second single and Jerry Dammers was persuaded by Frank Murray to produce it.

Another original they'd written was *Easy Life*, a feminist anthem. The song is a political statement which discusses women rejecting the easy life and actually challenging themselves. It also shows the potential that The Bodysnatchers had as a political band. This would be recorded alongside *Too Experienced,* a cover of a Winston Francis song. The songs were in the can before Dammers decided *Too Experienced* needed a tambourine on it and he played it himself!Only Jane and Nicky Summers were in the studio at the time. The single was pencilled in for a July release.

The Specials organised a seaside tour of the UK for June and The Bodysnatchers and The Go-Gos joined as the support bands. The tour spanned two weeks of June and saw them take in Skegness, Blackpool, Colwyn Bay, Portsmouth, Southend, Margate, Hastings, Bournemouth, Worthing, Great Yarmouth, Aylesbury, Barrow, Bridlington and Leeds although we are still trying to find the seaside in Leeds!

The second single, *Easy Life*, was released in July and despite being a cult favourite these days, it barely troubled the charts and peaked at a lowly No.50. The label was beginning to fade and The Bodysnatchers were starting to follow suit. Divisions began to develop in the band and Jane Summers was sacked in mid 1980. She was quickly replaced by Judy Parsons, who had been playing with The Mistakes, just in time for some shows. Parsons joined The Bodysnatchers full time shortly afterwards.

THE BODYSNATCHERS

The band appeared on their own sticker in 1980

Despite the low chart placing of *Easy Life*, another Peel session followed in September. Four songs were recorded; *Hiawatha, Mixed Feelings, Private Eye* and *The Loser*. The popularity of 2 Tone was waning as 1980 progressed resulting in falling record sales and a poor run in the charts. The Bodysnatchers became the first band not to hit the Top 40 but were followed by Rico and Swinging Cats who failed to chart with their singles, the two that followed *Easy Life*.

The Bodysnatchers headlined their own tour and also supported Toots & The Maytals in September. However, after a year of relentless touring and recording, Nicky Summers wanted to take a break to write new material and decide which direction they wanted to head in. Other members of the band were blinded by the fame and decided they wanted to be wealthy. Musical differences began to occur. Summers and Dakar wanted to continue being a political band but the rest didn't want to lose the momentum they'd gathered and wanted to be a pop band.

By October, it had started to fall apart, with arguments continually breaking out and this came to a head before a gig in Manchester with two members falling out. Nicky Summers was also at loggerheads with the label. Despite being on 2 Tone, Chrysalis were running things and they were marketing The Bodysnatchers as an all-girl pop group rather than the political band she'd originally intended. She has since spoken about this; "I felt there was a lot of pressure on us to 'perform', keep up a certain image, and churn out chart hits. We were not given space to develop. After one interview for a magazine I was reproved by a rep from Chrysalis for not wearing a short skirt (I was in jeans). It wasn't what I'd signed up for"[4].

Relations had broken down after that and they booked a farewell gig at Camden Music Machine in November. This marked the first anniversary of their first ever gig. The Bodysnatchers released a statement citing musical differences as the reason for the breakup. Some of them wanted to be more political whereas the others wanted to venture into the pop world. Rhoda Dakar and Nicky Summers went on to record *The Boiler* with The Special AKA and the rest of the band formed The Belle Stars so it's easy to work out who wanted to follow each path!

The Bodysnatchers featured twice on film following their breakup, firstly in December on *Alright Now* alongside The Selecter, where they performed a version of *What's This?* and this was followed by their appearance on the 1981 film and LP *Dance Craze* where *Easy Life, Let's Do Rock Steady* and *007 (Shanty Town)* were featured on the film. The footage demonstrates the band's talent and their frantic version of *Easy Life* is far superior to the studio version.

The Bodysnatchers is a fine example of "what could have been". Aside from the Peel sessions, *Dance Craze* and various bootlegs, they released just two singles and four tracks. There has never really been anything like The Bodysnatchers since.

Despite only being together for 14 months, they are still loved over 40 years later. That is quite something for a band that only released two singles. Rhoda Dakar was a great frontwoman and her commanding presence on the stage was something else. She looked great and inspired many a rude-girl thanks to her style and magnificent beehive hairdo. Many more avenues could have been explored musically and politically and the band's story is one of missed opportunities. In hindsight, they should have released *The Boiler*, and it would have had much more of an effect being released by The Bodysnatchers than the eventual release by The Special AKA. The Belle Stars went on to achieve moderate commercial success but mostly thanks to novelty songs although at least one Bodysnatchers original was recorded by them when *Hiawatha* was released as their debut single in 1981.

Dakar aimed to record the album that The Bodysnatchers should have recorded back in 1980 and recorded an album's worth of material. The album contained recordings of; *Easy Life, The Ghost of the Vox Continental, Happy Time Tune, 007, Private Eye, Too Experienced, The Loser, Mixed Feelings, Hiawatha, Let's Do Rocksteady*. She recruited her own band for the recordings; Lenny Bignell (guitar), Lynval Golding (guitar), Horace Panter (bass), Mark Claydon (drums), Sean Flowerdew (keyboards) and Karl Wirrmann (saxophone). Dakar played a number of shows off the back of the release and occasionally performed under The Bodysnacthers name for these shows though she was quick to dismiss the rumours of a reunion.

Releases on 2 Tone:

Let's Do Rocksteady (1980).

Easy Life (1980).

Ticket from Rhoda Dakar show, billed as The Bodysnatchers

The Bodysnatchers are one of the only 2 Tone bands that have never reunited in any form and after The Belle Stars broke up in 1986, the members went their separate ways. However, Rhoda Dakar reactivated the name in 2015 and launched a crowdfunding effort to fund the recording of an album to celebrate the band's 35th anniversary. She had been approached numerous times over the years to record the "lost" Bodysnatchers album and eventually decided to do it.

Where Are They Now?

Rhoda Dakar
Vocals, 1979-1980
Dakar has probably been involved with every band on 2 Tone at one point or another. Aside from The Bodysnatchers, she guested on The Specials second album *More Specials* and joined them on tour in 1981, also appearing on *Top of the Pops* when they performed *Ghost Town*.

Rhoda Dakar in 2016

She then released her second solo album (with Nick Welsh) *Back to the Garage* in 2008 and appeared on the Madness song *On The Town* from their 2009 album *The Liberty of Norton Folgate*. She continued to perform live for a number of years before she decided to record an album of Bodysnatchers material, including songs that were unreleased. This saw the release of *Rhoda Dakar Sings The Bodysnatchers* in 2015 and it has since been re-released in 2019 for the 40th Anniversary of the band. Rhoda also released the 7" singles *The Lotek Four Vols 1 & 2* in 2016 and 2018 respectively.

Rhoda has since toured with The Specials, as the support act and DJ on their 2016 UK tour (where she would join them on stage for their encore of *You're Wondering Now*) and The Selecter on their 2018 and 2019 tours of the world. She has also toured with her own band and in 2020 toured Australia and New Zealand for the first time as well as continuing with her DJ spots. She was going to support Toots & The Maytals in 2020 on their final tour before COVID-19 curtailed it.

Dakar remained with the band after the breakup and recorded *The Boiler*, credited to Rhoda & The Special AKA. She remained with the band until it was dissolved in 1985. Dakar also provided the backing vocals on *The Feeling's Gone* by The Apollinaires in 1982 and this led to a working relationship with the Swinging Laurels.

Dakar became involved with Red Wedge and was the chair of the steering committee. She seemed to leave the music business completely and only made occasional appearances on releases by Dr. Robert, Palm Skin Productions, The Communards and Apollo 440.

In the early 2000s, Pauline Black and Jennie Mathias asked Dakar if she'd like to work with them on a project, it was ultimately short-lived but she began writing new material and continued to tour, later releasing her own solo album in 2007, *Cleaning in a Another Woman's Kitchen* with Nick Welsh. She also joined Welsh's band Skaville UK appearing on both of their albums *1973* (2007) and *Decadent* (2008).

Nicky Summers
Bass, 1979-1980
Summers wasn't invited to join the Belle Stars and carried on working with Rhoda Dakar, playing bass guitar on *The Boiler*, credited to Rhoda & The Special AKA. She has had an online presence in the last few years, running her own blog talking about her career in the music business.

Miranda Joyce
Alto Saxophone, 1979-1980
Joyce left The Bodysnatchers in 1980 and formed The Belle Stars with Sarah-Jane Owen, Stella Barker, Judy Parsons and Penny Leyton. They recorded and toured for six years before breaking up in 1986. Since the band broke up, Joyce has had no involvement in recording music but remained in the music industry by doing the make-up for a number of bands. She had an extended period as the make-up artist for Tears for Fears before she went into the fashion industry.

Thanks to this, Joyce worked with Kate Moss in her early days and also Jenny Howarth and Naomi Campbell amongst others. Joyce continues to work as a freelance make-up artist in the fashion business.

Jane Summers
Drums, 1979-1980
Summers was the original drummer in the band played on the records but left to be replaced by Judy Parsons. Summers has proved elusive and there appears to be no trace of her since she left The Bodysnatchers in 1980.

Sarah-Jane Owen
Lead Guitar, 1979-1980
Miss SJ continued with The Belle Stars but left in 1986. Having studied Art at the Royal College in 1977 she went on to work as a clothing designer. She later relocated to California to run her own business SunJay's Medicine and is an artist, healer, teacher and medicine woman. Owen is also a certified shamanic practitioner and sound healer, a yoga and sacred dance instructor, naturalist, herbalist and aromatherapist.

Stella Barker
Rhythm Guitar, 1979-1980
Barker was one of the four members that left to form The Belle Stars shortly after The Bodysnatchers broke up. They enjoyed some short-lived success in the pop charts before they broke up in 1986. Barker was also in a relationship with Neville Staple in the early 1980s and they launched the record label Shack Records in 1981. Barker later worked as a corporate events manager in Cheltenham but is now living in France.

Penny Leyton
Keyboards, 1979-1980
Leyton joined The Belle Stars in 1980 and remained in the band until the breakup in 1986. She has since left music and has worked as a graphic designer, illustrator and digital artist at Dreamworks. Has also worked as an interface designer, portraitist, printmaker and mannequin painter but now works as a full time graphic designer and web developer.

Judy Parsons
Drums, 1980
Parsons joined the band after the departure of the original drummer Jane Summers, she had previously been playing with The Mistakes before being invited to cover for Summers' absence, she soon joined full time. However, this didn't last long as the band broke up and she joined the other members in forming The Belle Stars. Parsons remained in the band until 1984 and is now living in Scotland and is no longer involved in music.

(Pic. Gillian Flanagan-Jones)

Swinging Cats

Swinging Cats were formed in Coventry in 1979 by Toby Lyons and John Shipley after they'd met in the Hope & Anchor pub.

They decided to try and make some music together and Lyons played *Never On A Sunday* to Shipley, suggesting they cover the record. Shipley played the guitar and Lyons could play keyboards and they soon turned to Steve Wynne to play bass, up until recently he'd been playing with Neol Davies and Desmond Brown in Transposed Men.

"We first played together with a really tiny little drum machine at Toby's in Earlsdon, it was a laugh anyway. Then we got Billy in". Wynne is referring to Billy Gough, a local drummer who'd been approached to join the band. Gough's arrival had been preceded by the arrival of singer Jane Bayley, who remembers the time well; "At the time, the Swinging Cats were the most exciting thing that had ever happened to me! Until then, I'd only sung other people's songs at folk clubs in Coventry and Leeds".

Bayley was approached by Shipley to join the band; "John Shipley, a great guitar player in Coventry, asked if I fancied singing a couple of his songs with him that Jerry Dammers had said he could record on his 2 Tone label. Suddenly, talented local bass player Steve Wynne was on board and when a really good drummer called Billy Gough was persuaded to join us, we were a band!".

The origin of the band name is said to come from when they would rehearse in Billy Gough's garage where there wasn't enough room to swing a cat! They would also rehearse at the Green Shed, Coventry. Jane Bayley remembers the early days; "We rehearsed either in Billy's garage or in a friend's cellar in Radford and they all jammed and came up with more songs and chords. I felt a bit out of my depth because I couldn't jam, but I managed to put melodies and words to some of those songs".

Eventually the band started to get to somewhere and were producing a sound that they could identify with which had been drawn from their influences of muzak, Latin music, 1960s instrumental music and theme tunes.

"The result was a kind of dance-y ska with a tongue in cheek Latin flavour, and some fun cover versions like *The Avengers, Magic Roundabout, Never On A Sunday* and a Mantovani tribute tune".

The band started to venture out of Billy Gough's garage to play gigs around Coventry, The General Wolfe being a regular haunt of theirs. They played numerous gigs and began to get noticed.

They were soon joined by Chris Long who was a friend of Toby Lyons. "I have no idea of the date that I joined the band but Toby was my best mate so when he started out with John Shipley writing stuff I was aware of that. When they got the band together I somehow wangled my way in as a go-go dancer and percussionist!".

Swinging Cats continued to hone their craft and entered a Battle of the Bands contest, they ended up winning the heats of the competition but Jane Bayley departed soon afterwards. "The others played me a tape of my singing that sounded awful and they replaced me with a better singer, Val who was Jerry's girlfriend".

Val Webb was engaged to Jerry Dammers at the time and her arrival came just a week before the band were due in the final of the contest. Webb stepped in but had less than a week to learn and rehearse all the songs before the contest at the Latch Hall, Coventry. It was judged by Trevor Horn amongst others and Swinging Cats ended up winning, with their prize being a day's recording at Woodbine Studios, Leamington Spa. The competition also led to them appearing on the BBC show *Look Hear* where they performed, *Away* and *Never On A Sunday*, though the music appeared lost on the audience. Chris Long agrees; "The audience didn't get the band at all, they were young kids that were expecting the next Specials I guess".

The band had their first involvement with 2 Tone in February 1980 when Holly & The Italians pulled out of their support slot on The Selecter's Too Much Pressure Tour.

The band had experienced a torrid time with the audiences, being abused and suffering from constant crowd trouble. Swinging Cats replaced them, whilst The Bodysnatchers moved from bottom of the bill to second on the bill.

The lineup by now consisted of; Val Webb (vocals), John Shipley (guitar), Steve Wynne (bass), Billy Gough (drums), Toby Lyons (keyboards) and Chris Long (percussion & dancing). Various members also had highly amusing stage names, Val Webb was Pussy Purrfect, John Shipley was Vaughan Truevoice, Chris Long was Craig Guatemala, Toby Lyons was Tobi El Dorko and Steve Wynne was Wayne Riff.

The band were incredibly quirky and could have rivalled Bad Manners and Madness at the time for their on-stage antics, Chris Long's dancing had to be seen to be believed and he could even have been a precursor to Bez from the Happy Mondays, but with much more talent!

At the end of the tour, Val Webb left the band to be replaced by Jane Bayley; "The new line-up didn't work out and they asked me to come and sing again, they also said that they'd make sure we'd get foldback so I could hear myself!".

(Pic. Gillian Flanagan-Jones)

(Pic. Gillian Flanagan-Jones)

By now, Jerry Dammers had asked them to record a single on 2 Tone and were due in Woodbine Studios. Paul Heskett, an old friend of John Shipley, had returned to Coventry on holiday from university and Shipley asked him if he fancied playing saxophone with the band. Heskett decided to leave university and join Swinging Cats soon afterwards, joining them in the studio to record the single.

The sessions were thrown into turmoil with the shock departure of drummer Billy Gough, who decided to leave shortly before the recording. This saw The Specials drummer John Bradbury play on both sides of the record. Steve Wynne remembers it well; "I remember trying to get Billy to stay, he wasn't having it at all. John Bradbury stepped in for the single and did a great job...with no rehearsal!".

Gough had never really enjoyed the limelight, although the various members are complimentary of his musical talents, with Wynne comparing him to John Bonham.

The rest of the sessions went okay and the single was soon finished, though Wynne remembers it as a "messy take", and Dammers got to work mixing it though he took a while to do so.

The 'A' side was a tune called *Mantovani* and the Mantovani tribute tune that Jane Bayley mentioned they would play in the early days, it was credited to John Shipley but contained snippets of *Hear My Song Violetta* and *Speak To Me Of Love*. The flip side was a Swinging Cats original called *Away*, which they'd played on the *Look Hear* programme and was penned by John Shipley, Jane Bayley and Toby Lyons.

The single was eventually released in September as a double 'A' side and despite the first 20,000 copies being sold at the price of 50 pence, the record failed to reach the Top 40 and eventually sunk without a trace although Steve Wynne remembers that it hit No.96!

John Shipley, whilst being interviewed at the 2 Tone Village in March 2019, said that the band should have released a version of *Never On A Sunday* instead, Wynne tends to agree; "Yes I can see that logic, it's a good one!". Wynne is still complimentary about the single though; "It's good that we got that recorded, I'm glad about that, it sounds fresh".

Aside from The Specials releasing *Stereotype* in September, the single was a far cry from anything that'd been released on 2 Tone up to then and it's fair to say the critics weren't impressed. The *NME* rather unfairly asked the question; "Has the 2 Tone quality control gone on holiday or what?". If the critics and public alike were expecting another ska record then they were in for a shock. Swinging Cats didn't play ska in the same way The Specials and Madness did but opted more for muzak, with a lot of Latin influence. Where Jerry Dammers and The Specials had been influenced by the sounds of Prince Buster and Desmond Dekker, Swinging Cats took influence from 1960s pop and lots of different types of instrumental music. This is evident with *Mantovani* and Wynne has since revealed that they were influenced by The Harry Robinson Crew, their tune *The Bilbao Song* being a particular favourite of the band, their song *I Want To Be Happy* was based on it.

John Shipley later told the *NME*; "We want to make the sort of music you'd listen to while waiting for an ice cream in a cinema. Or in a dentist's waiting room. Having your teeth out needn't be so painful with The Swinging Cats"1. The Swinging Cats also contributed backing vocals to *Enjoy Yourself* on *More Specials* in the summer of 1980 but were uncredited. According to Steve Wynne, they were knocking around the studio at the time of recording and decided to join in the fun.

(Pic. Gillian Flanagan-Jones)

Jerry Dammers invited the band to support The Specials on the More Specials Tour which commenced in September. Before the start of the tour, the band had found their replacement for Billy Gough in the shape of Dick Burrows, better known as Dicky Doo! Jane Bayley was also replaced once again and Chris Long offered to step in, mostly because he knew all the words to the songs! Long remembers; "The More Specials Tour is memorable to me. Jane was replaced as the vocalist and like an idiot I put myself forward. I say "idiot" because it wasn't an easy job at all".

Long's first gig behind the microphone was held at the Hope & Anchor, London; "Most of Madness were there and it went okay for me in that small sweaty basement".

He had a shock on the first night of the tour though when he found that his surroundings were world's apart from that of the warm-up gig a few nights before. "The gig was at the Cornish Riviera in Newquay with a capacity of about 4,000, if I remember, it was massive anyway! When I stepped out in front of the crowd my breath was literally taken away and through nervousness I found it hard to breathe". Although after that initial shock he settled into his new role and remembers this was "ridiculously hard work, something like 36 gigs in 40 days".

The tour also led to a hilarious incident in Bristol where John Shipley was missing, the tour bus was ready and waiting but Shipley was nowhere to be seen. All of a sudden, Shipley appeared covered in oil as he'd been asleep under the bus all night!

The original concept for the cover of Mantovani though it was never used.
(Pic. Joe Kerrigan/John Shipley)

Unfortunately, the More Specials Tour was marred with outbreaks of violence and as the support band, Swinging Cats often bore the brunt of it, with violence breaking out during their set.

Perhaps the most documented incident occurred at Midsummer Common, Cambridge. Famously, The Specials refused to perform until the crowd calmed down and Terry Hall and Jerry Dammers were arrested and charged with inciting a riot. Before they took to the stage, Swinging Cats had been playing when a big gang of Cambridge United supporters broke into the gig and began to cause trouble. Steve Wynne takes up the story; "What a circus, it had the cops in. It wasn't usually violent, that gig was almost funny. Like watching goons on parade!".

Chris Long was directly involved in the trouble; "When we were on stage, I could see and hear a gang of about 30 Cambridge United fans, who had played Coventry the week before in the FA Cup. They'd rushed the door and were now heading straight towards me, arms raised, clapping and chanting". As the trouble worsened, one of the group jumped on stage to attack Long; "One jumped up on to the stage and was about to attack me but just in time, one of the roadies rushed out and clarted the attacker, he flew backwards in a reverse swan dive into the crowd - a vision I'll never forget!".

(Pic. Gillian Flanagan-Jones)

Swinging Cats promptly left the stage and didn't return though according to Wynne, it wasn't a factor in the eventual breakup; "it didn't cause the split, that just happened. We went on to the next gig okay". Despite this, Swinging Cats didn't last until the end of the tour, breaking up a few dates before the end. They were replaced by Team 23 for the last handful of gigs. The pressures and intensity of the tour and the failure of the single have since been cited as major factors in the breakup.

Unfortunately, because they only released one single on 2 Tone and broke up within a year, Swinging Cats are perhaps one of the least known 2 Tone bands, they also never really had a settled line-up, with numerous line-up changes throughout their short time as a band.

Their impact was significantly more than people realise, as Jerry Dammers has since credited John Shipley with influencing his change in musical tastes. With much of the early Specials output being ska, Dammers wanted to progress and move away from it. Shipley was heavily influenced by muzak, which is evident on the small number of recordings that are available of Swinging Cats. The Specials released *More Specials* in October 1980 and it was heavily influenced by muzak. Paul Heskett also contributed to the album by playing saxophone on *Sock It To Em' JB*.

As well as influencing The Specials, it is perhaps even less well known that Madness were also seemingly influenced by the Swinging Cats. John Shipley thinks that after some of the Madness lads had seen their gig at the Hope & Anchor, some of their songs had a more easy listening sound to them. Paul Heskett is of a similar opinion and thinks *Baggy Trousers* closely resembles *Mantovani* and has claimed that Chris Foreman and Lee Thompson told him that their 1981 single *Return of Los Palmos 7* was a tribute to the Swinging Cats. So despite only releasing one single, the Swinging Cats were far more influential and important than most give them credit for, hopefully this has now been put right!

There seems to be a consensus across the band members that there was so much more that they could have done. As the deal with 2 Tone had been a two-single deal, there was a follow-up single to *Mantovani* planned, but *Greek Tragedy* was never recorded due to the band splitting.

It has since been established that a version was recorded, albeit by John Shipley and a group of musicians including Rhoda Dakar in 1981, shortly before he joined The Special AKA.

Steve Wynne looks back with fondness; "It's a special band for me as we were experimenting. We laughed a lot, it was a train station of comings and goings". He firmly believes that Swinging Cats should have recorded an LP and has revealed that tapes still exist that the public have never heard; "We should've done an LP really, there are tapes though several need mixing". He also expresses regret at breaking up when they did; "Dennis Bovell was around at the time and still is as a reggae producer. He was an influence in the pirate radio stations around the Midlands. He wanted to produce Swinging Cats but the band split up in the middle of negotiations, some slight regret there".

No footage of the band is known to exist except the *Look Hear* performance although they were filmed for *Dance Craze* but were left out of the final cut. At least one Swinging Cats song ended up as a Special AKA song, *Night on the Tiles* appeared on the 1984 album, *In The Studio*, which featured John Shipley on guitar and he shared a songwriting credit with Jerry Dammers.

Reunion

The band remained dormant for almost 30 years before there was a reunion of sorts for 2 Tone's 30th anniversary in November 2009.

As part of the 2 Tone Trail, a plaque was unveiled at the site of the Hand & Heart, Coventry and the celebrations continued at The Dog & Trumpet when Paul Heskett and John Shipley performed on stage as Swinging Cats for the first time since 1980.

For the gig, Shipley recruited some local musicians; Dominic Hazell (bass), Terry Downes (drums) and Steve & Lindsay Eaton (vocals) to make up the rest of the band, Heskett took on keyboard duties as well as playing the saxophone.

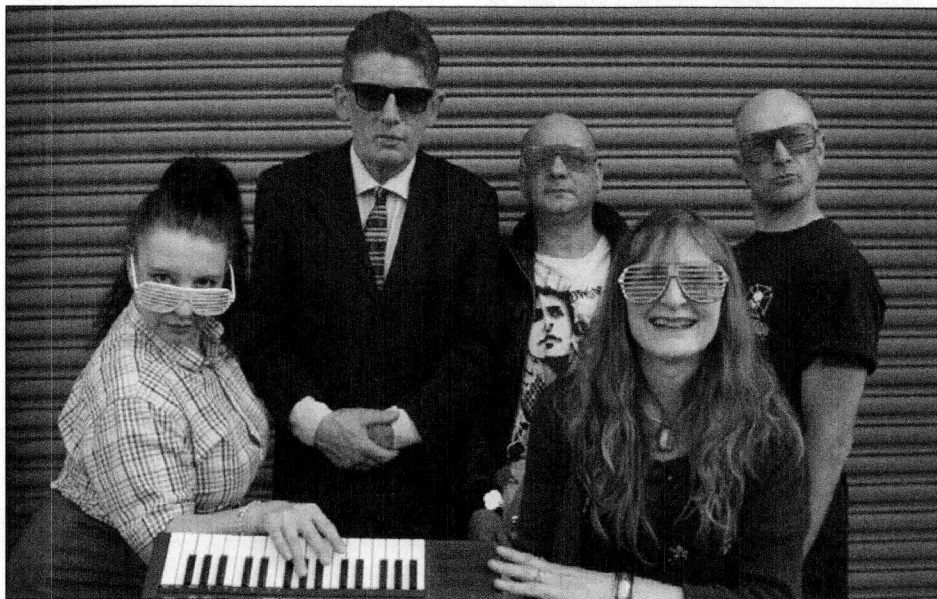

The Swinging Cats reunited in 2009 with John Shipley second from left. (Pic. Joe Kerrigan)

They played favourites such as *Away, Mantovani* and *Never On A Sunday* and it was hinted that the band could continue. Swinging Cats later played a number of gigs during the early 2010s in and around Coventry, with Shipley being the only original member at this point.

Releases on 2 Tone:

Mantovani (1980).

Where Are They Now?

John Shipley (Vaughan Truevoice)
Guitar, 1979-1980

(Pic. Joe Kerrigan)

John Shipley was once described as "the best guitarist in the world" by Jerry Dammers, he is certainly one of the most underrated musicians associated with 2 Tone. He formed Swinging Cats in 1979 with Toby Lyons and they drew heavily on Shipley's influences of muzak, John Barry soundtracks and other early 60s instrumentals, as well as some Mantovani thrown in for good measure. Shipley is often credited with influencing Jerry Dammers' decision to change the musical direction of The Specials for their second album *More Specials*, released in 1980. He later joined The Special AKA in late 1981 and first appeared on *The Boiler*, released in January 1982.

He remained in the band until it dissolved around 1985 and later played on Stan Campbell's 1987 solo album. Shipley remained in music and played with Pauline Black in The Supernaturals who became The Great Escape after a lineup change. Shipley saw out the 1980s playing with The Cosmics, co-founding them in 1988.

Shipley later reformed the Swinging Cats in 2009 for a one-off gig, eventually leading to more gigs in 2010 with a new lineup. He was also a member of Eletrik Custard, with his son Ethan until 2013 and also with Barb'd Wire and The Connections in the early 2010s. Shipley also guested with the Coventry band Ruder Than U occasionally.

Away from music, Shipley has worked in a variety of different professions over the years including as a chef, a scaffolder, a labourer, a pub cellarman and a cleaner as well as having his own record shop in Coventry Market. Shipley is sadly suffering from Parkinson's disease these days but can often be seen at the 2 Tone Village and is still a sharp dresser.

Toby Lyons (Tobi El Dorko)
Keyboards, 1979-1980
Lyons had been a co-founding member of the band with John Shipley and after the Swinging Cats broke up in late 1980, he joined the band Armalite with his former bandmate Billy Gough though soon joined forces with Terry Hall in 1984, forming The Colourfield with Karl Shale. The Colourfield recorded two albums and released some singles, the most successful being *Thinking of You* in 1985, before Hall pulled the plug in 1987. Lyons left music and went on to work in telesales before moving into design in 1992, teaching at Stockport College. He worked there until 2005 when he began to work at Sheffield Hallam University as a senior lecturer in graphic design until his retirement in 2018.

Valerie Webb (Pussy Purrfect)
Vocals, 1979
Webb was in a relationship with and later engaged to Jerry Dammers and lived at Albany Road at the height of 2 Tone.

The Specials 2 Tone | Rude Boy Two Tone Ska 2 Music Records Case & Skin for Samsung Galaxy
https://www.redbubble.com

She joined the Swinging Cats as singer to replace Jane Bayley though she only lasted one tour before she left, ironically her replacement was the woman she'd replaced! Webb later joined The Great Escape in the late 1980s, playing alongside her former bandmate John Shipley. She left Coventry some years ago and is now residing on the south coast with her husband but has recently been spotted at the 2 Tone Village.

Jane Bayley (Jane de la Swing)
Vocals, 1979, 1979-1980
Bayley was an original member of Swinging Cats but was replaced before the Battle of the Bands contest. She did rejoin but left again before the More Specials tour. Following her departure, Bayley moved to London and formed the band The Round-a-Way Round Chamber with her sister, Leigh, on clarinet, her partner Andre on trumpet and his sister Francoise on vocals, whilst Bayley played guitar and harmonium. Since 1990, she has been known as Jane Bom-Bane and has performed as a solo act with her songs, harmoniums and mechanical hats, which illustrate some of the songs. She collaborated with Nick Pynn for ten years before she opened her own music cafe in 2006, Bom-Banes in Brighton. She performs regular shows in the cafe as well as running the place and cooking!

Steve Wynne (Wayne Riff)
Bass, 1979-1980
Steve Wynne is another original member of the band and after the breakup, was invited to join Dexy's Midnight Runners in 1981. He only remained in the band for a short time, leaving in 1982, but did appear on *Top of the Pops* when the band performed *Jackie Wilson Said*, a now infamous performance with BBC showing a photo of darts player Jocky Wilson in the background! Wynne later played with the Blue Ox Babes in 1988 and also worked with Grande Fromage in 2008, directing their music video at Bom Bane's in Brighton, run by Jane Bayley! He continues to write and record his own music and is in the process of releasing some new material. Wynne is now living in London having moved away from Coventry some years ago and occasionally bumps into old friend Jerry Dammers.

Chris Long (Craig Guatemala)
Percussion & Dancing and later Vocals, 1979-1980
Chris Long was a DJ, having begun spinning the discs in 1979 under the name Rhythm Doctor. Long was good friends with Toby Lyons before he wangled his way into the band doubling up as go-go dancer and percussion player! Following the departure of the lead singer, he became the vocalist when they supported The Specials on the More Specials Tour in the latter half of 1980. After the band broke up, Long continued as the Rhythm Doctor and DJed all over the world. He teamed up with Jerry Dammers in 1986 to form the Artists Against Apartheid club in Covent Garden. Here, Long introduced house music and was one of a select few DJs that championed it in London, leading to the release of *Mister/Phuture* credited to Rhythm Doctor. He was also involved with 1988 house remix of *Nelson Mandela* which was released for Mandela's 75th birthday. The Rhythm Doctor can often be seen spinning his records in London and also ventures out to Estonia once a month for the same purpose. When he's not spinning discs, he can be found working in a record shop in London.

Paul Heskett (Vince Laredo)
Saxaophone, 1979-1980
Heskett joined the band quite late as he'd been away at university. Whilst in the band, he moonlighted with The Specials, playing saxophone on *Sock It To Em JB*, also appearing with them on the More Specials tour and later appeared on *Ghost Town* playing the flute. After The Specials broke up in 1981, Heskett left music and went on to work as Arthur C. Clarke's private secretary and even co-wrote his speech to the United Nations in 1982! He dipped his toes back in the water occasionally and played with Crunch, Imelda May, Pama International, Eletrik Custard, Roddy Radiation and even played with Hawkwind at a science fiction convention!

Heskett was also part of the Swinging Cats reunion in 2009 playing saxophone and piano. He later worked as a radiographer before his retirement and now lives in Evesham and can occasionally be seen at the 2 Tone Village, of which he is a patron. He has taken part in Sounding Off events in the past, the latest being in February 2019, he also made a guest appearance at John Shipley's in March 2019. He is currently working on some new music and hopes to release an album in the near future.

Billy Gough
Drums, 1979-1980
After the Swinging Cats broke up, Gough later joined the local band Armalite and was joined by Toby Lyons. They broke up in 1984 and he later went on to work in carpentry. He is now residing in Brighton and his daughter is the guitarist in the band Dream Wife.

Dick Burrows (Dicky Doo)
Drums, 1980
When Billy Gough left the band shortly before the recording of *Mantovani*, the Swinging Cats were left without a drummer. After John Bradbury had played on the record, they recruited Dick Burrows and he remained with the band for the rest of its life. After the breakup, Burrows went on to teach music for children.

Paul Heskett - Pic by Joe Kerrigan

Rico performing in 1977 - Pic by OC Roy

Rico

Rico Rodriguez had already been there and done it when he started working with The Specials in 1979, having played on a number of famous ska records from the 1950s onwards, working with Prince Buster, Dandy Livingstone and Laurel Aitken amongst others.

Rico had also recorded a number of solo efforts over the years, as far back as 1961 he'd released solo singles under his own name and that of Reco's All Stars, Rico And His Blue Boys and Rico All Stars.

His first solo album came in 1969 with *Reco In Reggae Land* where he paid tribute to Don Drummond, who'd passed away earlier that year, which was quickly followed by *Blow Your Horn*, credited to Rico & The Rudies. Rico was originally from Cuba but grew up in Jamaica before moving to London in 1961.

It would be impossible to list all the releases that he played on, but he was always busy and can be heard on ska records across the years. By 1976, he was signed to Island Records and released the solo album *Man From Wareika*. One of the contributors to the album was Dick Cuthell, he played on all the songs and also worked on the production of the album engineering some tracks, Cuthell and Rico were firm friends. The album was well received and is recognised as one of the first examples of a musician mixing jazz with reggae.

By 1979, Rico, still signed to Island Records, was approached by The Specials to play on their cover of *A Message To You Rudy*. Incidentally, he'd played on the 1967 original by Dandy Livingstone. This was released as a single and credited to The Specials featuring Rico. Rico also played on other songs on The Specials' first album and by the end of the recording process, was a member of the band, albeit an honorary member.Rico and Dick Cuthell would remain with The Specials until the breakup in 1981.

The purists would probably have been well aware of Rico but there were a lot of 2 Tone fans that were exposed to his music for the first time in 1979. His resurgence coming about thanks to his involvement with The Specials.

When he recorded with The Specials initially, he appeared with permission from Island Records, with whom he was still signed to. However, by 1980, he was no longer with Island and for the first time in a long number of years, was without a record deal. Jerry Dammers decided to release a Rico single on 2 Tone and the trombonist went into the studio to work on it. Dick Cuthell was also involved, working on the production of the single, co-producing and mixing the tracks.

Advertisement for Rico's 2 Tone single, Sea Cruise

From these sessions, a single emerged in October 1980 with a cover of Frankie Ford's *Sea Cruise* on the 'A' side and a cover of The Folks Bros' *Oh Carolina* on the 'B' side where Rico received a credit for the arrangement of the track. *Oh Carolina* had been produced by Prince Buster and released on Blue Beat Records in 1961 although Rico's version was simply titled *Carolina*.

Despite containing two accomplished tunes, the single failed to reach the charts, which followed the disappointment of the Swinging Cats' *Mantovani* performing poorly, the 2 Tone single that preceded *Sea Cruise*. The single was probably never expected to chart but it gave Rico the opportunity to put his music out there and it returned the favour for him playing with The Specials and giving them that authentic link to 1960s Jamaican ska.

In December, Rico joined The Specials for a Peel session where they recorded their own version of *Sea Cruise*, the song becoming a staple of their live set shortly afterwards.

The Specials would also occasionally play *Man From Wareika* and *Chiang Kai-Shek* during their live performances from 1980 onwards.

Soon after the recording of the single, Rico went into Joe Gibbs Studio in Kingston, Jamaica to work on a solo album, to be released on 2 Tone. By now, Swinging Cats and The Bodysnatchers had split up with only Rico and The Specials remaining on the label.

For *That Man Is Forward*, Rico recruited his own backing band involving both young and old musicians. As always, Dick Cuthell was on hand to mix and produce the tracks, with Rico himself helping out with production. The engineer for the sessions was the famous dub studio engineer, Errol Thompson. Rico played trombone, drums and percussion alongside Dick Cuthell who played flugelhorn, cornet, percussion and pick guitar on various tracks.

The rest of the album resembled a who's who of ska and reggae and saw the album split into two sections, Side One featured younger musicians such as Sly & Robbie (drums & bass), Mikey Chung (rhythm guitar), Robbie Lyn (piano) and Nambo (trombone) and they were joined by veterans Ansell Collins (organ) & Skully (percussion).Side Two featured a lot of the "old guard"; Santa (drums), George Fullwood (bass), Earl 'China' Smith (rhythm & lead guitar), Jah Jerry Haynes (ska guitar), Winston Wright (piano) as well as Oswald "Rasculture" Palmer (off mic repeater).

Advertisement for Rico's first 2 Tone album

Aside from those musicians, Glen Da Costa (tenor saxophone), Deadly Headley Bennett (alto saxophone) and David Madden (trumpet & flugelhorn) featured on the majority of tracks with Cedric Brookes (tenor saxophone) appearing on one song on each side.

Rico really did get some of the best in the business to join him for the sessions, even managing to convince Jah Jerry Haynes, from The Skatalites, to play on the album despite having no serious involvement with music for 16 years!

The album was released in March 1981 but was only ever going to be one for the purists and unsurprisingly failed to chart. It didn't really matter, the objective was to get Rico's music out there and those that did buy were treated to a decent album of eight instrumental tracks featuring some of the most talented musicians on the ska and reggae scenes.

Rico played some select dates to promote the album in March and April where The Rico Band played at Warwick University, Bristol Barclay Club and Birmingham Cedar Ballroom amongst others. The Bristol gig saw The Specials perform as Rico's backing band!

The solo stuff was then put on the backburner as Rico joined The Specials in the studio for the recording of Ghost Town and they also performed shows in Holland, Germany and the UK. Ghost Town hit No.1 in July and the band appeared on Top of the Pops to perform on two separate occasions, followed by a tour of North America in August, with the band breaking up shortly afterwards in October.

In the autumn, Rico embarked on a small tour of German universities and jazz clubs taking Jerry Dammers, John Bradbury, Horace Panter, Dick Cuthell, Anthony Wimshurst and Satch Dixon with him as his backing band. The tour began well and Rico went down a treat, it was also a welcome distraction for the members of The Specials who'd experienced the breakup of the band shortly beforehand.

However, the tour ended in crisis with the band not being paid and the last few dates being cancelled. Horace Panter has since described it as "one of the best musical memories of my life"[1].

Advertisement for the single Jungle Music

Shortly after the tour, Rico was back in the studio with sessions taking place at Woodbine Studios, Leamington Spa where three tracks were recorded.

It was decided to record the songs that'd gone down well on the tour and these were; *Jungle Music, Rasta Call You* and *Easter Island.* Jerry Dammers produced *Jungle Music* whereas Dick Cuthell produced *Rasta Call You* and they both produced *Easter Island.* The first two made it into the 7" release, whereas *Easter Island* was included on the 12" release.

Rico was joined in the studio by his backing band from the tour, Jerry Dammers, Horace Panter, John Bradbury, Dick Cuthell, Anthony Wimshurst, Tony 'Groco' Uter and Satch Dixon, they were also joined by John Shipley who was now part of The Special AKA.

The single was released in February 1982 credited to Rico & The Special AKA but it failed to chart and is now quite a rarity among the 2 Tone record collectors. The single was also the last on 2 Tone to feature Walt Jabsco, he'd appeared on the album complete with a trombone!

Rico, during his time with The Specials
Pic by Gillian Flanagan-Jones

It's unclear when the sessions for Rico's second album on 2 Tone occurred but they came at some point after the tour, with the album being recorded partly in Jamaica (Joe Gibbs Studio, Kingston) and partly in London (The Town House).

The album would be very much a 2 Tone affair as he enlisted some of The Specials to help him along, with Jerry Dammers (piano), Horace Panter (bass) and John Bradbury (drums) all playing on the record. Dammers also worked on the production of the album, co-producing *Easter Island, Destroy Them* and *Distant Drums* whilst Dick Cuthell produced and mixed the whole album as well as playing cornet, flugelhorn, funda drums, piano and percussion across various tracks.

Jama Rico was released in May and once again Rico was backed by some of the biggest names in the business with many of the musicians from the first LP contributing once again. Rico showcased his many talents by playing trombone, vibraphone, funda drums, percussion, rasta bass drum, repeater, cabasa and scraper on the album. The LP also saw the return of Sly & Robbie,

David Madden, Winston Wright, George Fulwood, Tommy McCook, Jah Jerry Haynes, 'Deadly' Headley Bennett, Ansell Collins, Robbie Lyn, Mikey Chung, Glen Da Costa and China, all of whom played on *That Man Is Forward*. It also featured first appearances from Satch Dixon, Tony 'Groco' Uter, Skully, Bo Peep, Lloyd Parks and Mick Jacques.

As with the first album, *Jama Rico* saw David Storey design the sleeve, he was now a 2 Tone regular and also designed the sleeve for *Too Much Pressure* (The Selecter) and *In The Studio* (The Special AKA) as well as the single cover for *Ghost Town* (The Specials). Glen Da Costa has since spoken about Rico and his involvement with the two albums; "To be honest, I don't even remember playing on Rico's albums but working with Rico was always a pleasure. What I admired about Rico more than anything else was that he had an insatiable desire to make a path for himself in the music business that would leave a legacy for him". Da Costa was also complimentary about Rico's desire to make his own music; "Although he wasn't as dynamic a soloist as Don Drummond, Vin Gordon or Carl Masters, he had confidence in himself to do his own music and I admired him very much for doing so. He was a very easy going person, very laid back and fun to be around".

Ultimately, *Jama Rico* failed to chart though by 1982, 2 Tone was heading in a different direction. The Specials had broken up and Jerry Dammers was trying to adapt the label to sign new bands that reflected the changing musical styles in the charts. Dammers opted to sign The Higsons and The Apollinaires who were both funk bands and was also concentrating on putting The Special AKA together.

Rico never released any more material on the label though he did feature on 2 Tone once more when he appeared on The Special AKA's *In The Studio* in 1984 playing on *Alcohol, Break Down The Door, Housebound* and *What I Like Most About You Is Your Girlfriend*.

Releases on 2 Tone:

Sea Cruise (1980) - Single
Jungle Music (1982) - Single
That Man Is Forward (1981) - Album
Jama Rico (1982) - Album

Rico's Backing Band
Where Are They Now?

Rico's backing band occasionally included Jerry Dammers, John Bradbury and Horace Panter from The Specials. They toured with Rico in 1981 and then appeared on some of the tracks on his second album *Jama Rico* in 1982. As they are covered in The Specials section they are not included here but it's right to mention their contribution.

Dick Cuthell
Cornet, Flugel Horn, Funda Drums, Piano, Percussion, Pick Guitar 1980-1982
See The Specials.

Satch Dixon
Funda Drum, 1982
Dixon has been involved with music since at least 1970, releasing his own single *Bonga Bonga* under the guise of Young Satch and also released a single with Rico in the same year. He went on to work with Mark Holder, Junior English and The Undivided before playing on Rico's *Man From Wareika*. Returned to work with Rico in 1982 on *Jungle Music* and on *Jama Rico* later in the same year playing on the tracks *Destroy Them* and *Some Day*. Dixon later appeared on the *Starvation* charity single in 1985. Aside from music, he worked as a cab driver in South London but is now living in Florida and still performs occasionally.

Tony 'Groco' Uter
Percussion, Shaker, Repeater, Rasta Bass Drum, 1982
Groco had been playing on ska and reggae records for decades, he'd already played on *Man From Wareika* before appearing on *Jama Rico* in 1982, as well as *Jungle Music*. He also appeared on The Special AKA's *In The Studio*, playing congas on *The Lonely Crowd*. Groco has enjoyed a long and varied career, playing with Bob Marley and The Wailers during the 1970s and also played with Diz Watson. Groco is still fit and healthy and into his 90s and still plays the occasional gig with Watson.

"Deadly" Headley Bennett
Alto Saxophone, 1981-1982
Bennett was a session musician that'd played saxophone since the 1950s and had worked with Prince Far I, The Abyssinians and Bob Marley. He had also released two albums worth of soul ballad instrumentals with Ossie Scott. Bennett played the alto saxophone on *That Man Is Forward* and *Jama Rico* and his contribution to the development of music was recognised in Jamaica in 2005 when he was awarded the Order of Distinction in the rank of Officer by the government. He continued to play the saxophone and worked with Junior Reid, U Roy and Bushman amongst others before he passed away in 2016, shortly after being diagnosed with prostate cancer.

Ansell Collins
Organ, 1981-1982
Collins had been playing keyboards since the 1960s and after working with Lee 'Scratch' Perry, teamed up with Dave Barker who was a session vocalist. They formed the duo Dave and Ansell Collins and released the song *Double Barrel* in 1970 which hit No.1 in May 1971, the second reggae song to hit the top spot. The follow-up, *Monkey Spanner* in 1971, reached No.7 although they later disbanded and went on to become session musicians.

Collins began working with Rico in 1977, providing some of the keyboards on *Man From Wareika* and continued the association in 1981 playing the organ on *That Man Is Forward* and again in 1982 on five tracks on *Jama Rico*. Collins has since worked with Jimmy Cliff, Gregory Isaacs and Barrington Levy and released his solo album *Ansel Collins* in 1986. Collins later reunited with Dave Barker in 2012 for several gigs in the UK and has continued to play occasional solo gigs.

David Madden
Trumpet, 1981-1982
Madden had been a member of The Wailers when he joined Rico's backing band, playing trumpet on *That Man Is Forward* in 1981. He returned to the fray in 1982 for the *Jama Rico* sessions. Madden has also recorded with Beres Hammond, Sean Paul, Jimmy Cliff and Peter Tosh. He has also ventured into production work over the years working with Dean Stone, Tanya Hudson and Michael Rutherford. Madden has continued to record, releasing his own solo work, the last of which was the 2015 EP *Nice We Met*. He now no longer plays the trumpet, choosing to concentrate on singing, and is currently living in Kingston, Jamaica.

Glen Da Costa
Saxophone, 1981-1982
Da Costa had worked with Bob Marley before he played saxophone on all but one of the tracks on *That Man Is Forward*. He continued the association with Rico, featuring on *Jama Rico* in 1982 though he appeared on just the one track, *We Want Peace*. He has since worked on his own projects and released an album with Zap-Pow in 2017. He has also been writing his memoirs on and off for years and is now living in Falmouth, Jamaica.

Mikey Chung (Pic. TimDuncan)

Mikey Chung
Rhythm Guitar, 1981-1982
Chung began his career in the late 1960s and was involved with a number of bands including the Mighty Mystics, The Virtues, Generation Gap and the Now Generation Band. He worked with Pete Tosh before he played on *That Man Is Forward* in 1981, playing on four tracks and also worked on a single track, *We Want Peace*, on *Jama Rico* in 1982. Has since moved into production and worked with artists such as The Rolling Stones, Joe Cocker, Grace Jones and Sinead O'Connor and is still working as a session musician in Jamaica.

Noel 'Skully' Simms
Percussion, 1982
Skully played on many ska records over the years working with Prince Buster, Peter Tosh and Jimmy Cliff. He also played percussion for a number of bands appearing on over 200 albums. His body of work was already impressive before he worked with Rico on *Man From Wareika* in 1977 and then on *Jama Rico*, playing on five tracks. Skully continued to work as a session musician featuring on albums by a whole host of names from Michael Prophet to Alton Ellis. Later in life, Skully began to lose his sight and eventually succumbed to glaucoma but kept on working until he was diagnosed with lung cancer in 2015, later passing away in 2017. Skully was honoured by the Jamaican government in 2004 for his contribution to Jamaican music.

Robbie Lyn
Piano, 1981-1982
Lyn was one of the younger members of Rico's backing band, and although he was only in his 30s when he appeared on *That Man Is Forward*, his body of work was already impressive, working with Ernie Smith, Al Brown, Peter Tosh and Bunny Maloney. Played piano on a number of tracks on both albums and continues to work as a session musician. Lyn also released his own solo album *Making Notes* in 2006 and has released a number of solo singles over the years. He is currently living in Jamaica and plays live occasionally.

Robbie Lyn (Pic. TimDuncan)

Robbie Shakespeare

Bass Guitar, 1981-1982

One half of Sly and Robbie, Shakespeare has been active since the 1970s and had a huge body of work before becaming involved with Rico in 1977, playing on *Man From Wareika*. Also featured on *That Man Is Forward* and *Jama Rico*. Shakespeare played bass on a number of tracks on both albums. Shakespeare continues to play as part of Sly and Robbie and they have since moved into production, working with the likes of Paul McCartney and Britney Spears.

Sly Dunbar

Drums, 1981-1982

The other half of Sly and Robbie, Dunbar played drums on *Man From Wareika* and continued his association with Rico by appearing on *That Man Is Forward* and *Jama Rico*. Dunbar continues to be a session musician with his musical partner Robbie Shakespeare and has also worked on production with him, working with Paul McCartney and Britney Spears amongst others. He has occasionally worked on music without Robbie and worked with Larry McDonald in 2009 on his album *Drumquestra*.

Winston 'Bo Peep' Bowen

Guitar, 1982

Bo Peep began his career in the 1970s, playing guitar with We The People and Dean Fraser amongst others. He was an in-demand session musician when he played three tracks on *Jama Rico* in 1982. Bo Peep later worked on the Havana Meets Kingston project in 2017, which spawned a tour, and also worked with Inna De Yard, playing lead guitar on their self-titled album. He later passed away in March 2019 after suffering a heart attack.

Carlton 'Santa' Davis

Drums, 1981-1982

'Santa' Davis, so-called because of a skating accident which left him with a red and swollen face, had been in Soul Syndicate during the 1970s, working with George 'Fully' Fullwood. Also played with Roots Radics and The Aggrovators and was drumming with Bob Marley and The Wailers before he worked with Rico on *That Man Is Forward* in 1981, drumming on four tracks and then drummed on three tracks on *Jama Rico* in 1982.

Robbie Shakespeare (Pic by Schorle)

He worked with Peter Tosh and his band before Tosh was murdered in 1987. Santa was injured in the shooting himself, being shot in the shoulder and the 9mm bullet is still in his back. Santa later joined the band Big Mountain in 1994 and has since worked as a session musician working with a number of non-reggae artists including Chaka Khan, Pink and Willie Nelson. He released his own solo album *Da Zone* in 2008 and is currently the drummer for Ziggy Marley's backing band. Santa lives in California with his wife Debra.

Lloyd Parks
Bass, 1982
Parks guested on *Jama Rico,* playing bass guitar on two tracks, *Love and Justice* and *Jam Rock*. He has played with his band, We Are The People for decades supporting Dennis Brown. Parks has also released his own material over the years, including some solo albums including the 1998 album *Wonder of You* and an album of songs originally performed by The Techniques, *Lloyd Parks Sings The Techniques* released in 2016. Away from performing music, Parks has worked in production sporadically over the years usually on his own work but not exclusively.

Tommy McCook
Saxophone, 1982
McCook was a founding member of The Skatalites and had recorded with many respected reggae artists before he played on *Jama Rico* in 1982. He played saxophone on *Jam Rock, Love and Justice* and *Do the Reload*. McCook continued to play with The Skatalites and was a well respected musician on the scene, leading his own band The Supersonics and releasing a number of solo efforts. Sadly passed away in 1998 from heart failure after suffering from pneumonia.

Winston Wright
Piano, 1981-1982
Wright played piano on four tracks on each album, he'd been a member of Tommy McCook's Supersonics and could play the Hammond organ as well as he played the piano. He played the organ on the Harry J All Stars' hit *Liquidator* in 1969, a role which went uncredited. After his work with Rico, Wright continued to work as a session musician and was a part of the supergroup of session musicians The Dynamites before he passed away in 1993 after suffering from a heart attack.

Sly Dunbar (Pic. by Schorle)

118

Cedric 'Im' Brooks

Tenor Saxophone, 1981-1982

Jamaican native Brooks was already a prominent session musician by the time he featured on *That Man Is Forward* in 1981 playing tenor saxophone. He also appeared on *Jama Rico* in 1982. After living in Jamaica, Canada and the US at various times in his life, Brooks relocated to New York and his musical output dropped somewhat. He later worked with The Skatalites in 1999 following the death of Rolando Alphonso and toured with them until 2010 when he was admitted to hospital suffering from diabetes, hypertension and this ultimately led to pneumonia. After suffering a cardiac arrest in 2013, Brooks passed away in hospital.

Oswald 'Rasculture' Palmer

Drums (Off Mic Repeater), 1981

Palmer had worked as an assistant engineer and in production for Dennis Brown, Johnny Clarke and Derrick Morgan before he appeared on four tracks on *That Man Is Forward*. Apart from an appearance on a Gregory Isaacs album in 1990, he has since exclusively worked in writing and production. He penned a number of tunes that were released in 1981, *Dem A Fight*

Chinna Smith (Pic. Joakim Westerlund)

by Barry Brown, *Boxing Around* by Cornel Campbell, *Party Time* by Mighty Diamond and *My Princess* by Sammy Dread. Has since produced artists such as Yellowman, Jackie Edwards, Tony Rebel, Keith Hudson and Joe Gibbs & The Professionals.

Earl 'Chinna' Smith

Rhythm and Lead Guitar, 1981-1982

Before working with Rico, Chinna was in The Aggrovators, also working with Bob Marley and The Wailers and The Upsetters, with Lee 'Scratch' Perry. Chinna played on four tracks on *That Man Is Forward* in 1981 and followed that up with an appearance on the track *Java* on *Jama Rico* in 1982. After his involvement with Rico, Chinna worked with Jimmy Cliff, even appearing in the 1986 film *Club Paradise* as part of the character Ernest Reed's (played by Cliff) backing band. He has also recorded solo efforts, the last of which, *Guitars on Top*, was released in 2009. Chinna continues to work as a session musician, lives in Kingston and was awarded a Silver Musgrave Medal by the Institute of Jamaica in 2013.

Ronald 'Nambo' Robinson

2nd Trombone, 1981

Nambo was a veteran in the business by the time he guested on *That Man Is Forward* in 1981, playing the 2nd Trombone on the opening track *Easy Snappin'*. He had already worked with Cedric Brooks, Sly Dunbar, Bob Marley, and Dennis Brown before he appeared on the album. He went on to work with Jimmy Cliff, The Four Tops and Gladys Knight amongst others. As time went on, Nambo ventured into jazz, classical and rhythm & blues as well as continuing to play reggae. He went on to work with a number of young and upcoming Jamaican musicians and had put on a series of shows that featured them. He also released four solo efforts, *Reggae in My Bones*, *Nambone Ska*, *Nambo Sing and Play* and *Raw Roots Rock Reggae* and also continued with his session work before he passed away in Jamaica in 2017.

George 'Fully' Fullwood

Bass, 1981-1982

Fully Fullwood had formed his own band, Soul Syndicate in the early 1970s and boasted of other members of Rico's backing band, Chinna and Santa. The band were one of the best known and well respected reggae session bands in Jamaica, performing on literally hundreds of tracks during the 1970s and 1980s. Fullwood played bass on four tracks on That Man Is Forward and one track on Jama Rico. Since his work with Rico, Fullwood has worked with Mikey Dread, Peter Tosh and Ken Boothe amongst others. He has reunited with some of his Soul Syndicate band members on occasion, the last of which was in 2016 at the Reggae on the River festival in California. He has also recorded three albums worth of solo material and continues to play live, usually at the Golden Sails PCH Club in Long Beach, California and also works as a mentor and coach to up and coming musicians.

Jah Jerry Haynes

Guitar, 1981-1982

Jah Jerry had been a member of The Skatalites before their breakup in 1965 and was a session musician playing on a number of classic ska hits, playing with Prince Buster, Fred Locks and The Abysinians amongst others.

He hadn't played seriously for 16 years when he was approached to play on That Man Is Forward in 1981. Haynes played guitar on four songs on the first album and one on the second, Jama Rico in 1982. He continued with session work until he rejoined The Skatalites in 1983, remaining until 1986. He continued as a session musician, working with Lee 'Scratch' Perry amongst others. He later lived in relative obscurity before passing away in 2007 aged 86. Haynes was posthumously inducted into the Jamaica Hall of Fame in 2008 and was further recognised in 2010 by the Jamaican Government on National Heroes Day, receiving the Order of Distinction for his contribution to the development of Jamaican music.

Mick Jacques

Guitar, 1982

Jacques was a member of Curved Air before he featured on Easter Island on Jama Rico in 1982 playing guitar on the track. He later worked with Rico again on the 1995 release What A Wonderful World. Away from his association with Rico, Jacques has worked with The Mother Station and featured on some recordings with Chaz Jankel in 2007.

Ne-Ne Na-Na Na-Na Nu-Nu

Bad Manners

Bad Manners began life as Stand Back in 1976 at Woodberry Down Comprehensive, Stoke Newington and their first gig came at a hippy convention at Stonehenge led by the larger than life Dougie Trendle.

The band featured former pupils of Woodberry Down but not exclusively. They went through a raft of musicians before they settled on a lineup, which by 1979 consisted of; Dougie Trendle (vocals), Alan Sayag (harmonica), Louis Cook (guitar), David Farren (bass), Brian Tuitt (drums), Chris Kane (saxophone), Paul Hyman (trumpet), Andy Marson (saxophone) and Martin Stewart (keyboards).

It is important to refer to each band member as their stage name, Trendle was known as Buster Bloodvessel, Sayag as Winston Bazoomies, Cook as Louis Alphonso, Farren as David Farr-in, Kane as Crust, Hyman as Gus "Hot Lips" Herman, Marson as Marcus Absent, Tuitt as Brian Chew-It and Stewart was known by his own name although was referred to as Mr Bogingong on occasion!

Stand Back became Stoop Solo and the Sheet Starchers but they settled on the name Bad Manners, which had been shortened from Buster Bloodvessel and his Bad Manners.

Bloodvessel took his name from Ivor Cutler's character in the 1967 film, *Magical Mystery Tour*. They were regulars on the pub scene in the early days and were heavily influenced by the Bonzo Dog Doo-Dah Band but the various members had eclectic tastes which shone through in their sound. By 1979, Bad Manners were playing their own style of ska mixed with r'n'b and this coincided with the 2 Tone explosion towards the end of the year where The Special AKA, Madness, The Selecter and The Beat had all reached the Top 10. Although these bands had hit the big time, Bad Manners continued to play the smaller venues of London and remained unsigned. Jerry Dammers was soon spotted at a gig at Dingwalls and he approached the band, offering them a single on 2 Tone. There were similarities with the music that the 2 Tone bands were playing and they were also a multi-racial band, with Brian Tuitt being the sole black member. However, Bad Manners steered clear of politics and very few songs contained political references.

Aside from 2 Tone's interest, EMI were also circling but the band went for Magnet after being invited to their Christmas party. They went into the studio with Roger Lomas, who'd already produced The Selecter's *On My Radio*, to record an album. As Coventry was booming in early 1980, the album was recorded at the city's Horizon Studios. Lomas agreed to produce Bad Manners without even listening to them, he'd had such a good time with them at the party. "Buster Bloodvessel was brilliant. He was larger than life. I knew that the band couldn't fail, because he had so much charisma"[1].

Buster Bloodvessel declared 1980 as Year of the Fatty and it was his size that set the band apart from the other 2 Tone bands. Buster was a proud fat bastard and also sported a rather large tongue, which he wouldn't stop wagging, and a skinhead, attracting a huge skinhead following in the early days. This saw violence occasionally break out at gigs, although they were quick to pile into the audience if it did occur.

Similar to Madness, Bad Manners were tarred with the skinhead brush and suspected of agreeing with the NF's warped views. However, with Brian Tuitt being black and some of the band being Jewish, they were anything but racist. Bad Manners were not a political band, they simply wanted to have fun and their music reflected that. The first single *Ne-Ne-Na-Na-Na-Na-Nu-Nu* was released in February. The 'A' side had been released in 1958 by Dicko Doo and the Don'ts and this particular single was in Alan Sayag's famous record collection.

The single had a slow start before it hit No.39 in early April, remaining in the 30s before they were invited to perform on *Top of the Pops* and on April 24th, Bad Manners were projected into the nation's front rooms for the first time. The British public would've been shocked to see a fat man wagging his massive tongue and bouncing around on the stage like his life depended on it, along with the equally crazy Winston Bazoomies hitting a cowbell!

The single peaked at No.28 before dropping out after 14 weeks. *NME* discussed the single with the band in April with Buster Bloodvessel alluding to 2 Tone's offer; "We didn't have a demo tape or anything, so we got one together, and by the time 2 Tone came back to us there were other companies after us. And because we thought 2 Tone was more of a stepping stone for groups who couldn't get a good contract, and we already had Magnet and others offering us a lot of money...we let it pass". Louis Alphonso pondered the possibilities on 2 Tone; "We would've been famous now if we'd have gone on 2 Tone. But there again, we're making it on our own merits not on the label's merits"[2].

Gig advert from March 1980

Bad Manners were now gigging extensively across the country and they were a hit, helped by Buster Bloodvessel's obvious charisma, their willingness to have a lot of fun and despite being fine musicians, they didn't take themselves seriously. Those early shows were summed by a Brian Harrigan review; "It wasn't just the excitement of the show that they put on - you expect them to be excellent on that score as a matter of course. No, it was also the depth of musicianship they displayed - a collective ability which only now I'm becoming more aware of. Overall Bad Manners were outstanding". They were occasionally joined on stage by Den Hegarty, former member of Darts and friend of Roger Lomas, playing bass saxophone and joining in the lunacy on stage. Thanks to the links with 2 Tone, they began to pick up gigs with other 2 Tone bands, including one at the Electric

Ballroom in March where they shared the bill with The Bodysnatchers and the Swinging Cats. Here, all three bands were filmed by filmmaker Joe Massot who was making a 2 Tone film.

The debut album was released in April and titled *Ska 'n' B*, although it was ultimately a disappointment, reaching No.34. The title perfectly described their brand of music which combined ska with r'n'b and it contained a mixture of originals and covers, with the covers being brought up to date in their own weird and wacky way. It was fun-filled and they didn't take themselves too seriously, the only remotely serious track on the album was *Inner London Violence*, their version of *Concrete Jungle* by The Specials.

The single was on it, along with covers of *Monster Mash, Fatty Fatty, Caledonia, Wooly Bully* and the *Magnificent 7*. The rest of the tracks were all originals, *Special Brew, Here Comes The Major, King SkaFa, Lip Up Fatty* and *Inner London Violence* and perhaps the best songs on the LP except for *Wooly Bully*.

The album also saw the start of a tradition where the final song on the LP would be 'off the wall'. The track that received this honour was *Scruffy Was A Huffy Chuffy Tugboat*, a cover of *Scruffy The Tugboat* from 1956, a record that was in Winston Bazoomies' vast record collection. *Fatty Fatty* is also notable for a trombone solo from Buster Bloodvessel, which he still performs to this day on stage!

The second single to be released was *Lip Up Fatty* in June. This is perhaps the band's best known song and it performed well, reaching No.15 and it was hilariously backed up by *Night Bus To Dalston*, their response to *Night Boat To Cairo* by Madness! The release led to their second *Top of the Pops* appearance where they were introduced by Elton John.

There was one final single to be lifted from the album in the form of *Special Brew*, a love song about their favourite beer! This release silenced some of the critics that had begun to accuse the band of hanging on the coattails of 2 Tone.

Buster Bloodvessel unveils a plaque at the site of Horizon Studios in 2009 - Pic by John Coles

It also got the record company off their backs as they'd been expecting better chart positions with the album and previous singles. *Special Brew* was released in September and by November it had reached No.3. Not bad for a song written in about two minutes after they'd sunk a few cans of the stuff!

Just to touch on the criticisms of the band in the early days, although they played a similar style of music, Bad Manners were a great band in their own right. They weren't a carbon copy of The Specials, The Selecter or Madness and played their own fusion of ska and r'n'b in their own wacky style. They also boasted a fantastic horn section and had the craziness of Winston Bazoomies blowing his many harmonicas in his own unique way.

They had been picking up support slots with the 2 Tone bands and the association definitely helped them on their way during this period. They headlined their first tour in June, with the band Headline supporting them. Bad Manners would later cover one of their songs *Don't Knock The Baldhead*. Shortly after the tour, they visited Finland to play the Olou Festival where they played in front of 40,000 people and performed six encores! They were even joined by Iron Maiden on *Ne-Ne-Na-Na-Na-Na-Nu-Nu*!

This was the beginning of a love affair between Bad Manners and Finland.

Despite the relentless touring schedule, Bad Manners found time to squeeze in the recording of their second album, *Loonee Tunes!* which was released in November, again recorded at Horizon with Roger Lomas. Some copies even came with a free Fatty Man earring although most of them were recalled due to people getting infections!

It wasn't unlike their first effort but featured only three covers, although it only reached No.36, it was an improvement on the first album. The silliness was still there with *El Pussycat* and *Ivor The Engine* but *Just A Feeling, Lorraine* and *Doris* were highlights, as well as a great version of *Tequila*. Once again, the final track on the album was a weird one, *Gherkin*, which saw Buster Bloodvessel singing into a drainpipe about little pieces of gherkin!

The chart position was once again a disappointment but it led to the single *Lorraine,* which peaked at No.21. Its popularity was helped by the *Top of the Pops* performance, where Buster dressed as Henry VIII (wearing Charlton Heston's costume from the 1977 film *Crossed Swords)* and sang to a blow up doll!

Alan Sayag's gold disc for Dance Craze alongside a signed edition of the LP

The second single *Just A Feeling* was a bigger success, reaching No.13, leading to another hilarious *Top of the Pops* appearance with Buster dressed as a human spot! Sadly, the second outing of the song on *Top of the Pops* was marked with tragedy as Alan Sayag had fallen ill and made the first of his numerous departures from the band. For this performance, Louis Alphonso played harmonica and has since said that the band were "playing through pain" during this performance due to Sayag's enforced absence.

The reader may be wondering why Bad Manners are featured in a 2 Tone book, despite never being signed to the label. The band had been filmed back in March 1980 for an upcoming film about 2 Tone and after some delays, *Dance Craze* was released in February 1981 with an accompanying LP. Bad Manners appeared in both the film and on the LP, performing *Ne-Ne-Na-Na-Na-Na-Nu-Nu*, *Wooly Bully*, *Inner London Violence* and *Lip Up Fatty* and the LP featured the latter two songs.

The *Dance Craze* version of *Lip Up Fatty* later found its way onto the 1989 compilation *The 2 Tone Story*. The footage shows how tight Bad Manners were at the time and far more than the novelty band people think they were. The album sold over 500,000 copies and all the band received a gold disc.

During the same month, Bad Manners were involved in a hilarious incident at the Italian Sanremo Festival which was broadcast live on Italian television. At the end of their set, Buster, who was by now stripped to his underwear, pulled down his underpants and flashed his backside at the cameras. He was unaware that the Pope was watching and it was seen as a great insult! This incident led to them being banned on Italian television for ten years! He also did it in 1982 on Irish television and earned a lifetime ban!

The relentless touring led to an Irish tour being cancelled in May due to ill health though they released a new single in June, *Can Can*.

It was released at the same time as *Ghost Town* by The Specials. The two bands couldn't have been any different, with The Specials providing a soundtrack of a generation, Bad Manners providing some fun in and amongst all the doom and gloom of 1981. It performed well too, hitting No.3, while *Ghost Town* was at No.1. Roger Lomas spoke about it in 1999; "Buster wanted to do it but the rest of the band thought it was a crap idea. Buster knew he could sell it and I knew he could, he'd already convinced me. Bad Manners ran out of things to record so I suggested trying to record a demo of *Can Can*. In the absence of anything else, the band eventually agreed. We played it to the record company and they were knocked out by it. Even the band thought it was good".

The finished recording highlights the talent in the band; "*Can Can* is a classical music piece which would normally be played by a 50 piece orchestra, so it was a difficult recording task. I had to make the song sound as big as an orchestral piece. I ended up using 40 or 50 tracks on a 24 track tape machine, so I had to bounce lots of tracks together. It took me a day and half to mix it. I just knew it was going to be a massive hit"[1].

The release led to another famous *Top of the Pops* appearance with Buster Bloodvessel performing a can-can dance wearing a dress and Doc Marten boots! He has since said that he had the idea for the *Top of the Pops* performance before they'd even recorded the song. Despite the success, it is this particular release which probably placed the band in the "novelty" section of bands, a judgement that is grossly unfair.

Alan Sayag also made a welcome return to the band for the song. *Can Can* was originally written by Jacques Offenbach for his 1858 opera, *Orpheus in the Underworld* and when the Bad Manners version went into the Top 40, it became the oldest melody to hit the charts since Waldo De Los Rios charted with Mozart's *Symphony No. 40* in 1971.

June also saw the band record their next album at Rockfield Studios, Monmouth.

The album's release was preceded by a short tour of England and the release of the single *Walking In The Sunshine* in September. It performed well and peaked at No.10 and even saw the band record a video. It was their seventh consecutive Top 40 hit, although they'd originally intended to release *Ben E. Wriggle*, even going as far as pressing the singles. However, they decided to release *Walking In The Sunshine* instead, Roger Lomas still feels that *Ben E Wriggle* would've been a certain hit!

The single was followed by their third album, *Gosh! It's Bad Manners* in October. This is their highest charting album, reaching No.18 and Lomas was on hand once again to produce. *Gosh! It's* was also their highest selling album and it went silver, selling over 250,000 copies.

The album shows them at their best and showcases the musical talent in the band. Some of the originals on the album such as *Never Will Change, Weeping And Wailing, Runaway* and *Walking In the Sunshine* are classic Bad Manners songs and proved they could also write serious songs as well as the fun stuff. Shortly afterwards, readers of *Record Mirror* were treated to a free Bad Manners single with *Runaway* being chosen as the title track, which had featured on the album. The album led to the Gosh It's Tour which toured the UK in October and November.

Bad Manners, with their willingness to send themselves up, became famous for their appearances on the children's TV show *Tiswas* between 1980 and 1981. Some of these appearances are still remembered, including one where Buster Bloodvessel crushed pickled onions and pork pies into a jar and drank the contents!

They were also happy to have their music featured on television programmes; Thames Television produced a children's TV series *Educating Marmalade* which first aired in November 1981, with Bad Manners providing the theme tune.

This track featured Den Hegarty on bass saxophone alongside the usual horn section of Chris Kane, Paul Hyman and Andy Marson. Hegarty also featured with the band on an episode of *Tiswas* performing *Monster Mash* and Hegarty, who was presenting the show, guested on vocals.

Following on from the success of *Walking In The Sunshine* and the *Gosh! It's* album, Bad Manners released *The R'N'B Party Four* EP in November, featuring *Buona Sera, Don't Be Angry, The New One* and *No Respect*. *Don't Be Angry* had appeared on the album but the other three tracks were brand new. Despite containing the brilliant *Buona Sera*, the EP was the lowest charting release by Bad Manners since *Ne-Ne-Na-Na-Na-Na-Nu-Nu* though it reached a respectable No.34. It also led to another memorable *Top of the Pops* performance of *Buona Sera* which saw Buster Bloodvessel going absolutely crazy while Winston Bazoomies pushed a pram around in the background!

More touring followed before they were back in Rockfield Studios to record their fourth album.

The band were quiet until April 1982 when they released the single *Got No Brains*. It would be their lowest charting single at No.44. The sleeve is particularly memorable for depicting Buster Bloodvessel with a bright green head and was painted by David Farren; he'd designed the original Bad Manners logo and also painted the cover of *Ska 'n' B*. It wasn't a surprise when he became an artist after leaving the band.

Despite the low chart placing, the reviews were generally favourable. The band were trying to be more serious but had found this difficult due to their reputation as a novelty band. Buster Bloodvessel bemoaned the band's image in August; "This band has been together for seven years, which is five years longer than most. The problem with *Got No Brains* was that people didn't want us to be educated. Plus it was well-played and produced and the public don't want us to be clever musicians".

Fatty continued; "Because we do silly songs on the telly, it doesn't mean we can't play properly. It's hard to be respected for being both silly and serious as the Bonzo Dogs once were. Bad Manners being deep isn't what the fans want".

Following the disappointment with the previous single, Bad Manners planned to release another single *Samson and Delilah*, which was originally entitled *Rub It Up Delilah* until the chorus was changed to suit radio airplay. However, Magnet decided to release *My Girl Lollipop* in July.

Millie Small had originally sung *My Boy Lollipop* in 1964 and it became one of the first ska songs to make an impression on the UK charts. Unbeknown to some, Small's version was also a cover, Robert Spencer had originally written *My Girl Lollypop* and it had been released by Barbie Gaye in 1956.

The single is another one of the band's most famous songs and it eventually peaked at No.9. Despite being a success, it was not the band's choice to release it. Buster Bloodvessel discussed this in *Record Mirror* in October; "We were only advised to put out *Lollipop* by our record company. It was a record to keep us in the public eye. Even now we don't all agree if it was the right decision although it did make the Top 10"[3].

The band began to experience disagreements with Magnet, the decision to release *My Girl Lollipop* instead of *Samson and Delilah* being a factor but the label also wanted to release a greatest hits LP ahead of the next album. Buster Bloodvessel discussed this in an interview in August; "Magnet want to release a "Greatest Hits" album for Christmas while we want to release an album of new material. We've been working on songs for the last couple of months and we're ready to go". Fatty ended with a swipe at the label; "Magnet are more into making money than sense. They want us to record singles to slap on a "Greatest Hits" album but won't pay for us to make videos for our singles - even though we're a visual band"[4].

The band eventually got their way and *Samson and Delilah* was released in October, the 7" on clear vinyl with a clear sleeve, David Farren has since said that this is his favourite Bad Manners song. The single didn't fare too well, eventually reaching No.58 though it was granted a music video which saw Buster Bloodvessel dressed as King Kong!

The band released their fourth album, *Forging Ahead* in November which coincided with a tour. The album had mixed reviews and only reached No.78 in the charts. It featured a guest appearance from old friend Den Hegerty.

He played bass saxophone on *Exodus* and *Educating Marmalade*. It was a marked change from previous albums as they wanted to be taken seriously but it didn't really work. *Samson And Delilah, My Girl Lollipop* and *That'll Do Nicely* are perhaps the only notable songs with the others being merely fillers, although two songs became theme tunes. *Educating Marmalade* has been mentioned previously but the other was *Your*, used as the theme for children's television show, *Hold Tight* in 1982. It was presented by Pauline Black and the band appeared on one of the shows. *That'll Do Nicely* was released as a single in April 1983 but only reached No.49 and was the band's last single to get near the Top 40. *Forging Ahead* was the final album of original material on Magnet before they parted company, it was also Roger Lomas' final involvement with the original band; "I did their last record in 1982, after the fourth album Bad Manners got very serious. They thought their fourth album was the best, but I think it's the worst, because the character we got in the first album was lost by then. Suddenly they wanted to be taken seriously, because they were fed up with being seen as the 2 Tone joke band"[1].

The label released the compilation album *The Height of Bad Manners* in May in association with Telstar. Although it was viewed as a farewell, the band had no intention of finishing. However, it was now 1983 and the whole 2 Tone movement had more-or-less died. The Specials and The Selecter had broken up and The Beat were also on their way out and would split by the end of the year. Only Madness remained on top of their game although they'd changed musical direction by now.

This is when the "golden period" of the band came to an end, and despite being overlooked as one of the top bands of the 1980s, they spent 111 weeks in the charts between 1980 and 1983, scoring nine Top 40 hits during that time as well as three Top 40 albums. Shortly afterwards, Winston Bazoomies left for good due to health problems and was replaced by Jerry Trimaine.

However, he didn't last long due to his bluesy harmonica playing being at odds with the band's sound and he was replaced by Stevie Smith. Jimmy Scott, a conga player, also joined the band around this time.

Following the release of *The Height Of Bad Manners*, the band seemed to almost disappear and although they toured relentlessly abroad, taking in Europe, the Middle and Far East, America and Australia, they remained out of the spotlight. In 1985 they signed to Portrait Records, a label owned by CBS.

This came as a surprise though they were soon in the studio recording a new album in May and the tracks were completed by June. The label spent a fortune on it and would even pay to fly the producers over to work on it. It was produced by John Walters, Nick Garvey, Steve Thompson (who also played bass marimba on *Blue Summer*) and Mike Barbiero.

The single *Blue Summer* was released in August though it failed to chart. This was followed by the next single in December, *What The Papers Say*, another that failed to chart. The album, *Mental Notes,* was released with the single but anyone in the UK would have been hard pushed to hear it as it was only released in the US due to legal wrangles. The album represented a change in direction for the band, the brass was still there but there was a soul/funk fusion evident across the album, a change that didn't last long but was perhaps necessary in the mid 1980s. A third single, *Tossin' In My Sleep* was released in January but again failed to chart.

The band quickly became disillusioned with Portrait and it was on a tour of the States in 1986 when their relationship came to an end. The band were relentlessly touring all over the States and it was before a gig in Los Angeles when they visited Portrait's office and were shocked to discover that they didn't know who Bad Manners were.

The tour was starting to take its toll and they decided it was time to go home. Buster Bloodvessel tore their contract up at Portrait's head office in New York, he is said to have sat on the bosses desk to make sure he knew who he was and then tore the contract up in front of him!

The worst was still to come as tragedy struck when they returned to the UK as Jimmy Scott passed away. He was strip-searched at the airport upon his return and left naked for two hours, while suffering from pneumonia, and he later died. This affected the band greatly but they threw themselves into raising money for his family by playing benefit gigs.

Scott had originally coined the term "Ob La Di Ob La Da" and knew Paul McCartney, the band managed to make contact with him and the story goes that he donated £1000 to the benefit fund.

Around this time, the band were also landed with a huge VAT bill, the debt being left by their previous manager. Disillusioned with the whole thing, the band went underground, with the gig fees being cut drastically and the members weren't even sure whether to carry on anymore.

By 1987, the band had gone through some wholesale changes with Brian Tuitt, Martin Stewart and Paul Hyman all departing and David Farren was in and out of the band while he completed his studies. Nick Welsh joined to cover Stewart's absence on keyboards and also occasionally deputised on bass.

Bad Manners were almost dead by this point, with some of the band working full time jobs and only playing the occasional gig and even when they did, it was usually to pay off the VAT. By now, Buster had formed his own sideline group Buster's All Stars, who would play Bad Manners songs but also covers of ska classics as well. He wanted his new band to challenge those in Bad Manners and to give them a kick up the arse and eventually merged the two.

Andy Marson and David Farren didn't survive the merger though Martin Stewart rejoined. Buster's All Stars actually recorded some material, *Skinhead Love Affair* and *Pipeline*, which were released on a ska compilation. *Skinhead Love Affair* has become a popular Bad Manners song, despite originally being a BAS release!

Buster had also been trying to launch his own label and in 1988, took over the trademark of Blue Beat Records, the original ska label from the 1960s. The new Bad Manners were soon in the studio and these sessions resulted in the release of *Eat The Beat*, which featured new material for the first time since *Mental Notes*, with some of the highlights being *Sally Brown* (a cover of the ska classic by Laurel Aitken), *Since You've Gone Away*, *Return of the Ugly* and *Rosemary*, all of which were original tracks mostly written by Nick Welsh with some input from other band members.

The release was a failure and sold very little though the band had emerged from the wilderness with new members and renewed energy. By 1989, they had a settled line-up consisting of; Buster Bloodvessel (vocals), Louis Alphonso (guitar), Martin Stewart (keyboards), Chris Kane (tenor sax), Alan Perry (alto sax), Nick Welsh (bass) and Perry Melius (drums).

Once Buster had got the label off the ground, it was time to record an album. *Return of the Ugly* was the result of this although the release was delayed for the single *Skaville UK* to be released in April. The single managed to hit the charts, charting at No.87, and was the band's highest charting release since 1983. The low chart placing didn't matter as the public now knew that Bad Manners were back and producing quality original material, mostly driven by the songwriting talents of Nick Welsh.

Away from Bad Manners, Buster and Welsh became involved with Longsy D, who had recorded the acid house single *This Is Ska,* and they worked on one of the remixes for the eventual single release in May.

Buster even appeared in the music video! The song was adopted by Bad Manners and was included on the album, also becoming a staple of their live shows from then on.

They released another single in July, *Gonna Get Along Without You Now*, featuring guest vocals from Verona Davis. Bizarrely, Buster Bloodvessel didn't appear on either side of the record! The single failed to chart and is now quite a rarity among the collectors, although not quite as rare as the next single.

It was intended for *Sally Brown* to be the follow-up and a number of 7" and 12" singles were pressed before the release was pulled! Finally, *Return of the Ugly* was released and although much of the album's material was already out there, it's a decent listen and popular amongst the fans. It contains a number of classics that are still spun by ska DJs and still performed by Bad Manners today, including *Sally Brown, Skaville UK* and *This Is Ska*. *Sally Brown* and *Hey Little Girl* featured ska legend Laurel Aitken on keyboards and both are covers of his songs.

The album also saw the return of Alan Sayag, who'd been away since 1983, he rejoined and would continue to perform when his health allowed. One more single was released in 1989, *Christmas Time Again*, which was backed with a new version of *Skinhead Love Affair*. Released just days before Christmas, the single failed to chart.

The band soon decided to record a follow-up to *Return of the Ugly* in the form of a covers album, similar to UB40's *Labour of Love* albums. They intended to release it on Blue Beat but it collapsed in 1990 due to bankruptcy. The sessions continued intermittently and saw Longsy D and Buster Bloodvessel co-producing. It would continue to be recorded over the next few years in a number of different studios on a number of different continents! Rico Rodriguez, former trombonist with The Specials, joined Bad Manners in 1990 after being invited into the fold by Nick Welsh and would remain until the mid 1990s, playing on a number of tours.

This period was also notable as it led to the departures of two long serving members. Buster's All Stars were still playing the occasional gig and had been inviting Neol Davies and Pauline Black from The Selecter to join them on stage. These cameos had been going down well and led to some serious interest in The Selecter reforming, something that Martin Stewart and Nick Welsh had discussed with them.

Stewart, through his day job as a band booker, secured a short tour of the UK and a three week tour of the US, with Nick Welsh, Perry Melius and himself making up the rest of The Selecter. This caused a rift between Buster Bloodvessel and Martin Stewart, with Stewart never playing with the band again.

Welsh took in three more shows before he left for the tour and had every intention of remaining in Bad Manners. Buster had other ideas and told Welsh that he was either in Bad Manners or The Selecter. Welsh opted to leave and join The Selecter and those two departures left a gaping hole in the band with Stewart's keyboard playing integral to the Bad Manners sound.

Likewise with Welsh, his songwriting saw the band release some of their best material in years and it's sad to reveal that Bloodvessel hasn't spoken to either of them since. They were both quickly replaced and the band continued with Mark Pinto on bass and Dave Welton on keyboards. Finally, the album that'd been in progress since 1990 was released in 1992 though *Fat Sound* was limited to release in Germany. It had taken that long to make, it featured long departed members Chris Kane, Martin Stewart, Perry Melius and Nick Welsh. Sadly, a year later, Alan Sayag left once again due to long-term illness and has not appeared on stage since, though is an honorary member of the band. Mr. Bazoomies was replaced by Dave Turner, a fan of the band.

After a couple of years touring the world, the band were back in the studio with old friend Roger Lomas. This led to the release of *Fatty's Back in Town* in 1995.

A slimline Buster Bloodvessel - pic by Joe Kerrigan

It was a CD containing new recordings of *Special Brew* and *Lip Up Fatty*, new songs *Feel Like Jumping* and *Lager Delirium* as well as old favourites, *Sally Brown* and *Skaville UK*. The CD was released on the band's new label BAD Records and it's release helped to put the spotlight back on them and they were soon booked for a huge tour of the UK and Europe. They took in Finland on the tour and they were given a hero's welcome when they arrived, many of the people here were still fans after they'd played there originally in 1980!

Following the tour, the band recorded a new album in 1996. Louis Alphonso was heavily involved in the production and provided most of the new material. The album became *Heavy Petting* and featured some of the best recordings from the band since the release of *Return of the Ugly*. Unfortunately, the album was only released in Germany (as *Don't Knock The Baldhead)* and America and sadly the last involvement that Louis Cook had with the band. Dismayed at the band's lack of enthusiasm for playing songs from the new album, he left in January 1997.

As the 20th Century came to a close, some more recording took place and the band released *Millennium Knees Up* in 1999, backed by *Come On England*, a medley of football songs. This was followed by the release of *25 Years of Being BAD* where the band re-recorded every single released by the original line-up.

One thing that blighted the band in the late 1990s was a number of compilations that were released and credited to the band. A number of them included new or condensed recordings of earlier classics such as *Special Brew, Lip Up Fatty* and *My Girl Lollipop* which are pale imitations of the original releases. Some of these were recorded on tour buses or at venues the band were playing whilst on tour. Finally, in June 2003, they released an album of original material, *Stupidity*, though most of it had been recorded in the years prior, much of the material featured Louis Cook who had left in the last century!

The album is a mix of original material and cover versions, Cook had written *Happy* and *I Don't Care* for the *Heavy Petting* album but they'd been left off the final cut. *Stupidity* also contained covers of *Do Nothing* by The Specials, *Way Out Mummy* by The Fall and a version of *Teddy Bear's Picnic*! Surprisingly, a new version of *Tossin' In My Sleep* is included on the album, as well as *Millennium Knees Up* and *Come On England*. This was followed by *The Ultimate BAD Collection* in November 2003, a 10-CD box set of individual albums; *Crooners, Fat, Football, Skinhead, Rock, Alcohol, Instrumentals, Sex, Cowboys* and *Girls*. As with much of the band's output in the last 20 years, it seems to have been limited for sale at gigs and the Internet.

By 2004, Buster Bloodvessel, who'd been dogged by health problems for years, had remove two-thirds of his stomach removed. He had a habit of collapsing on stage and eventually found a surgeon willing to operate. This gave him a new lease of life and he was more energetic than ever!

Bad Manners appeared on the Christmas edition of *Never Mind The Buzzcocks* in 2004 and launched their own festival Badfest in July 2005. They also recorded a live DVD of a gig in Essex, *Don't Knock The Baldheads Live*, which featured a guest appearance from Jerry Trimaine. Buster Bloodvessel has continued to tour as Bad Manners and performs across the UK each year. The last original release to surface was *What Simon Says* in 2012. The song, an attack on Simon Cowell's influence on the music business, was released with a Facebook campaign to get it to No.1 though it failed to chart.

It's difficult to describe Bad Manners, in the early days they were a criminally underrated competent set of musicians. Not unlike Madness, they seem to have been lumped into the "novelty" section and this in part due to their less than serious songs like *Can Can*. The serious compositions such as *Inner London Violence, Walking in the Sunshine, Suicide, Got No Brains* and *Just A Feeling* are often overlooked.

Despite the band's image, there was much more to them than just pissing about. Louis Alphonso discussed this in *Record Mirror*; "Doug may be the frontman, but eating hamburgers and sticking out your tongue isn't the extent of Bad Manners, we all know that. Making silly appearances on *Top of the Pops* is something we're very good at, unfortunately, but there's a lot more to us than that"3.

Despite various lineups over the years, the original lineup of the band has never been surpassed and the period of success between 1980 and 1983 has never been bettered.

Buster Bloodvessel is one of the best frontmen of the 2 Tone era but often overlooked is the craziness of Winston Bazoomies, as well as the great musicianship from the rest of the band, including the fantastic horn section.

Anything that followed that original lineup has been a pale imitation, although their resurgence in the late 1980s steered by the songwriting abilities of Nick Welsh pushed it close. Once Welsh and Martin Stewart left the band in 1991, the changes were noticeable. Buster has continued to tour as Bad Manners but its now a nostalgic knees up, the trap that many a good band have fallen into in their later years.

His version of Bad Manners are still going strong and although there are no other originals left, the band itself has a revolving door of musicians, and although they haven't recorded any new material for years, they still perform around the world and are one of the hardest working bands in ska. The current lineup is; Buster Bloodvessel (vocals), Tom Massey (guitar), Lee Thompson (bass), David Edwards (keyboards), Adrian Cox (saxophone), Tony Richardson (saxophone), Mark Hamilton (drums), Colin Graham (trumpet) and Russell Wynn (percussion). The band also regularly have people deputising, although there is one man that can never be replaced!

Buster Bloodvessel (Douglas Trendle)
Vocals, 1976-present

Buster Bloodvessel is famous for his large stomach and his even larger tongue, with his larger-than-life personality being at the forefront of the band. In 1987, he formed sideline project Buster's All Stars and also set up his own label, taking over the trademark of Blue Beat Records. He also tried to start a solo career, signing a deal with Innocent Records, though before the release of his debut album, the project was pulled. A single was released in 1998, *Stop Messin* and credited to Ay Caramba starring Buster. Another solo effort was released in 2001 when a cover of David Bowie's *Laughing Gnome* managed to find its way onto a compilation of Bowie covers, *Diamond Gods: Interpretations of Bowie*.

Away from music, Trendle owned a kebab shop before he opened Fatty Towers in 1996, a bed and breakfast hotel in Margate which catered for the larger people, offering extra large beds, lard arse pudding and cow pies amongst other things! This collapsed in 1998 and Trendle filed for bankruptcy. He also joined the board of directors at Margate FC, with Bad Manners sponsoring the club shirts. He hit the headlines in 1997 when they reached the FA Cup 1st Round and played Fulham and he entertained the crowd before the game, cartwheeling around the pitch!

In 2000, Trendle launched a bid to be London Mayor but stood aside when he realised he had to pay a deposit to stand. He also had a brief acting career in the late 1980s and early 1990s, appearing in *Sammy and Rosie Get Laid* and *Out of Order* as well as an episode of *Boon*. Trendle's weight carried on to balloon until he collapsed on stage in Italy during a show in 2001 and was seriously ill, suffering a strangulated hernia. He collapsed again a year later in Northampton and was booked in for surgery at the Nuffield Hospital, Leeds in 2003 for a gastric bypass, where 2/3s of his stomach was removed. Not so Fatty Fatty anymore, Trendle now lives in Bulgaria with his partner Angie and still tours with Bad Manners regularly and is in the process of moving his bandmates to his adopted homeland to record some new material in his custom built studio.

Winston Bazoomies (Alan Sayag)
Harmonica 1976-1983, 1988-1993
Sayag was known for his crazy harmonica playing, wiggly dance and just general bizarreness! He remained in the band until 1981, when he left due to illness, but returned shortly afterwards. Sayag departed once again in 1983, this time for good. He'd been showing worrying signs for a while until he succumbed to illness in Dublin in the middle of a tour and was sectioned.

Alan Sayag in 2019

He then disappeared off the face of the Earth for a couple of years before appearing on David Farren's doorstep one day, much to Farren's surprise. Sayag was diagnosed as schizophrenic and spent some time in recovery before he rejoined the band in 1989 and remained until 1993, when he once again left due to illness. He later worked as an antique trader but is now living the quiet life in Stoke Newington where he is doted on by his sister Louise and enjoys getting out and about when his health allows. Sayag's favourite moment with the band was playing to the Queen of Denmark!

Martin Stewart
Keyboards, 1976-1991

Stewart joined the band after they'd stolen some sandbags out of his van to soundproof their studio. They were looking for a keyboard player and discovered he played them! By 1987, he was working in insurance and left the band briefly before rejoining in 1988. He also worked as a band booker and left Bad Manners in 1991 to join The Selecter, a reformation with Neol Davies and Pauline Black along with fellow Bad Manners bandmate Nick Welsh. While in The Selecter, Stewart also played in Big Five with Welsh, John Bradbury and Jennie Mathias. By 2006, The Selecter had split and Stewart joined Skaville UK in 2007. He has since played with The Skatylsts but now plays with Sax on Fire and lives in London with his family.

Gus "Hot Lips" Herman (Paul Hyman)
Trumpet, 1976-1987

Hyman was an old school friend and rugby teammate of Buster Bloodvessel and Winston Bazoomies and an original member, having played at the band's first ever gig at Stonehenge. Towards the end of his days in the band, Hyman started working in the finance industry and eventually left Bad Manners in 1987. He continues to work in the finance industry and lives in Enfield with his wife and family.

Chris Kane (Crust)
Saxophone, 1976-1989
Chris Kane left the band in 1989 and toured with Lee 'Scratch' Perry before he worked as musical director on *Elvis-The Legend.* This led to him playing with the Jordanaires, Louis Lymon and the Teenagers and The Chevrolets. His 'A' level in Music has since come in handy as he has worked as the Head of Music at the Swedish School of London and as the orchestral arranger of Jewish choir music. Kane is now working as a music teacher in Cambridge and plays in a rock 'n' roll tribute show, Be Bop A Lula.

Brian Tuitt (Chewit)
Drums, 1976-1985
Tuitt was the original drummer in the band and remained until 1985. After attempts to try and start his own band and managing the folk guitarist Psalm, Tuitt founded Backline Rehearsal studios in Guildford in 1993. He has since relocated to Ramsgate and has played in a number of local bands as well as running a local recording studio. Tuitt is also involved with running a cafe with his partner and plays in Soul of Santana, a Santana tribute band.

Andrew Marson (Marcus Absent)
Saxophone, 1976-1987
Marson eventually left the band in 1987 after he failed to survive the cull when Buster's All Stars merged with Bad Manners. Marson became a carpenter in London and is still living in the capital. He's had an occasional involvement with music, playing in the country and western band The Drawbacks and is also involved with bell-ringing with partner Maureen. Marson remains in contact with his former bandmate David Farren.

Chris Kane with the author, Scunthorpe 2019

David Farren performing as Keith Retched
with The Rollin' Stoned - Pic by Yve Paige

He had to be based in France a lot of the time, though was allowed to come and go from the band as he pleased. He eventually left in 1997 and hasn't been involved since, despite appearing on the 2003 album *Stupidity*. Cook ventured into school-teaching but left the profession after a couple of years. He later joined forces with Martin Stewart and Nick Welsh to form Skaville UK in 2007 and has since released his own solo stuff, including album *A Noir* in 2013. He later formed Poison Hearts before going into the studio and releasing the album *Outside Everything* in July 2020. Poison Hearts can often be seen playing around Paris, where Cook is currently living with his partner.

David Farren
Bass, 1976-1987
Farren left the band in 1987 and became an artist. Not surprising really as he'd designed the band's logo as well as some of the record sleeves. He became a freelance illustrator and spent 20 years producing commissioned work for reproduction, including book covers, record covers and posters and continued his obvious musical talent playing with a number of bands and musicians including The Jam Professors, The Incredibly Strange Film Band and Tinda Pinder. Farren is a freelance artist, running his own business David's Pictures and he also plays in a Rolling Stones tribute band, The Rollin' Stoned playing Keith Retched!

Louis "Alphonso" Cook
Guitar, 1976-1997
Louis Cook was the original guitarist and remained in the band throughout the various incarnations until he started a degree in French philosophy and language during the 1990s.

136

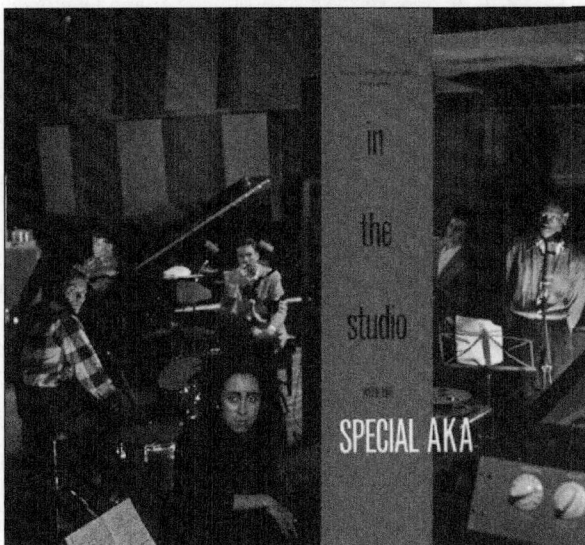

One of the only photographs of the rarely seen The Special AKA

The Special AKA

The Special AKA were formed from the remains of The Specials, after the Fun Boy Three and Roddy Radiation left the band towards the end of 1981, with Jerry Dammers, John Bradbury, Horace Panter and Dick Cuthell remaining.

Finding themselves at a loose end, they went to Germany to play a short tour with Rico, touring universities and clubs. Once they returned, the departed members needed replacing and Dammers recruited John Shipley and Rhoda Dakar, Shipley was an adequate replacement for Radiation and Dakar had been playing live with The Specials since early 1981.

On the last Specials tour, Rick Rogers had ceased to be the band's manager after being sacked by Dammers so he turned to his own manager Pete Hadfield to manage them.

Due to legal constraints, he couldn't use The Specials name so reverted to The Special AKA, a moniker that'd been used various times between 1978 and 1980. The band went underground and headed into the studio with Dammers wanting them to continue as a rhythm section and to see what would turn up vocally. He was determined for the new band to carry on where The Specials had left off and was disappointed that they hadn't followed on from *Ghost Town*.

Towards the end of 1981 they began recording with the intention of releasing a single in the New Year. By now, Dammers had full control and produced everything in the studio. While Fun Boy Three released *The Lunatics Have Taken Over Asylum* in November, Dammers and the remaining Specials stayed silent for the rest of 1981.

Signed edition of The Boiler

The Special AKA emerged in January 1982 with *The Boiler*, a song about date-rape that'd been written by The Bodysnatchers and played by The Specials during their final tour. Dammers had been trying to record it since early 1981 but postponed the sessions whilst The Specials recorded *Ghost Town* and toured on the back of the release.

After the Rico tour, he went into the studio with some new recruits and got the sessions completed. The single was credited to Rhoda & The Special AKA, featuring a guest appearance from co-writer Nicky Summers on bass and was also John Shipley's first appearance with the band, and according to The General; "the best guitarist in the world".

It has since been described as a song that is only supposed to be heard once and anyone that has heard it would surely concur, Dakar's terrifying screams in the final minute of the song make the exact impact that was intended. Dammers has even described it as "the "listen once only" single, the story of a rape too harrowing for repeated listens"[1].

Due to the lyrics, it is quite easy to ignore the music, which is underrated itself, but the full instrumental track *Theme From The Boiler* was included on the 'B' side with Dick Cuthell's cornet playing being particularly startling.

Despite the disturbing content of the song, it managed to reach No.35 in the charts, though it received a stony response from commercial radio and after brief airplay from John Peel and Richard Skinner at Radio One and also Peter Young at London's Capital Radio, it was soon banned and dropped from the playlists. "Rape Disc Banned" screamed *The Sun*.

The release date coincided with the court case of rapist John Allen, who was convicted of rape at Ipswich Crown Court but was only fined £2000, the case being memorable for the backlash against Judge Bertrand Richards who had presided over the case and suggested that the 17 year old victim "was guilty of a great deal of contributing negligence" as she was hitchhiking to try and get home.

The song appeared on television just once when Rhoda Dakar appeared alone singing to a backing track (which was in fact the 'B' side *Theme From The Boiler*) on *Oxford Road Show* where she was also interviewed. There was also a music video for the song which briefly featured Dakar as well as a montage of passive women and violent men from mainstream media, this too was rarely shown on mainstream television. A follow up single was planned but *Female Chauvinist Pig* was never recorded.

The Special AKA also worked with Rico and released *Jungle Music* in March, credited to Rico & The Special AKA. This came after Jerry Dammers, Horace Panter, John Bradbury and Dick Cuthell had joined him on a short German tour towards the tail end of 1981.

After the tour, they decided to record three of the most popular songs on the tour, *Jungle Music* got the nod and the 'B' side was *Rasta Call You*. For the 12" release there was an extra track, the fabulous *Easter Island*. Alongside Dammers, Panter, Bradbury, Cuthell and John Shipley, Rico was joined by old friends Tony 'Groco' Uter and Satch Dixon on percussion and Anthony Wimshurst on guitar, all three had also been on the tour and were friends of the trombonist.

Unusually, Rico performed lead vocals as well as blowing his trusty trombone on the 'A' side. Despite being a decent enough single, it became yet another 2 Tone release not to reach the Top 40 (something that was becoming all too often by 1982) and is one of the lesser known releases on the label. All of three of the tracks are almost lost 2 Tone classics but were released on the 2000 compilation *Specials - A's, B's and Rarities*. Interestingly, it was the final release on 2 Tone to feature Walt Jabsco - the end of an era!

By April, Horace Panter decided he'd had enough and handed in his notice, having been with the band since 1977. At the time, Panter was involved with Exegesis, a religious cult, which led to some tensions between him and Dammers. Panter discussed this period in his book; "He (Dammers) started to look progressively worse and became more difficult to be around. It seemed to me that he showed all the signs of meltdown but he was fine and battled through it". He also discussed how the recording sessions would go, describing quite a miserable experience; "The atmosphere was unbearable, and I just couldn't cope with it. It was like attending a funeral every day of the week. Eventually it was worth losing the £100 I got every week not to be there. I was not happy creating music in such circumstances"[2].

Panter tried to convince Dammers and Pete Hadfield to halt the sessions to attempt to change the atmosphere in the studio but this was ultimately unsuccessful. The following day he decided to quit and ended his five year working relationship with The General. Panter was quickly replaced by Gary McManus, he'd played bass in The Defendants, and had been a student at Warwick University. The sessions continued and The General continued to look for new talent to recruit as he still hadn't replaced Terry Hall from the previous year.

By the end of 1982, Dammers had put his band together which already consisted of himself, John Bradbury, Gary McManus, Dick Cuthell, John Shipley and Rhoda Dakar, also adding Stan Campbell on vocals and Egidio Newton on backing vocals. Campbell's inclusion came after Dammers spotted him in a Coventry cafe and observed that he was a Grace Jones lookalike! He'd originally auditioned for The Selecter before their demise and his previous experience came in the Coventry band Channel A. Newton was an old friend of Rhoda Dakar, they'd both met whilst camping outside David Bowie's house in their teens! The band were now locked in the studio, working on the sessions for the new album.

The first release with the full line-up was *War Crimes*, a song which compared the killing of Palestinians to the Holocaust and begged the question; why was nothing learned? It was a highly provocative song, although we wouldn't expect anything different from Jerry Dammers. It'd taken a long time to put together, with the rhythm track recorded almost a year before the lyrics were added. The lyrics were his response to the Lebanon War, which had begun in June 1982. The song contained some of the most hard-hitting lyrics The General has ever written;

"Bombs to settle arguments, the order of the boot.

Can you hear them dying in the rubble of Beirut?

I can still see people dying, now who takes the blame?

The numbers are different, the crime is still the same."

War Crimes was similar to *The Boiler* where Dammers was happy to sacrifice the commercial opportunity to get his message across to the public. Dammers commented on this in the *NME*; "I suppose there's a conflict there between songs like *The Boiler* and *War Crimes* and pop music. Pop is giving people what they want to hear, we're giving people what they don't want to hear".

Ironically, the Fun Boy Three had been experiencing similar problems with their latest release *The More I See The Less I Believe*; "A lot of people don't want to hear about rape or Beirut I know. It's the same thing with the Fun Boys' new one - people don't want to hear about Northern Ireland. In that sense it isn't pop music"[3].

Similar to *The Boiler*, the single struggled for airplay as by 1982, the New Romantic scene was in full flow and radio stations had no interest in playing a song about bombs being dropped on innocent people and the massacre of refugees in Lebanon, meaning that this was the first release by The Specials/Special AKA not to reach the Top 40. This was despite airplay from John Peel and Kid Jensen although Capital Radio went as far as to ban the record completely. Dammers did pass comment on those Radio One DJs; "It seems ridiculous to me that those DJs on Radio One have got so much power; it's like with Frankie Goes To Hollywood - although everyone's said it, why should Mike Read be the person to decide what millions of people should listen to?". It's important to note that Radio One didn't ban *The Boiler* or *War Crimes*, they just didn't play them. Dammers even joked; "I wish they'd ban our songs, but they don't - they just ignore them! The best thing that can possibly happen is to get a record in the charts and then get it banned"[3].

The lineup of the band was now settled; Stan Campbell (vocals), Rhoda Dakar (vocals), Egidio Newton (vocals), Jerry Dammers (keyboards), Gary McManus (bass), John Shipley (guitar), John Bradbury (drums). Horace Panter appeared on the recording but had left by the time the single was released, Gary McManus was thanked on the back of the record sleeve. The single saw a guest appearance from violinist Nick Parker and he has since spoken about his involvement; "One day, Dammers' agent asked me to come into the studio to work on a new track together with Jerry which was all about the outrage of the Beirut bombing". The track was nearing completion at this point.

"Most of the track was already in the can and Jerry had semi-conceived an elemental fiddle-part; he had vague ideas as to what he wanted playing, but didn't specify particular notes. We played around with the track with me on the fiddle in the control-room for half an hour during which he told me what he liked and what he didn't want and then he made me comfortable alone in the studio with a feed and spun the track at me several times while I improvised and he produced me".

Parker is also complimentary of The General, The Special AKA and 2 Tone in general; "He was extremely polite and articulate in his coaching and I was really quite surprised how quickly we got it done. It all felt very creative and I think the track still sounds full of atmosphere and is still relevant even today. I think they were a brilliant group who promoted some fairly seminal political messages and I do still actually quite enjoy listening to some of the 2 Tone legacy".

Parker remembers that after having a coffee with Dammers, he revealed that he was the son of a Jewish refugee from Germany much to The General's surprise; "As it happens, I had myself been appalled by the recent Israeli bombings and didn't actually altogether disagree with the sentiment of the lyrics so I was both intrigued to be involved on a musical level and was also quite prepared to be partially identified with the message. However, Jerry was sufficiently worried by this conundrum as to ask me courteously whether I was sure I was happy to be on the disc at all. I remember being quite impressed at the time that he'd handled that issue so sensitively".

The accompanying video featured Gary McManus on bass and a different violinist in Parker's place, with Johnny Taylor getting the nod. Parker also spoke about this; "A few months later, I remember feeling slightly miffed to find that I'd been given the name "Nicky Parker" on the extended play cover and then I was summarily replaced by one of the other members of the band who was filmed playing my improvisation in the pop video. I'd have happily obliged but sadly was not invited. The other guy probably looked more the part I think". Following the brief publicity of the single, the band went back into the studio to work on more material for the album.

Following the release of the single, Jerry Dammers and Rhoda Dakar conducted a rare interview in a January 1983 edition of *NME* where Dammers talked about how he'd spent most of 1982 in the studio working on new music for the band. He was unsure how to launch the band into public consciousness and seemed content with letting it grow at it's own pace.

Dammers was also keen for the band to be more of a democracy than The Specials had been, commenting; "Part of the reason for The Specials split was the amount of attention that was paid to me, and the other three resented it. I can understand why, it was Jerry this and Jerry that". He also dismissed the notion of having a settled line-up for the band; "It will be a lot more fluid, it's a bit like Rip Rig & Panic in that respect, though not musically. It won't always be the same people doing lead vocals, there'll be plenty of guest musicians, though it will be based around me, Brad, John, Gary and Rhoda".

The lack of live performance was alluded to by Dakar; "It would have been better to play live before making the records" which Dammers appeared to agree with; "Too many bands become obsessed with the idea of making records once they're involved with the business, whereas recordings should just be recordings of what the group plays live. I've fallen into that trap myself, you're thinking in terms of what's produced, whereas what you should do is go in a place and play"[3].

Despite some of the band seeming to hint at their intention of playing live, there was hardly any trace of them throughout 1983 until the release of *Racist Friend/Bright Lights* in August on both 7" and 12", the latter containing instrumentals of both tracks as 'B' sides. *Racist Friend* began as a Dick Cuthell instrumental before the lyrics were written.

Dammers had found himself surrounded by hangers-on after the success of The Specials and realised he was spending more time with them than his 'real' friends. One day, he decided to go through his address book and cross out anyone that was racist. The song drilled home the message that it wasn't enough to just be anti-racist, you had to do something about it. Dammers commented in a 1985 issue of *Sounds*; "Overnight you suddenly get thousands of friends and you have to start making decisions about people. You can't spread yourself so thinly you have no time for nobody. So you have to start working out who you are going to blow out in a way. My life became crazy and hectic with the phone ringing every minute, so one of the criteria I decided on was, who has any racist tendencies, blow them out for a start"[4].

John Bradbury and Dick Cuthell were credited as co-writers alongside Dammers, who co-produced with Cuthell. *Racist Friend* even featured Roddy Radiation on guitar though he didn't rejoin, Dammers just pinched a guitar solo from an earlier Specials demo! The flip side of the single, which was released as a double A-side, was *Bright Lights,* a song dealing with the myth that London is a city with streets paved in gold. It also contained a reference to Colin Roach, a 21 year old black man who was shot dead at Stoke Newington police station in January 1983. This came after Jerry Dammers happened across a demonstration where Roach's father was arrested. Dammers was of the opinion that pop music was all about glitter and had lost touch with important issues.

"I got down to London and what did I see?

One thousand policeman all over the street,

The people were shouting and looking at me,

They say "the Colin Roach family demand an enquiry".

The single reached the charts but only peaked at No.60 before it faded away after a couple of weeks, although it was an improvement on the last single. As with *War Crimes*, *Racist Friend* contained a strong political message but had managed to chart on this occasion. On the day of the release, the band appeared on Channel 4's *Switch* and performed *The Lonely Crowd*, *Alcohol* and *Bright Lights*. Although it'd been two years since The Specials split, this was the first time the viewing public had seen the new look band, which now included saxophone player Andy Aderinto and Dick Cuthell had returned to the fray, having been absent on the previous single, although he didn't appear on *Switch*.

By now, the last three releases by The Special AKA, excluding the Rico single, had been strong political messages that weren't commercial in the slightest. Dammers planned to move away from this and produce more commercial music without diluting the subject matter to further the cause of commercialism, something he alluded to in an interview with *Sounds*. He spoke about the planned follow-up single *The Lonely Crowd*, which had been part-written about Lynval Golding being attacked in Coventry and Dammers felt particularly strongly about this; "The second verse is about Lynval getting stabbed. In London, the nightclub scene is quite nice and safe but in Coventry it is quite seedy and a bit nasty. There were all the articles in the papers about the great London nightlife and the reality in Coventry was Lynval nearly getting his bloody throat cut. And that was sickening in the extreme"[5]. The single was never released, with *The Lonely Crowd* eventually surfacing on the album.

Shortly after the release, The Special AKA recorded their one and only Peel session in late August when they performed versions of *Alcohol*, *Lonely Crowd* and *Bright Lights* and it was later aired in September. Jerry Dammers and Stan Campbell then appeared on *The Saturday Show* to promote *Bright Lights* where they were interviewed by David Rappaport, in character as

"Shades", although the conversation was limited to discussions about the band name and the upcoming LP with poor Stan Campbell not even getting a look in!

The band continued to work on the album, with the world not hearing another peep from them for the rest of the year. The album sessions were becoming expensive and with the band seemingly not making much progress, Chrysalis decided to move them into one of their own studios to save on the cost. The sessions were also notable for the growing tension between Dammers and Campbell, with the latter threatening to leave on numerous occasions.

Despite being active for almost two years, the band had still not played a live gig but did appear on Channel 4's *Play at Home*, recorded in early 1984 (although not broadcast until September). The show saw live performances and also some videos but the programme is most notable for its premiere of the song *Nelson Mandela*.

Dammers acknowledged that the song was still a bit rough around the edges and claimed he'd written it specifically for the programme. And although the finished song was slightly different, with 2 Tone's powers having waned in the previous two years, there was one glimmer of hope with the release of *Nelson Mandela*. The song was an anti-apartheid tune penned by Dammers about Nelson Mandela, a member of the ANC who'd been imprisoned since 1961 as a political prisoner. As hard as it is to imagine, Mandela was pretty much unknown in the UK in 1984, his name having been suppressed in the media. Dammers only became aware of him when he attended an anti-apartheid event. He'd started writing the song as The Specials were collapsing and eventually finished it off with the new band, Rhoda Dakar also has a credit on the original single.

The song featured a raft of guest musicians, Elvis Costello came in to produce the record and also provided some backing vocals, also on backing vocals were Afrodiziak, Molly & Polly Jackson, Dave

Wakeling, Ranking Roger and Lynval Golding. David Heath played flute and Paul Speare played the penny whistle.

Heath remembers the recording well; "I was going out with Caroline Lavelle at the time who was playing with Fun Boy Three and I met Jerry, who wanted me to play on *Nelson Mandela*. Two of the backing singers were overheard talking about Elvis Costello over the mikes "I thought Elvis was supposed to have a massive head but he looks quite normal!" and Elvis just said over the mike "that'll be all girls!" and they hadn't even sung anything!". Heath has been complimentary about working with The General; "I loved working with Jerry. My biggest problem working with him was trying to stop laughing. It turned into a real problem, we'd both start laughing uncontrollably and wouldn't be able to play anything for ages!".

The record was popular, reaching No.9, and helped to raise awareness about Nelson Mandela and the struggle against apartheid in South Africa. The single is the band's biggest achievement as it changed the political landscape and for the first time brought worldwide attention to Nelson Mandela and the fight against apartheid in South Africa. The song was banned in South Africa almost immediately but gained worldwide exposure and hit the charts in no fewer than five countries, including No.1 in New Zealand. South Africans could even be arrested for owning the record, such was the desperation for the message not to be heard. The UK government and Prime Minister Margaret Thatcher were of the opinion that Mandela was a terrorist but the tide began to change after the single was released and more people became aware of the trouble in South Africa.

Due to the success of the record, the band were required to do the obligatory TV performances to promote it, including appearances on *The Tube* and *Top of the Pops*. It was around this time that Stan Campbell left the band, he'd had interest from record companies and left to chase

the bright lights of stardom. He had to be persuaded to rejoin for the two performances on *Top of the Pops* and by the time of *The Tube* appearance he'd left the band completely with Elvis Costello taking on lead vocals. Dammers commented; "Leaving like he did was unnecessary, he could have waited until the LP came out and promoted it properly. What he did was obviously intended to fuck everything up, which to me is pointless"[6].

The success of *Nelson Mandela* brought attention to the band and Jerry Dammers in particular, who became a go-to name on anti-apartheid politics and was regularly interviewed on such matters. *Nelson Mandela* was the final song to be recorded and Dammers approached Elvis Costello after he'd praised the previous single *Racist Friend*. Costello was brought in to produce a song quickly in order to complete the album, leading to it being completed in just four days. However, Dammers decided to remix the album once again with more time and costs being run up in the studio. Costello was quoted at the time as saying "I don't want to be like my friend Jerry Dammers who stays in the studio forever in a day remixing your album 'till you don't know whether it's good or bad anymore. I've heard a rumour that he's going to remix it AGAIN, I can't believe he's going to be so foolish to do that because it sounds really good!".

The question of touring was again raised in an interview with The General in April's *Record Mirror*; "I wish I could say we'd tour, but unfortunately I can't promise anything like that at the moment. I hate to admit it, but the LP has been quite a studio production job and it'd be very difficult to translate live".

He toyed with the idea of playing a small venue but this posed its own problems; "I'd love to play in a pub but there would be so much attention from the press and everything that everyone would get too nervous. We did the *Switch* TV show to an audience of twenty people and we were really nervous".

He also touched on the previous albums by The Specials and went some way as to explain why the LP was taking so long to produce; "You have to realise that the first Specials LP took two years before it was made. We were playing for two and a half years before the public ever got to hear about The Specials. This band, after the original one broke up, has had to go back to square one. Start all over again"[7].

Shortly before the album's release, the band appeared on *Earsay* performing *Alcohol,* giving the public an insight into the upcoming album. Due to the success of *Nelson Mandela*, the LP was highly anticipated and after two long years in the studio, The Special AKA finally released *In The Studio*, in June. It couldn't have had any other name could it? Dammers had spent months slaving away at the mixing desk trying to perfect the album, remixing it a number of times before the release though he was now heavily in debt to Chrysalis. Because of the huge delay, there was very little promotion of the album as the label were unwilling to spend any more money. It was rumoured at the time that it'd cost around £500,000 to make! The General was contracted to provide another four albums but there was no money left to make them.

The album itself is a decent record, although it went over the heads of a lot of the public and music press. It was far removed from either Specials LP. David Storey returned to the fray to design the sleeve, as he'd done with Rico's releases and it was based on the cover of *Blues in the Closet* by Bud Powell, released in 1958. As The Special AKA had released a number of singles since 1982, there were only five songs on *In The Studio* that the public hadn't already heard. The singles *War Crimes, Racist Friend* and *Nelson Mandela* were included along with their respective 'B' sides, *Bright Lights* and *Break Down The Door*. The album marked a return for Rico, who played trombone on *Alcohol, Break Down The Door, Housebound* and *What I Like Most About You Is Your Girlfriend*. His friend Tony 'Groco' Uter also played the congas on *Break Down The Door*.

The unheard songs were *Housebound, Alcohol, Night on the Tiles, The Lonely Crowd* and *What I Like Most About You Is Your Girlfriend*. *Housebound* was based on Terry Hall, who became reclusive when he first became famous, struggling to cope with his new found fame and *Alcohol* was based on The General's struggle with alcohol and his experiences in stopping drinking.

The Special AKA released one final single in September, *What I Like Most About You Is Your Girlfriend*, featuring Jerry Dammers on lead vocals singing falsetto style. Laughably it featured Horace Panter two years after he left! It was backed by *Can't Get A Break*, which didn't appear on the album, and was released on both 7" and 12" and even featured on a special picture disc of Dammers dressed in a spacesuit!

The video sees him as an alien beamed down from space who goes into a pub and falls in love with a man's girlfriend. When he's rejected, he can be seen leaving and getting back into his spaceship! The band performed it on *Crackerjack* but only it reached No.51 in the charts.

To make up for the lack of live performance and to try and claw some money back, they released a VHS, *The Special AKA On Film*. It contained videos of most of the songs from the album, some of the videos had already been released previously, some were new recordings and a couple were taken from the *Play at Home* show. Barney Rubbles was involved in a couple of the videos and Dammers took a major role in the direction of them. As the band weren't performing live, he took a big interest in videos and recognised the power of them; "I think it's quite important because those videos are a bit more than promotional devices, they are the only performances of those songs by the people". He also told *Melody Maker*; "If videos are done well they can be the actual performance of the record"[8].

Although most publications claim that The Special AKA disbanded shortly after the release of the single, it's not really possible to put an exact date on when they ceased to exist.

We do know that Chrysalis gave Dammers a budget to make four albums but he used it all on *In The Studio*. He conducted a rare interview in *Melody Maker* in January 1985 where he spoke about the future of the band, making it clear they hadn't broken up and was on the lookout for a new singer to replace Stan Campbell. In another publication, he mentioned plans for a new single entitled *You Can't Take Love Seriously* which dealt with the idea that if you take relationships in their infancy too seriously, they'll usually end in tears.

Dammers never did find a new singer and although The Special AKA disbanded, there was no actual confirmation. Chrysalis were still wanting the four albums they were owed but with no budget to make them he had to sit tight until they came to an arrangement. Dammers remained in debt to Chrysalis until the late 1980s when he was finally released from the label.

The Special AKA are one of the only bands to never play a gig and it's fair to suggest this hampered them, they never had a chance to build up support by performing live and gathering an audience. Jerry Dammers was reluctant to go out on the road as he felt the media attention would be difficult but it could be argued that the lack of media attention was the band's downfall.

Although they released a number of singles and an album, promotional content was limited, partly due to the lack of funds available and partly because its very difficult to market songs about rape and war in Lebanon!

They were also very much a studio band, a lot of the sounds on the records would have been difficult to reproduce live. The songs had been worked out in the studio and featured a number of musicians on each song, a number of which played multiple instruments on the same track. Unlike The Specials, who had built up a rapport whilst playing live before they hit the big time and knew each other inside out, The Special AKA went through various line-up changes and some of the members never really got to know each other. Rhoda Dakar later commented in an article that she'd only met Stan Campbell on a couple of occasions and didn't know him. The sound of the singles also didn't help, this shows how cynical the music business is, both *The Boiler* and *War Crimes* were pretty gloomy whereas *Nelson Mandela* contained a similarly political message but because it sounded like a fun song, it gained much more exposure than the other two. *Nelson Mandela* was more radio friendly if you like. *The Boiler* and *War Crimes* would never have aired on *Top of the Pops* like *Nelson Mandela* did.

Nelson Mandela changed Jerry Dammers' life, as he became disillusioned with music due to his legal wrangles with Chrysalis, he threw himself into anti-apartheid campaigning founding the organisation Artists Against Apartheid in 1986 to try and engage people politically as well as organising music events. These events got bigger and bigger, culminating in a huge concert on Clapham Common in June 1986.

Two years later, in June 1988, Nelson Mandela's 70th birthday was marked by a concert at Wembley Stadium which was organised by Tony Hollingworth with a lot of help from Dammers. The concert saw *Nelson Mandela* get an airing with Dammers on keyboards and Dick Cuthell on cornet alongside a number of prominent South African musicians. There was also a specially remixed version released as a single and credited to The Special AKA. Mandela was released from prison in 1990 and a concert was held at Wembley in April, where the song was performed at the conclusion of the show.

Mandela later became the President of South Africa and the song was also played at his 90th birthday concert in 2007, with Amy Winehouse on vocals and Dammers playing the keyboards. Finally, when Mandela passed away in December 2013, Channel 4 News invited Jerry Dammers and his orchestra to play a special instrumental version of the song to close their news bulletin.

The label's powers may have waned by 1982 but there was one glimmer of what it once was in 1984 when The Special AKA released *Nelson Mandela*. Dammers brought attention to Mandela's plight and made the world sit up and listen. As hard as it is to believe, very few people had ever heard of Mandela in the UK in 1984 and his name had NEVER been mentioned in the Houses of Parliament up until that point. With *Nelson Mandela*, The Special AKA achieved something on a worldwide scale, which eventually led to his release in 1990.

Releases on 2 Tone

Singles:
The Boiler (January 1982)
Rhoda & The Special AKA
Jungle Music (March 1982)
Rico & The Special AKA
War Crimes (1982)
The Special AKA
Racist Friend (August 1983)
The Special AKA
Nelson Mandela (April 1984)
The Special AKA
What I Like Most About You Is Your Girlfriend (September 1984)
The Special AKA

Albums:
In The Studio (1984).

Where Are They Now?

Jerry Dammers
Keyboards 1981-1984
See The Specials.

Stan Campbell
Vocals, 1982-1984
Stan Campbell had been in the Coventry band Channel A before Jerry Dammers offered him the job of singer in The Special AKA. With aspirations of hitting the big time, Campbell was only too willing to join. Dammers and Campbell first met in a cafe when someone remarked that Campbell was a Grace Jones lookalike! He sang the lead vocals on a number of the songs on *In The Studio* and *Nelson Mandela*, in 1984.

Shortly after the release and subsequent success, Campbell left the band for good and tried to hold the band to ransom by demanding huge fees to appear with them on TV to promote the record. Although he appeared on *Top of the Pops*, his place was taken by Elvis Costello for a subsequent appearance on *The Tube*. Campbell signed a record deal in 1986 and recorded a self-titled solo album, *Stan Campbell*, released in 1987. Despite being an impressive piece of music, it didn't chart and Campbell never really fulfilled his promise. Later fell on hard times, arrested for harassing and attacking women in London, Coventry and Birmingham and sectioned indefinitely in 2002. However, he is now out and back living in Birmingham and has been seen busking in the past few years.

John Bradbury
Drums 1981-1984
See The Specials.

John Shipley
Guitar 1981-1984
See The Swinging Cats.

Dick Cuthell
Cornet, Flugelhorn, Bass, 1981-1984
See The Specials.

Gary McManus
Bass, 1982-1984
McManus had been the bassist and vocalist of Coventry band The Defendants in the late 1970s before he replaced Horace Panter on bass in 1982, although he didn't play on the record, he was thanked on the sleeve of *War Crimes* and played bass on the video. McManus remained with the band until the breakup and later passed away in 1999.

Andy Aderinto
Saxophone, 1983-1984
Aderinto joined the band in 1983 and played saxophone for the rest of the band's life, including on the biggest hit *Nelson Mandela*. After seemingly leaving the music business, Aderinto is now working as a photographer in London and is a volunteer with Meanwhile Gardens, a group in North Kensington.

Rhoda Dakar
Vocals, 1982-1984
See The Bodysnatchers.

Egidio Newton
Backing Vocals, 1982-1984
Newton was a friend of Rhoda Dakar after they'd first met whilst camping outside David Bowie's house! She was recruited by Jerry Dammers in 1982 as a backing vocalist and featured on a number of the songs on *In The Studio*. Afterwards, Newton moved away from music and hasn't featured on any releases since. She later worked as a creative practitioner offering interactive workshops for schoolchildren with her company Young Music Explorers and has worked as a photographer and artist based in Lambeth, South London.

Guest Musicians

The Special AKA featured a raft of guest and session musicians on their releases. Some of the musicians are not included here as they are already included in the sections for other bands. Rico Rodriguez appeared on a number of songs on *In The Studio* and also featured on *Jungle Music* in 1982, Tony 'Groco' Uter and Satch Dixon also appeared on *Jungle Music* and are covered in Rico's section, Horace Panter left the band in 1982 and is covered in The Specials. Elvis Costello, Ranking Roger, Dave Wakeling and Lynval Golding also sang backing vocals on *Nelson Mandela* and can be found under Elvis Costello & The Attractions, The Beat and The Specials respectively. Roddy Radiation's guitar playing was featured on the single, *Racist Friend* and he is covered in The Specials.

Anthony Wimshurst
Guitar, 1982
Wimshurst appeared on *Jungle Music* in 1982 and had been on tour with Rico during the latter stages of 1981. When they returned, they recorded *Jungle Music* and *Rasta Call You*. He later went to art college in Huddersfield and now runs his own stained glass window workshop, Anthony Wimshurst Stained Glass Workshop in Ruislip, Middlesex.

Afrodiziak
Backing Vocals, 1984
Afrodiziak were formed in 1982 and consisted of Caron Wheeler and Claudia Fontaine, later being joined by Naomi Thompson. The first record they featured on was the *Beat Surrender* single by The Jam, providing the backing vocals for one of the 'B' sides, *War*. They also provided backing vocals for The Jam on *The Tube* in November 1982, singing on *Beat Surrender*.

The band still consisted of Fontaine and Wheeler at this point with Thompson joining in 1983, by this time the trio had recorded backing vocals for Elvis Costello's *Punch The Clock*. After recording with Hayzee Fantazee, Afrodiziak recorded *Nelson Mandela* with The Special AKA and appeared on *The Tube* and *Top of the Pops* performances. They provided the backing vocals for the Madness single, *Michael Caine* and also worked with Heaven 17 and contributed backing vocals to the *Starvation* record in 1985. They later worked with Howard Jones and Julia Fordham before eventually disbanding in 1988.

Claudia Fontaine
Claudia Fontaine had originally performed as a duo with Caron Wheeler before Naomi Thompson joined Afrodiziak to make it a three-piece. She continued to be heavily involved with music afterwards, working with The Beatmasters in 1989 on their single *Warm Love* and with Serious Chocolate on their release *If You Wanna Lover* also in 1989. She had a long and distinguished career as a backing vocalist for a whole host of artists, working with Jimmy Somerville, Baby Ford, Maxi Priest and EMF although she most famously worked with Pink Floyd on their 1994 Division Bell Tour and with Robbie Williams performing backing vocals on *Let Me Entertain You* in 1997 and *Millennium* in 1998.

Fontaine later worked as a vocal arranger & vocal performance tutor as well as working with Geri Halliwell and Jools Holland before she passed away in March 2018 at the age of 57.

Caron Wheeler

Wheeler had been singing for a number of years, already being a member of the group Brown Sugar in 1976, a band that didn't last long but made an impression on the reggae charts. Wheeler remained a part of Afrodiziak until 1988 when she moved on to Soul II Soul, who are best known for their 1989 hit *Back To Life*. She remained with them until 1990, when she embarked on a solo career, resulting in the release of the album *UK Blak* which spawned the singles *Don't Quit*, *UK Blak* and *Livin' In The Light*. She later released her second solo effort, *Beach of the War Goddess* in 1993 and then rejoined Soul II Soul a year later in 1994. Once again, she didn't last very long and left in 1995, later releasing a duet with Toshinobu Kubota and moving into production work as well as providing the odd guest vocals and releasing her own solo stuff. Since 2007, Wheeler has performed live with Soul II Soul and continues to tour with the band.

Naomi Thompson

Thompson has remained in music and after Afrodiziak disbanded in 1988 she sang backing vocals on Erasure's 1988 song *Chains of Love* and also worked with World Beat Club on their single *Johannesburg*. She also worked with Betty Boo in 1990, appearing on *24 Hours*. Thompson was last known to be working with Dick Groves, a singer, songwriter and producer. She has appeared on some of his releases and also released her own solo work.

Paul Speare

Penny Whistle, 1984

Speare played the penny whistle on *Nelson Mandela* in 1984 and had previously been a member of Dexy's Midnight Runners between 1981 and 1982 before he formed a horn section with Jim Paterson and Brian Maurice from the band, called The TKO Horns and they worked with Elvis Costello in 1983. Speare worked as a music and media lecturer in further education until 2005 and has since worked as a freelance arranger and session musician. In 2020, he worked on a production project for a composer but this is yet to be released.

David Heath

Flute, 1984

Heath had been going out with Caroline Lavelle, who was working with Fun Boy Three, and was asked by Jerry Dammers to come along and play the flute on *Nelson Mandela*. They also worked together on the sessions for *Absolute Beginners* but Heath's contributions didn't make it past the demo stage. He has worked as a composer for many years and has worked with a number of prominent artists including; Nigel Kennedy, James Galway and Richard Blake. Heath has also worked in schools and continues to work in music, The Ulster Orchestra played some of his work in Belfast in February 2020, a performance that was broadcast on BBC Radio 3.

Molly & Polly Jackson

Backing Vocals, 1984

Molly & Polly were two sisters that John Bradbury had met in a bar in Camden and they sang backing vocals on *Nelson Mandela*. They had previously sung backing vocals with JB's Allstars and also sung backing vocals with The Boomtown Rats and Status Quo before leaving the music business. Polly has become a qualified lawyer and is now working in London at Strictly Law, having been a partner in the business since 2011. Molly also works with her sister and has written two novels and a screenplay which as yet are unpublished.

Nick Parker

Violin, 1982

Following his brief involvement with The Special AKA, Parker played with Madness on their 1983 tour, having previously played with the Fun Boy Three on their 1982 release *Summertime*. He has since played violin with the Academy of Ancient Music, the English Baroque Soloists, London Early Music Group and the Capella Coloniensis and these associations have involved tours all over the world. Parker has also played stage music for a number of productions at the National Theatre and his music has featured in television and film. He is currently working as a recording producer of classical music productions on CD.

Pic by Stephen Leonard-Williams

The Apollinaires

The Apollinaires were born out of the ashes of a post-punk band from Leicester called Il Y A Volkswagens with Paul Tickle (vocals), Kraig Thornber (drums), Francis Brown (guitar), Dave Allonby (guitar) and James Hunt (bass) making up the original band.

After numerous gigs, they were booked in for a Capital Radio session after being spotted in London. The session was heard by Geoff Travis from Rough Trade and he got them into the studio to record two singles. *Kill Myself* was released on Rough Trade in 1981, although it didn't make an impact on the charts and the other single remains unreleased.

The original band were dark, moody and electronic but had become disillusioned with the music they were playing as it didn't resemble what they were dancing to in clubs and decided to disband. The band then quickly reformed as The Volkswagens in July 1981, on the day of the Royal Wedding.

The Volkswagens began as a 6-piece consisting of; Paul Tickle (vocals), Tom Brown (guitar), Francis Brown (guitar), Kraig Thornber (drums & backing vocals), James Hunt (bass) and Simon Kirk (percussion). Kirk and Tom Brown were recruited to try and add some danceability to the band, with both of them adding new ideas to the group, with funk being their biggest influence.

Tickle declared in an interview that they were a funk group, whereas Tom Brown felt it was a reaction to the old group, which had more intensity and anger than the new one.

The band also experimented with brass and the early days saw The Swinging Laurels join them on stage. The Laurels were a Leicester based horn section containing the seasoned saxophone players Gaz Birtles and John Barrow. Barrow remembers it well; "The Apollinaires were a group of guys we'd been friends with for a couple of years prior to their 2 Tone association. When they formed the band, they recruited us in on brass for their live shows".

The Laurels were in demand as session musicians and it was becoming increasingly apparent that the arrangement wouldn't last forever and the band started to look for their own brass section, firstly recruiting Peter Millen on saxophone. Millen says; "Someone told them that I owned a saxophone and so one night Paul and James turned up at my door and asked if I'd like to audition. I showed up at their house on Turner Street where they rehearsed in the basement. I couldn't play very well but they must have liked something because they asked me back". Millen found himself becoming part of The Swinging Laurels for a while and is complimentary about their involvement; "So I became for a short while an extra Swinging Laurel at gigs which was terrifying as I'd never really played in front of people but the Laurels were great and really supportive - really nice guys".

With 2 Tone on its knees after The Specials split up in late 1981, Jerry Dammers set about trying to unearth some new talent.

By now, the ska explosion had finished and the charts were dominated by New Romantics, new wave and funk. Dammers decided to sign something different to try and move the label on. A mutual friend had told him to go and watch The Volkswagens at the Horsefair, Leicester. John Barrow fills in the blanks; "We did a number of gigs with them when Jerry Dammers was scouting them. Jerry was dating a Leicester girl at the time and we bumped into him a number of times at the Prohibition Club in Leicester. In fact, he took a look at the Swinging Laurels too and came to a couple of our gigs".

Dammers turned up at the Horsefair and was impressed with what he saw. He introduced himself and told them he was interested in seeing them play in unfamiliar surroundings. He organised a gig in Coventry, which was treated as an audition, it went well and they sent Dammers a demo tape to listen to.

He soon offered them a two-single deal with the option of a third and they were

happy to accept as he'd shown a genuine interest in them and saw them as a band rather than just a product. Dammers has since said; "Ska exhaustion had definitely set in so 2 Tone were searching for a new direction. There was a bit of a twisted 'whiteboy funk' thing emerging, which seemed like it might have potential".

Simon Kirk and James Hunt share a cig!
(Pic. Stephen Leonard-Williams)

The band were soon in the studio at Woodbine, Leamington Spa and Dammers would be producing. It was also here where the name changed to The Apollinaires, Peter Millen says; "Somewhere here too the name had to change to The Apollinaires as I think someone else had the Volkswagens name. Who'd have thought it!". The Swinging Laurels also took part in the sessions. John Barrow has since said; "They asked us to play on their first single for 2 Tone. The song *The Feeling's Gone,* had become a live favourite during our sporadic live appearances with the band and this gave us a unique opportunity to work with both factions after The Specials split, having already worked with the Fun Boy Three"[1].

The recording began but after a couple of days, Dammers decided the song needed a flute on it and Millen suggested that his and Thornber's housemate, Stephen Leonard-Williams would be a good choice. Leonard-Williams was thrown in at the deep end, as he'd never even been in a studio before, but was reassured by Dammers.

He says; "Jerry was both patient and supportive and made it relatively easy for me. I played some repeating riffs, some parts of the brass backing and a short solo which I was given free rein to do as I liked". Millen also describes a similar situation; "Once again I learned a lot from the Laurels but also got the chance to write some of the brass lines which gave me a lot of confidence".

The Laurels had only expected to be in the studio for a couple of hours but ended up spending two days there! Barrow says; "Jerry was a fascinating, complex character, but he was one of those pedantic perfectionists that insisted on twenty takes to record a line that was perfect on take one".In a bizarre twist of fate, The Laurels had played on Fun Boy Three's single *The Telephone Always Rings* in May, although Dammers didn't hold this against them! Barrow remembers; "When we recorded the brass for *The Telephone Always Rings* it coincided with The Apollinaires' release which was a potentially prickly point!".

The band's first single, *The Feeling's Gone* was released in July and it saw a guest appearance from Rhoda Dakar on backing vocals. The 'B' side was an instrumental version entitled *The Feeling's Back*. Paul Tickle told the Leicester Mercury; "I suppose it's a love song. It's about the degeneration of a relationship, people getting fed up with each other and deciding to split up before it gets any worse"[2]. The single failed to chart and the reviews were chalk and cheese, with one reviewer describing it as "a mess from start to finish" whereas the *NME* described it as "particularly impressive"[3]. Barrow sums it up perfectly; "*The Feeling's Gone* was a fabulous slice of pop/funk and should have been a hit in my opinion". Dammers commented on the single in *Record Mirror* but was critical of his own work; "I don't think I did a particularly good production job on *The Feeling's Gone*. I thought that was a really good song, maybe someone should do a cover of it"[4]. Dammers had taken influence from Curtis Mayfield's *Move On Up* and was aiming to produce his version of the song.

Simon Kirk, Tom Brown, Paul Tickle, Kraig Thornber, Francis Brown (Pic. Stephen Leonard-Williams)

By now, The Apollinaires were being compared to bands such as Pigbag and Haircut 100 with their fusion of funk, jazz and melody. One review described the band as "Britain's newest, tightest percussive-funk outfits who're gonna make you forget Pigbag and Haircut 100 ever existed". It's easy to see the comparisons with Pigbag, who took the charts by storm with *Papa's Got A Brand New Pigbag* in March 1982, as they had an eclectic mix of brass musicians including alto, tenor and baritone saxophones, a trombone, clarinet and steel drums, similar instruments to what The Apollinaires boasted at the time. However, The Apollinaires played at a much faster pace and were more of a funk band than a post-punk band like Pigbag. The comparisons with Haircut 100 are less understandable, although they had a saxophonist in the ranks, they sounded nothing like The Apollinaires.

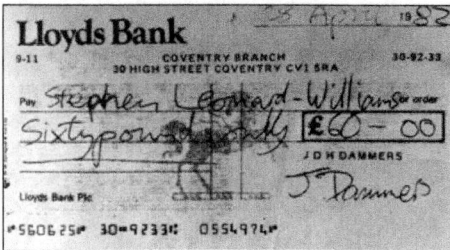

Cheque paid to Stephen Leonard-Williams
signed by Jerry Dammers

After the experiments with brass on the first release, it was decided to keep the brass section, with Peter Millen and Stephen Leonard-Williams remaining in the band. However, The Swinging Laurels mutually agreed to part ways with the band and were replaced by Laurence Wood, Paul Hood and Chris Freestone, making the group an 11-piece.

Gaz Birtles has since called The Apollinaires "Leicester's coolest ever band". Wood remembers joining the band; "I was a Fine Art painting student at Leicester Polytechnic, and I co-formed a band from the Fine Art department called Farm Life. There were Andy Mosquera, Mark Thompson, James Hunt and myself on clarinet and sax.

We played a kind of experimental music. Paul Tickle, also in the Fine Art department asked if I was interested in joining his new band emerging from the Volkswagens. I decided to join". Interestingly, the brass section were paid as session musicians and as Leonard-Williams says; "In the end this probably meant that we did better financially than the original core band members!". Once the brass section was complete, the band started to write and rehearse new material. Millen looks back fondly; "We seemed to gel really quickly and sounded really tight. It was really fun working out all the brass lines and harmonies - some based on stuff the Laurels had been doing and a lot of our own stuff".

The brass section in action during a gig
(Pic. Stephen Leonard-Williams)

After the single release, The Apollinaires recorded their one and only Peel session in July, recording versions of; *The Feeling's Gone, Envy The Love, First Degree* and *Dance With Your Heart*. The session was broadcast August 25th. The line-up by this point consisted of Paul Tickle (vocals), Tom Brown (guitar), Francis Brown (guitar), Kraig Thornber (drums), James Hunt (bass), Simon Kirk (percussion), Peter Millen (alto saxophone), Laurence Wood (tenor saxophone), Paul Hood (trombone), Chris Freestone (trumpet) and Stephen Leonard-Williams (flute). The 2 Tone connection also helped them with gigs and things had developed pretty quickly, as Millen remembers; "Fast forward a couple of months and the first single was out, we did a Peel session and the connection with 2 Tone got the band on a good booking agency and gigs around the country".

The Apollinaires also toured with label mates The Higsons towards the end of 1982, a band that were playing a similar funk sound and had experienced similar hostility from 2 Tone die-hards and the music press in general, due to the fact they weren't remotely ska.

The band in full flow
(Pic. Stephen Leonard-Williams)

The band were soon back in the studio to record the next single and they knew that this was their chance to kick on, especially after the disappointment with the first single. Wood says; "Recording the second single was really exciting as in many ways it could have been the single that launched a whole different level of success, and we knew that. I think we also all learned a great deal about recording and trying to capture some of the energy that everybody said was a feature of our live gigs".

The band were now playing a unique fusion of funk, jazz and melody and as Millen says; "We were playing two or three times a week and rehearsing new material so we improved rapidly and really sounded good live". The new arrivals settled in well and added a new dimension to the band as they now boasted a five-piece brass section, all of whom added their own little bit to the mix. Warne Livesey was approached to produce the single. Livesey is now a respected producer but back then was very much a rookie.

As the first single had been experimental, the decision was taken to make a more radio friendly single this time around. Millen says; "*The Feelings Gone* had been a little experimental with Jerry referencing his love for Curtis Mayfield's *Move On Up* so I think the decision was made by 2 Tone to go a bit more pop hit/radio friendly with the next one".

While Livesey's talents as a producer are not in doubt, some of the band think he held them back. Millen says; "You could tell this meant a lot to him, he took his role seriously and was a perfectionist. In retrospect I feel he was a little too precise and sanitised our sound a bit. It was a slick production but lacked some of the grit and soul of our live sound". Laurence Wood shares a similar view; "I think that the production made us less distinctive and less experimental, even if much funkier. It's always a difficult balance to try and tap into a mainstream trend and yet retain some quirkiness".

Wood has since pondered the possibility that the band were ahead of their time; "Maybe the production style and timing was also slightly behind the 'curve' in terms of trends". When *Envy The Love* was released in November, Wood's observations were definitely evident though The Apollinaires aren't the first band to have struggled to transmit their live performances on to record and certainly not the last. Dammers has since said of The Apollinaires; "Unfortunately, although they were all very nice lads, and very nice records, with the funky sounds, 2 Tone never again reached the dizzy heights of the ska period"[5].

The band in London on their way to record *Envy The Love*
(Pic. Stephen Leonard-Williams)

Paul Tickle and Kraig Thornber in the studio
(Pic. Stephen Leonard-Williams)

Despite the band's disappointment with the finished product, the single was indeed more radio friendly than the first and received a lot more airplay. Rumours were swirling at the time; "The rumour was that if we sold enough records to break the Top 60 we were going to get a slot on *Top of the Pops*. Never happened though, sales dipped off after two or three weeks I think" says Millen. *Envy The Love* fell away after a few weeks and never did manage to break into the charts.

A third single was discussed briefly but never materialised and the band left 2 Tone shortly afterwards. Millen remembers; "There was talk of a third single but I don't think 2 Tone had the same clout with their major label partners to take a further risk. Shame because we did have a couple of newer songs that might have gone somewhere". Paul Hood looks back fondly on that period; "It was an exciting time and looking back, the whole 2 Tone thing was fairly great music...more than that, more like a movement". It is important to note the affection and gratitude that some of the band have for Jerry Dammers with Millen describing him as; "a lovely bloke, very regular and open and happy to join us in the pub for a pint! I bumped into Jerry again one evening on a London Street and was gratified to be recognised".

When the band played live, they strived to recreate the sound of the records on stage and seemed quite proud of the fact that they didn't make any money from playing live due to paying all the musicians. They felt it was important to present their sound in its entirety and the lack of money-making was a burden they were prepared to shoulder.

The live performances are remembered fondly by the various members and a number of them maintain that they were a better live band than the records seem to suggest. A number of gigs took place in Leicester including their local, The Prohibition but the band branched out and played all over the UK mainly in colleges and arts centres but also venues that are shrouded in history and coolness such as The Canvey Island Gold Mine and The Hacienda in Manchester, as well as travelling to Paris to play a show at Club Gibus! They travelled to these gigs in a 1960's Bedford bus they bought from the British Shoe Corporation!

Laurence Wood remembers some of the gigs; "I loved all our gigs! As the momentum grew, they became increasingly exciting and we had real dynamism as a live outfit and you could always see the audience could feel that. I remember fans at one gig gesturing us to slow the tempo down as it was so fast! The tour to Paris gave us all a taste of what might come next...but it didn't turn out as planned when we got back to the UK!".

Stephen Leonard-Williams in front of the famous tour bus
(Pic. Stephen Leonard-Williams)

154

The bus got them to Paris as Peter Millen says; "We drove there in our 20 seat coach that we bought from a shoe factory and that Kraig and I drove everywhere", it also led to a strange incident where he lost his saxophone! "I left my saxophone under my hotel bed by accident after too many beers at the gig and thought it was gone forever until we found out that the manager had given it to label mates The Higsons (who we performed with on a few occasions as a double bill) who had played Paris a few days after".

Paul Hood, Laurence Wood and Peter Millen recording *Envy The Love* (Pic. Stephen Leonard-Williams)

They also recorded a session for Kid Jensen in March featuring another three original compositions, *Ideal Couple, Give it Up* and *Shape Up*. Laurence Wood feels this material had potential; "Within the sessions we did for John Peel and Kid Jensen, there is a huge amount of musical material that could have been further exploited. I think we were a band that should have done an album which could have demonstrated the depth of musical creativity and the ambitious range of our music".

The Apollinaires made their only appearance on television in April, appearing on Channel 4's *Switch*, performing *Envy The Love* and *Ideal Couple*. The clip is the only known footage of the band performing live, it shows a frantic performance and one can imagine how exciting some of those live gigs must have been with the fusion of 2 Tone funk. However, this period wasn't all plain sailing as Millen remembers; "After a while though I think it all started to lose it's appeal. Keeping a large band together became difficult and the feeling was gone!

People start to get on each other's nerves. Ironically we did our one and only TV appearance as things were starting to wind down in 1983, on *Switch*, a Channel 4 pop show with Tears for Fears".

By 1983, Margaret Thatcher had been Prime Minister for four years and Thatcherism was at its most powerful. The Conservative government's continued assault on the public sector was being opposed by the Stop The Cuts campaign and had been since the mid 1970s, however the campaign had become stale. The National and Local Government Officers' Association (NALGO) had decided to change tact and they launched Put People First, a £1 million campaign which was designed to alert the public as to what the government were doing and to try and stir up a reaction.

By now, the band's association with 2 Tone had finished after the release of *Envy The Love* but they continued to perform and were soon back in the studio where they recorded *Put People First*, an anti-privatisation tune. It was also believed to be the first record to record to be commissioned by a trade union. Laurence Wood says; "We did another single, for the Put People First Campaign which I think is much stronger in terms of musical inventiveness, irrespective of the politics. If we could have taken that direction back into 2 Tone for a third single I think the Apollinaires would have become very distinctive and could have expanded the musical boundaries for 2 Tone too".

Soon after, the band had started to fragment with different members pulling in different directions and they intended to carry on but with a different name, The Apollinaires had broken up by mid 1983. Wood remembers those final days; "I can't recall the details of the last gig we played...I think in London perhaps..but I remember the trouble between some members of the band during and after the gig. I guess there were conversations with 2 Tone as well, that I was not party to, concerning the size of the band and the plans for a third single".

Soon after, most of the brass section had left the band and The General Idea emerged as Leonard-Williams remembers; "The General Idea had the same core line-up but most of the brass section wasn't involved. It never really took-off but I've got a fantastically pretentious mission statement that was issued at the time". Millen is also unsure of the specifics; "As to post Apollinaires, some of the guys, Frank, Tom and Paul had a band called The General Idea I think but I don't think it went very far. I pretty much lost touch after I moved". Many months followed before The General Idea played their first gig as a five piece at De Montfort Hall in May 1984 and their second and final gig occurred a week later at the Recession/Spectrum Club in Leicester but the project never really got off the ground and the new band had broken up by the end of 1984.

Releases on 2 Tone

The Feeling's Gone (1982)
Envy The Love (1982)

Where are They Now?

Paul Tickle
Vocals, 1981-1983
Tickle was one of the original members of the band and left the music business after The Apollinaires disbanded. He had studied Fine Art and was a talented artist, joining Next as a graphic designer. Tickle spent over 25 years in the graphics team at Next and sandwiched between this was a 4 year spell at Futurebrand. While at Futurebrand he designed the famous Walls Ice Cream logo and also worked on the British Airways logo when it was redesigned. He was a respected artist at Next, respected and well-liked by his fellow colleagues. Away from work, he was a keen cyclist and had completed the amateur leg of the Tour de France on several occasions, even earning a medal on one of those occasions. He continued to work for Next until 2018 before he sadly passed away in July 2019.

Tom Brown
Guitar, 1981-1983
Brown joined the band when they became The Volkswagens and his brother Francis was already in the band at this point. Brown remained in The Apollinaires until the breakup in 1983. A talented artist, Brown now works for himself as an artist and has spent over twenty years working in the specialist painting and interior design industry. He also worked with his brother Francis until 2010 when he passed away. Brown is still living in Leicester.

Francis Brown
Guitar, 1981-1983
Brown was an original member of the band when they were known as the I I YA Volkswagens and remained when they became The Volkswagens. When the band went their separate ways, he moved into art and became an interior designer and worked with his brother before he passed away in 2010 after a battle with cancer. He had been living in Leicester before his untimely passing.

Kraig Thornber
Drums, 1981-1983
Thornber was an original member of the band and remained until the breakup in 1983. He enrolled at East 15 Acting School and graduated in 1987. His first television appearance came on *The Bill* in 1988. He has since made the occasional appearance on TV and film but his acting is mostly on stage. Thornber has been a consistent performer for many years and is constantly in work, he has appeared in a number of West End productions and other stage productions including numerous pantomimes. Aside from his acting career, Thornber has worked as a choreographer on a number of stage productions and is noted for his work with Bowjangles, a comedy string-quartet that have been touring the world for over a decade.

James Hunt
Bass, 1981-1983
Hunt went on to work as a journalist for the Leicester Mercury and has gone on to be very successful in television.

He worked on *This Morning* as an editor and later executive producer. Hunt later worked for Sky Arts as the Channel Director before he stepped down in 2014. He is now a TV Executive and involved with production company, Subtle Productions.

Simon Kirk
Percussion, 1981-1983
Kirk joined the band in their early days and remained throughout. He left the UK in the 1990s to relocate to New Zealand where he now works and resides with his family.

Peter Millen
Alto Saxophone, 1981-1983
Millen joined the band just before the first single and remained when they decided to recruit their own brass section. After the split in 1983, Millen moved into graphic design at Shoot That Tiger. The studio designed record sleeves and he worked on covers for stars such as David Bowie, Aretha Franklin and Tina Turner. Ironically, it was the very studio where The Apollinaires covers had been designed! After a couple of years here, Millen moved to New York with his girlfriend in 1985 and was a director of Corey Edmonds Millen until 1993. He then founded his own design agency in the city, Peter Millen Design. The company boasts clients such as HBO, EMI and BBC Worldwide amongst others. He also occasionally plays the saxophone with friends, just for fun though!

Laurence Wood
Tenor Saxophone, 1981-1983
When Wood left the band, he was offered a place at the Royal College of Art, London where he studied a full time Masters degree in Painting for three years. While he was at the RCA, he played tenor saxophone at some live gigs and also recorded with the band Champion Doug Veitch in 1986, even playing a Peel session with the band. During the same year, Wood won a scholarship in Venice where he studied painting. It was around this time he started to become involved in martial arts, later becoming a semi-professional Kung Fu instructor.

He has since worked in arts and design and has worked as a writer, illustrator, contemporary painter and academic. He was the Dean of the University for the Creative Arts in the UK but retired from the role in 2012 to concentrate full time on his painting career. However, he was unexpectedly offered a professorship in Hong Kong in a department that specialises in art and music.

He now works as an academic and a painter and has had some solo shows and exhibitions in the UK and across Asia. Wood now rarely plays the saxophone but concentrates on learning the electric guitar and divides his time between Hong Kong, Germany and the UK with his wife and child.

Paul Hood
Trombone, 1982-1983
Hood joined the band when they were recruiting their own brass section in the build up to the second single release. He remained in the band until the split in 1983 and has since moved to Cologne, Germany where he now lives and works.

Chris Freestone
Trumpet, 1982-1983
Freestone joined the band along with Paul Hood but appears to have dropped off the face of the Earth since the breakup of the band. There is no information of Freestone's current whereabouts and none of the band appear to have kept in touch with him.

Stephen Leonard-Williams
Flute, 1982-1983
Leonard-Williams left music and moved to Cornwall with his girlfriend (now wife) in 1984 to try and start a business. He'd trained as a silversmith at college but ended up in engineering, a world he stayed in for 20 years. He set up his own business in 2002, Composite Integration and has recently semi-retired. He still plays music and enjoys making his own stuff and is still living in Cornwall with his wife.

Guest Musicians

The Swinging Laurels
Horn Section, 1982-1983

The Swinging Laurels were formed in 1980 by saxophonists John Barrow and Gaz Birtles, Barrow had been playing with Black Gorilla and Birtles with The Wendy Tunes. As well as their session work, they released six singles of their own. They were recruited by The Apollinaires to play on their first single *The Feeling's Gone* but the association was later ended by mutual agreement. The duo continued their session work throughout the 1980s, featuring on releases by Fun Boy Three, Musical Youth and Norman Beaton before becoming Happy House, a couple of years after they'd formed their own record label Happy Records based at their Happy House studio! They worked with Rhoda Dakar on the track *School of Faith* and she joined them for live performances regularly. By 1989, the band were known as The Swinging Laurels once again and had added Tony Robinson to the mix. Paul Heaton was looking for a brass section for his new group The Beautiful South and asked Birtles, Barrow and Robinson to attend an audition. Due to work commitments, Barrow was unable to attend so Kev Brown went in his place. Heaton liked the three of them and they were in the band, an association which carried on until 2007! The Laurels remained on hiatus throughout the 1990s until Birtles and Barrow released the CD *Be Someone* in 1997. Another eight years followed before they were invited to play on some tracks for Leicester band Ist in 2005 and also played on some live dates with the band. They later continued the association by providing the brass on Ist's 2009 album *Toothpick Bridge*.

Gaz Birtles
Saxophone, 1981-1982

After The Swinging Laurels disbanded, Birtles joined The Beautiful South in 1989 and remained in the band until 2007. He carried on with some of his former bandmates and formed the tribute band, The South in 2009. When the lead singer of The South, Dave Hemingway left the band in early 2017, Birtles replaced him as the lead singer and remains so to this day. Away from his work with The South, Birtles has been involved in music promotion at Leicester venue The Donkey since 2006 and also books the bands and deals with the front of house sound for gigs. He has also ventured into production, working with Babygenius in 2000 and Kevin Hewick on his 2007 single *Something To Do On The Bus*.

John Barrow
Saxophone, 1981-1982

The other half of The Swinging Laurels, Barrow has a CV as long as your arm and it's probably easier to name the artists that he hasn't played with over the years. Boy George, Bananarama, The Clash, Iggy Pop, Radio Riddler and Culture Club are just some of them. Barrow continues to work in music and released his memoirs in 2007, *How Not To Make it in The Pop World*. These memoirs have recently been updated and were re-released in 2020.

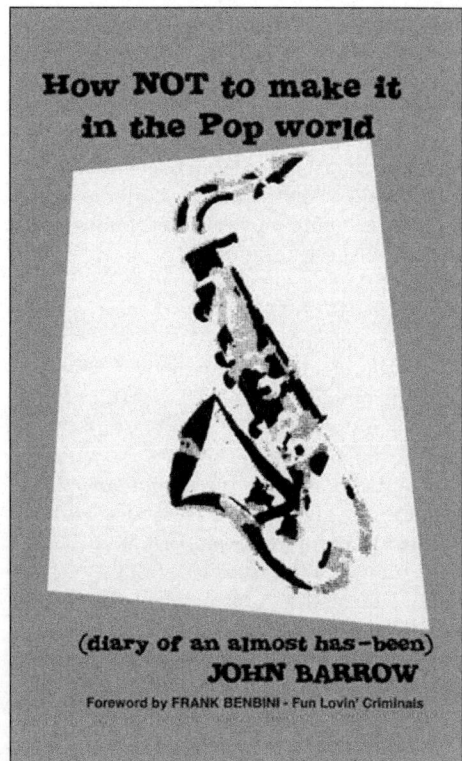

How NOT to make it in the Pop world

(diary of an almost has-been)
JOHN BARROW

Foreword by FRANK BENBINI - Fun Lovin' Criminals

The Higsons

Charlie 'Switch' Higson enrolled at the University of East Anglia in 1977 to study English and American Literature with a minor in Film Studies. While he was there, Higson wanted to form his own band, it was the height of punk and if there was one thing that punk had told people it was that anyone could have a go at forming a band.

Higson remembers it well; "When I went to university in 1977, the first thing I wanted to do was form a band. It seemed to be the best way to arse about on stage under the spotlight, impress your mates and get off with girls". He soon formed The Right Hand Lovers, which featured Paul Whitehouse amongst others and they played punk/fast rock and roll. They played a number of gigs but as time went on, most of the band members were kicked out of university and went home. Higson, unfettered by this, decided to form a new one with a fresh intake of students.

Punk was now on its last legs and this was now the era of post-punk, Higson wanted his band to represent these changes in musical styles and he formed a new one in January 1980. Whilst 2 Tone was taking the country by storm, there was also an emerging hip music scene which the band latched on to.

The University of East Anglia had a permanent ENTS officer and this meant that a lot of bands would play on campus and this led to the opportunity of local bands securing support slots, which Higson's band managed to do, including a gig supporting The Fall. The band consisted of himself (lead vocals, percussion), Terry Edwards (guitar/saxophone/trumpet), Dave Cummings (guitar), Colin Williams (bass) and Simon Charterton (drums).

After experimenting with the name of the band, Higson Brothers, Higson 5 and the Higson Experience being some of the early names before they eventually settled for The Higsons. Their early gigs were performed on campus and in and around their adopted home city of Norwich, including the Gala Ballroom and Jacquard Club.

As the band were learning their craft, they experimented with their sound, although it took them a while to find their groove. They eventually started to fuse punk with funk and disco as well as adding lots of percussion and African influences topped off with elements of jazz. This style was eventually branded "punk funk", Charlie Higson remembers; "What we did was spiky, jerky and rhythmic, with choppy guitars and lots of brass and percussion, I used to 'play' a bit of trumpet and hit a metal waste bin".

The Higsons weren't alone in playing this fusion of white punk with funk, disco and percussion, Pigbag, Rip Rig & Panic and A Certain Ratio were also playing similar music at the time. A 1982 press release stressed that The Higsons were reluctant to be associated with The White Funk Boy tag and this led the band to insist that their music was dance music to be enjoyed and thought about.

Charlie Higson and Dave Cummings were a year older than the rest of the band and they graduated in 1980. This culminated in the departure of Cummings, who moved to London in December of that year. "After graduating I left the band and moved to London into a flat with Paul Whitehouse". The band turned to Stuart McGeachin to replace Cummings on guitar and he would feature on all but one of the band's recordings over the next few years. Terry Edwards remembers; "The original line-up included Dave Cummings on guitar who was replaced by Stuart McGeachin when Dave moved to London. It was with Stuart that we found our punk/funk sound".

The band's first experience of a recording session came in 1981 with the band hiring

some equipment and recording it in Terry Edwards' parents house; "Our first recording session took place in Hornchurch at my parents' place where we hired an 8-track machine which a friend of mine, Ian McDonald engineered. I'd made a few demos on a 4-track with him before going to university and it was the cheapest option at the time. There were no recording studios in Norwich at that time believe it or not!".

The Higsons appeared on *Welcome To Norwich - A Fine City*, a compilation featuring various Norwich bands released on the independent label Romans In Britain. Charlie Higson takes up the story; "Similarly inspired by the punk, can-do ethos and our growing local success, other bands started forming around Norwich.

A couple of enterprising mates started a label and put out a compilation called *Norwich A Fine City*, on which we had two tracks". The two tracks they contributed were; *My Love Is Bent (At Both Ends)* and *We Will Never Grow Old*.

John Peel heard the album and he became aware of The Higsons, he was living in Norfolk and took an interest in the emerging music scene in Norwich which also contained Screen 3, The Mohair Twins, The Panic Parade, The Farmer's Boys and The Happy Few amongst others. Simon Charterton spoke about John Peel in the *NME* in August 1981; "Peel said there was nothing going on in Norwich so we wrote a letter to him and he came to see us at the Gala Ballroom. He played the album tracks. He's the only person playing good stuff on the radio". Peel soon became a fan and offered them their first Peel session in May 1981. The session saw them record five of their songs and anyone listening to the John Peel show on June 1st 1981 would have been treated to versions of *(I Don't Want To Live With) Monkeys, Got To Let This Heat Out, A Dash To The Shops* and *Surrender*. This session became the most repeated debut session on Peel's radio show, until The Smiths broke that record in 1983.

The Peel session encouraged the band's friends at Romans In Britain to put out a single. They recorded *I Don't Want To Live With Monkeys*, which would be the 'A' side and *Insect Love* appeared on the 'B' side. The 'A' side was the band's response to *Oops Upside Your Head* by The Gap Band which had been released in 1979. The single, released in July, performed well and after being championed by John Peel, it managed to hit the top of the Indie charts just months after its release. Despite selling over 10,000 copies of the single, they were tangled up in a dispute with the label over unpaid royalties. The success encouraged The Higsons to form their own independent record label and with the help of a local record shop (Banks Records) and The Cartel (a co-operative record distribution organisation), they formed Waap Records.

The band were becoming popular on the live music scene and were now playing beyond Norfolk. The Higsons were also pretty unique in the fact that they would make their living by playing live. They wouldn't use roadies, spend the night kipping on people's floors, and make a profit each time they toured or played gigs.

Shortly after the first Peel session, the band recorded a BBC Radio One session with Richard Skinner in August with recorded versions of *The Lost And The Lonely, (My Love Is) Bent (At Both Ends), Crash* and *It All Goes Waap!!* all getting an airing.

The session was soon followed by their second Peel session in October, recording versions of *We Will Never Grow Old, Conspiracy, Where Have All The Club A-Go-Go's Went?* and *Touchdown*. This session was later broadcast in November and repeated in December.

Shortly after the Peel session was first aired, the double 'A' side *The Lost and the Lonely/ It Goes Waap* was released in November. This release was quickly followed by a 12" single release, *Got To Let This Heat Out*, in December which featured a re-recorded version of the B-side of the previous single *It Goes Waap*. These singles didn't make a dent in the charts but did well in the Indie Charts. Ultimately they didn't replicate the success of the band's first single.

More live shows followed before The Higsons released their fourth single *Conspiracy* in April 1982, backed by *Touchdown*, which later featured on a Fortuna compilation that borrowed the song's name and was released later in 1982.

The single was followed by the release of *Live At The Jacquard Club,* a cassette of a show that'd been recorded in February. April also saw the band record a session with Kid Jensen at BBC Radio One, which saw them record versions of *Burn The Whole Thing Down* and *Ha! Ha!* amongst others.

To give you an idea of what a typical Higsons show would be like, here's a review from April 1982 when Roy Bainton reviewed their show at The Warehouse, Leeds; "There's a lean, stripped quality to their brand of fun-funk. Their sheer energy overwhelms and sucks you to the front of the stage. Switch's almost casual voice style is deceptive - he bursts with musical aggression which he pours into every trumpet note, every thrash with a stick on those Higsons trademarks, the empty paint tins". Bainton finished off the review with; "It's bands like The Higsons which show just how healthy and creative the British music scene is, and what a flaccid beast the American music machine has become".

By 1982, Jerry Dammers was looking for new blood to sign to 2 Tone after the breakup of The Specials while also recognising that for the label to move forward, it was necessary to try and move away from ska. Simon Charterton and Stuart McGeachin had already met Dammers at a party, with Charterton remembering; "we were all drunk and went on the rampage in this big house".

Terry Edwards confirms the story; "The Specials were all quite keen on our debut single *I Don't Want To Live With Monkeys* and Jerry happened to be at a party that Simon and Stuart were at and the idea was sprung there".

Dammers was interviewed in early 1982 and when asked who he thought the best new act were, he said The Higsons. Dammers signed The Apollinaires and The Higsons, both on two-single deals. Unlike most of the other bands that'd been on 2 Tone, The Higsons had a back catalogue behind them before they signed to the label. Charlie Higson remembers; "Dammers really liked our early records and I think that by 1982 the whole ska thing was coming to a natural end. Jerry wanted to reinvent 2 Tone and keep it moving forward, so they gave us a two-single deal".

The Higsons were booked into the studio and the song *Burn The Whole Thing Down (Before The Yanks Do)* was the overwhelming choice to be recorded and Dammers would oversee the production.

"That was our first and last 'proper' record deal" says Higson. "We were very excited and honoured that Dammers wanted to produce our first single himself, and he selected the songs he wanted to work on. This was the break we'd always been hoping for. As I remember it, we recorded it somewhere in the Midlands. We spent a couple of happy days recording two tracks". The tracks were indeed recorded in the Midlands, Coventry to be exact and as some of the band were still at university, the recording sessions had to be slotted in amongst their final exams!

Burn The Whole Thing Down (Before The Yanks Do) had been in the band's live set for a while and Dammers liked it. Despite this, he changed the title and told Charlie Higson to rewrite the lyrics to it! "The first thing Jerry did was change the title of the A-side and get me to rewrite the lyrics. It was a protest song - a call to arms at a time when (Ronald) Reagan was making very bellicose pronouncements about Russia and the like and we were getting involved in The Falklands. It was one of those times when things felt quite dangerous and unstable".

Dammers quickly realised that the song wasn't really compatible for the band and this is when he decided to change it. "Dammers realised we were actually a mild-mannered, middle class bunch of ex students and probably wouldn't be inclined to start an actual revolution and start burning shit down. So the message was diluted and it became *Tear the Whole Thing Down (Before The Storm Breaks)*".

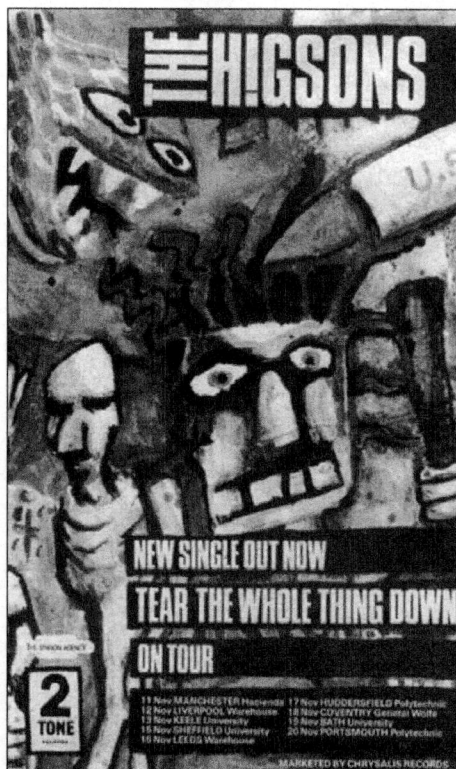

Advert for the first 2 Tone single

162

Higson believes Dammers could've had an ulterior motive for the change; "The change might have also partly been because Jerry had some cool recordings of thunder and had always wanted to use them on a recording". Jerry Dammers did mention this particular tidbit in a 2009 article in *Record Collector*; "I always wanted to put a thunder clap on a record since The Doors' *Riders On The Storm*, so I recorded one from my front room window".

Charlie Higson has since described a happy studio experience; "The recording was fun and pretty quick. For the guide track, Terry Edwards laid the brass parts down on his guitar, plucking the melody line. When we listened back to the first rough, desk mix, at the end of the recording it sounded pretty good, except for one thing…Terry had by then recorded actual brass, but for the playback Jerry accidentally left the plucked guitar guide up in the mix, which, when played alongside the saxes and trumpets, created a weird, tinny, Casio keyboard type of sound, and we all laughed".

Edwards has a slightly different take; "The song was edited down in the studio as we went until it was single length. I remember saying to Stuart at the time that I didn't know why we were there because we didn't have a good enough song for a single, but we ploughed on anyway. I think my favourite element of the single is Colin's wilfully unconventional bassline".

The band left Dammers to work on the remixing of the track and waited in anticipation with days and weeks going by before they heard from The General. They continued to wait in anticipation as Charlie Higson recalls; "Jerry seemed to be taking an inordinate amount of time in the studio mixing, which won't be news to anyone who worked with him, and our excitement and anticipation grew and grew. With all that extra time and effort, this thing was going to sound amazing - a complete transformation". However, when the track did arrive, the finished product was ultimately a disappointment; "eventually, the final mix arrived.

We were touring and we stuck the tape on the van's sound system. We listened in reverential silence and then looked at each other - it sounded exactly the same as the original, rough desk mix, right down to having that bloody plucked guitar line sitting on top of the brass". Higson concludes; "I was a bit nonplussed. In the end, I guess we were what we were and there wasn't much Jerry could do with us". Edwards says; "*Tear The Whole Thing Down* was a bit of a mistake to be honest. There had been some consensus amongst the other members of the band in my absence that this monolithic one-chorder should be the first single on 2 Tone".

The Higsons' first 2 Tone single received mixed reviews, "we always got mixed reviews after the first single" says Higson. "But a couple of them said what a shame it was we hadn't used real brass instead of the tinny Casio thing. For a long time I carried around a review by the legendary Charles Shaar Murray, which said that the song had a good beat to it, a strong melody, etc. etc. etc. but what a shame that the whole thing was sabotaged by a singer who hadn't got a clue".

A similar review featured in *Melody Maker*; "Thanks, one would assume, to the keen ear of producer Jerry Dammers, The Higsons have produced a record which at times sounds lovely - particularly the Stax-tinged horns. It slightly spoils it though when you've got some bloke whining away who has not the foggiest idea of how to sing". Perhaps they were on a hiding to nothing as Terry Edwards says; "The press had it in for anything on 2 Tone that wasn't ska". Looking at some of those reviews it's hard to disagree.

Following the recording of the single, The Higsons were invited for another Peel session, the band's third, which saw them record versions of *You Should Have Run Me Down, Gangway, Annie And Billy, John Peel's New Sig Tune* and *Put The Punk Back Into Funk*. This was broadcast on October 11th, the same day that *Tear The Whole Thing Down* was released.

The single received regular airplay on Peelie's show and was snapped up by the diehards but it failed to reach the Top 40. The Higsons also played a short nine date tour in November to promote the release playing venues such as the Manchester Hacienda, Leeds Warehouse and Huddersfield Polytechnic. On selected dates, The Higsons were supported by The Apollinaires, the other funk band on 2 Tone at the time. Another Kid Jensen Radio One session followed in late November, which aired in early December.

The Higsons were back in the studio to record their second single on the label and this time they were working with their own producer, Warne Livesey.

THE HIGSONS

new 12" and 7" single

RUN ME DOWN
C/W PUT THE PUNK BACK INTO FUNK

2 TONE

AVAILABLE NOW

Advert for the second 2 Tone single

The realisation had started by now that maybe they were never going to hit the big time but they carried on regardless, throwing themselves into the recording of the next single. *You Should Have Run Me Down* was chosen as the 'A' side and *Put The Punk Back Into Funk Parts I and II* were on the 'B' side. Charlie Higson is complimentary about the single; "Our second 2 Tone single, *Run Me Down,* was technically the most accomplished track we ever recorded and after *I Don't Want To Live With Monkeys*, is my favourite of all our singles".

Terry Edwards is also approving; "*Run Me Down* was a superior song and really should have got further up the charts than the frustrating place it got to - 101! The B-side was good, *Put The Punk Back Into Funk* stands the test of time, even if some of the bands Charlie was tilting at are lost in the mists of time, along with us!".

The single was released in February 1983, but failed to chart, although wasn't a complete failure as Higson remembers; "It's a big, funky epic that we recorded in London with our own producer. It went down well and was quite popular but failed to revive 2 Tone's fortunes. It was probably all too late by then".

Once again, reviews were mixed, Robin Smith was complimentary; "Blow me down with a feather, the Higsons have put the "F" into tired old funk, and jump and smash around in the most pleasing way. Even the 12 inch version doesn't run out of steam for a minute. Take me, I'm yours".

The *NME* were harsh; "Here they temper their bare boned clatterfunk with a few rudimentary constraints and bring themselves into line with the standard requirements of the class of '81-'82. But it's a bit late in the day as those with any style or talent have moved on past routine work-outs like *Run Me Down*". They finished off the rant with an attack on the band; "The Higsons have sounded careless, superficial in the past, and now seem to be in a terminal stupor".

Another review was equally as damning; "The Higsons could no doubt out-theorise the likes of Lakeside, but this doesn't compensate for the fact that their scratchy sound is about as funky as beef tea". *Melody Maker* were just as scornful; "There's something insidious about the Higsons' attitude, they drag everything around them down to their level and *Run Me Down* is the same old boring Higsons song - babbling bravado disguising guilty fraud. How desperate they sound as they sense the likelihood of a hit slipping further away!". They finish off the review with the most bizarre comparison ever heard; "They deserve to be remembered - if remembered at all - as the Freddie and the Dreamers of the brief Brit-funk revival. Sorry Freddie".

Despite the reviews, The Higsons' 2 Tone singles represent something different in the label's history and shows that, despite the overwhelming success with the ska releases, Jerry Dammers was willing to release other music rather than the tried and tested ska stuff. He was willing to try and move on when he could've just signed another ska band and knocked some stuff out that sounded like The Specials' first album. Dammers deserves respect for daring to experiment.

In March 1983, The Higsons appeared on Channel 4's *Whatever You Didn't Get*. The programme featured a live performance from the band as well as some reporting and in-studio discussion. Shortly afterwards, The Higsons parted ways with 2 Tone at the conclusion of their two-single deal and returned to independent status with their own label, Waap.

They were invited to record their fourth Peel session in May and recorded *Push Out The Boat, Clanking My Bucket, Round And Round, and Attack Of The Cannibal Zombie Businessmen*. This was broadcast in June and The Higsons wasted no time in recording another single, with *Push Out The Boat* becoming the band's fourth single released in November. The single saw the band renew their association with producer Warne Livesey.

The Higsons continued to play live but they were becoming aware that their time had probably passed, the audiences were dwindling and the band were getting older.

Their fifth and final Peel session took place in June 1984, where they recorded versions of *Walk On Water, 1958, Keep The Fire Alight* and *It's A Wonderful Life*. The band then signed with Upright Records and set about recording their first album, something that was talked about whilst they were on 2 Tone, but ultimately never happened. They would be working with producer Warne Livesey and the first thing to emerge from these sessions was the single *Music To Watch Girls By*, released in September, a 12" was also released but featured a song called *Music To Watch Boys By*!

The 'A' side of the 7" release was a cover of the 1966 Andy Williams hit and though it did slightly better in the charts than the 2 Tone releases, it still fell well short. Charlie Higson remembers; "It seemed our dreams of finally making it big weren't going to amount to anything. As the 1980s dragged on, recorded club music gradually eased live music out. The sort of small and medium sized venues we played in started favouring DJs over live bands and the rave scene was just over the horizon".

The Higsons' debut album *The Cure of The Higsons* was released in October to limited success. The band saw a change in the lineup when Stuart McGeachin was sacked and replaced by the man he'd replaced back in 1980, Dave Cummings. Cummings featured on the band's final single, *Take It*, which was released in 1985 on R4 Records.

With the changing scene and the lack of real success, the band started to fragment. Charlie Higson remembers; "In retrospect, we could have struggled on and changed into a club band. We could have got in some electronic drums and started using loops (like our contemporaries The Farm) and maybe revived our career as a rave act, but I'd had enough. I didn't have the heart for it. I wasn't a technically good enough singer to want to carry on and at 28 felt too old for rock and roll.

I wanted to do other things and the gigs became fewer and farther between". Terry Edwards backs this up; "Our cover of *Music To Watch Girl By* got us a little further up the charts, but by then our time had gone. We attempted a radio-friendly single called *Take It* with Dave Cummings back in the band at the expense of Stuart, but it was our swansong".

The band continued to perform on the university circuit but it was felt that they weren't really getting anywhere and played their last gig in March 1986. Dave Cummings says; "I told Charlie that I thought we were going around the UK college circuit in ever-diminishing circles. Upon reflection the rest of the band agreed with me and packed it in. We all remain friends".

Charlie Higson remembers it slightly differently; "Colin and I had started doing decorating jobs when we weren't touring to earn some proper money and realised we'd make a whole lot more if we stuck to decorating and knocked the music on the head". The Higsons are perhaps one of the only bands, especially 2 Tone related, that didn't break up acrimoniously. "There were no arguments or fallings out. One day we all sort of realised independently that the band probably didn't exist anymore. We played our last gig in 1986, I think, although we've never officially split up". Terry Edwards remembers the specifics, "Our last gig was at Nottingham University in March 1986, although we reformed for a one-off for Colin's 50th birthday".

Charlie Higson looks back fondly on the 2 Tone period; "I'll always be glad that we were a very small part of music history and the 2 Tone story. The label is rightly regarded with some reverence these days and was historically important. And there were some great songs!". However, he feels that Jerry Dammers' talents may have laid elsewhere; "2 Tone couldn't adapt and change and I'm not sure that, in the end, Jerry was really cut out to be running a record label. It wasn't what he was put on this earth to do.

The guy's a maverick". Terry Edwards shares a similar view; "Jerry was good to work with, got us moving along to get the tracks recorded - though I think he probably took quite a while getting the mixing right". Edwards has since worked with The General post-The Higsons; "In more recent years I've played on several shows in Jerry's Spatial AKA Orchestra and it's a thrill. He's got great ideas and a maverick idea of where the music should be coming from. I'd love to do more with him and I think it's essential that he gets another record out". He feels that 2 Tone was "a great label which deserves to be remembered for more than just ska".

The Higsons have since taken on cult status, partly because of the fame of Charlie Higson and partly due to the retrospective albums and performances that have surfaced since the breakup.

Just a year after playing their last gig, they released a singles compilation *Attack of the Cannibal Zombie Businessmen* on Waap and this was followed by *It's A Wonderful Life* in 1998, which was a compilation of BBC Radio One sessions, including the five Peel sessions they recorded and others for Richard Skinner and Kid Jensen.

A live DVD was released in 2006, *The Higsons - I Don't Want To Live With Monkeys*, containing a live show from 1984 when they played the Camden Palace Theatre, London. All the band members remain friends but have no intention of ever reforming. Terry Edwards has since said;

Later version of The Higsons, shortly before they broke up

"We won't be reforming, unless a very eccentric multi-millionaire rears his or her head!". Edwards has the last word on The Higsons; "We gave it our best shot but we ran our course and that was that. Not a bad track record - five John Peel sessions plus another five or so for an assortment of Radio One presenters, a lot of growing up in public and three tours of America along the way. I think the band probably had a fair amount of built-in obsolescence…".

Releases on 2 Tone

Tear The Whole Thing Down (1982)
Run Me Down (1983) 7" and 12" singles.

Where are they now?

Charlie Higson
Lead Vocals, Harmonica, Piano, Percussion 1980-1986.

Following the breakup, Higson squatted in London and worked as a decorator before he started to write comedy for Paul Whitehouse and Harry Enfield, co-creating Enfield's character Loadsamoney. He also has a songwriting credit for the 1988 single, *Loadsamoney (Doin' Up The House)*.

Higson then worked with Craig Ferguson in the early 1990s and became a writer on *Harry Enfield's Television Programme* in 1990 before he created *The Fast Show* in 1994 with Whitehouse. *The Fast Show* was incredibly successful and saw Higson come to public attention for his comedy writing and also his acting skills, appearing in various sketches on the programme. He then worked on the remake of *Randall & Hopkirk (Deceased)* between 2000 and 2001 and ventured into acting, appearing in *The Smell of Reeves of Mortimer, Fun at the Funeral Parlour, Marple, Broadchurch* and *Grantchester*. Higson also began writing novels in the 1990s and in the 2000s wrote a number of *Young Bond* novels, a series of James Bond books for children. He has since written a number of post apocalyptic, zombie-horror novels including *The Enemy* (2009), *The Dead* (2011) and *The End* (2015) and is now living in London with his wife and three children.

Terry Edwards
Guitar, Trumpet, Saxophone, Piano & Vocals, 1980-1986.

A talented multi-instrumentalist, Edwards is equally adept at playing saxophone, guitar, flugelhorn, trumpet, flute and keyboards. When the band broke up, Edwards worked with Yeah Jazz, producing and playing on their 1987 album *Six Lane Ends*. He moved into session work and has worked with a number of artists including Billy Bragg, Madness, The Blockheads, The Jesus and Mary Chain, PJ Harvey and Tom Waits. He is still involved with music both with his own bands and his session work and also has a number of releases under his own name.

Edwards is currently in Near Jazz Experience with Mark Bedford from Madness and Simon Charterton. Away from making music, Edwards penned a book about Madness, focusing on the period when they released their first album, *One Step Beyond…* as part of the 1/33 series of publications in 2010 and is currently living in London.

Simon Charterton
Drums, Vocals, 1980-1986.

After the band broke up in 1986, Charterton remained in music and collaborated with Terry Edwards on occasion, including the 1994 release *Well You Needn't*. He also formed his own band The Aftershave releasing *The Last Resort EP* in 1998 and continues to perform with them. He also formed Simon&thePope, who he also plays with regularly and also plays with Near Jazz Experience with Terry Edwards and Mark Bedford. In the daytime, Charterton is currently the Music and Live Events Manager at Kino-teatr in St. Leonards.

Dave Cummings
Guitars & Vocals, 1980, 1984-1986
Cummings was a founding member but left in 1980 after graduating. He rejoined in 1984 and remained until the breakup. Cummings went on to join Lloyd Cole and the Commotions for a year before joining Del Amitri in 1989, remaining until 1995. He began screenwriting in the early 1990s with Charlie Higson, culminating in *The Fast Show* in 1994, and has remained in the profession since.

While still in music, Cummings worked on some scripts for the 1988 television programme *Hey Dad…!* and *Harry Enfield and Chums in* 1994. He has since written a number of television programmes for the BBC including *Alexei Sayle's Merry Go Round, Happiness, Hustle* and the 2008 comedy *Parents of the Band,* starring Jimmy Nail.

Colin Williams
Bass & Vocals, 1980-1986.
After The Higsons disbanded, Williams became a speech therapist, before he decided to change careers and began to work for the NHS treating severely autistic children. He has since retired and is living in London. The one and only Higsons reunion occurred at his 50th birthday party!

Stuart McGeachin
Guitar & Vocals, 1980-1984.
McGeachin was brought in to replace Dave Cummings when he left the band in 1980. He appeared on the majority of the band's recorded output. He was later fired and replaced by his predecessor Cummings. McGeachin then ventured into writing and broadcasting before changing careers in 1989, moving into the in-flight entertainment and communications industry making destination videos in Hong Kong. He then formed his own company Phantom Media in 1999 and then co-founded Bluebox Avionics in 2006. Both companies were later acquired by DMD in 2011 and McGeachin served as creative director until 2017. He is now an independent travel media consultant, living in Brighton.

Anton Hilton, Eddie Eve, Abe Brooks, Adele Winter, Mike Hodges,
Terri Bateman, Graham Whitby Pic by Abe Brooks

The Friday Club

The Friday Club hailed from Scarborough and were formed there in 1984 although founder members Mike 'Hidge' Hodges, Andy 'Abe' Brooks and Graham Whitby had been playing together since the late 1970s.

Brooks' father owned a hotel in the town and they would rehearse on the ground floor, this would double up as a space for ballroom dancing lessons! In the beginning, Hodges was into punk whereas Brooks was into Northern Soul, leading to conflicting directions as Hodges wanted to form a new wave band and Brooks wanted to form a strict soul band. Eventually, a compromise was reached and they incorporated both sounds.

They soon recruited Adele Winter, Terri Bateman and Eddie Eve into the band, although Eve didn't know the band but bought "the only synthesiser in Scarborough" after spotting it in the window of a music shop. The band heard that Eve had bought it and approached him to join as they'd wanted a keyboard player anyway. Interestingly, The Friday Club were without a drummer in the early days, using a Roland drum machine instead!

The Friday Club played their first gig at the Warehouse Club, Leeds soon after their formation. It was organised by Ian Dewhirst, a popular DJ on the Northern Soul scene and someone who almost became the manager of the band. The musical direction had been decided, taking influence from the Northern Soul scene all the members had witnessed growing up in Yorkshire with the music of Wigan Casino, The Torch Club and Blackpool Mecca being used as a template.

The line-up for the first gig was; Abe Brooks (guitar/vocals), Michael Hodges (percussion/vocals), Terri Bateman (saxophone/vocals), Adele Winter (vibes/vocals), Graham Whitby (bass) and Eddie Eve (keyboards). They began playing gigs in Scarborough and ventured further down the country, taking in places like Leeds and Hull. This saw them become very popular, building up quite a following, leading to some riotous gigs! Later member Clint Golding says; "at their best they were anarchic, soulful and great fun".

Though Mike Hodges remembers one not so joyous performance; "the worst gig we ever did was in Hornsea playing an empty club and someone set the smoke machine off. As the smoke faded away we saw the guy who'd done it with his pants around his ankles pointing his backside at us!" Hodges continued; "in the early days, we weren't very professional but as we kept building up the following, we started taking things more seriously". Eddie Eve has since described the early days as "a messy affair" and recalls; "We used to roll our equipment across Scarborough on skateboards before we bought a Bedford van for £25!".

Eve was also the inspiration for the band's name as he used to run a club on a Friday night in Scarborough. Due to the violence back in the mid 1980s, he wanted to go somewhere to get drunk rather than having a punch up! Before they had a manager, he would organise the gigs and do all the publicity, such as designing the posters. Some members seem to have better memories of the drinking sessions that followed some of those early gigs rather than the shows themselves! Eve remembers travelling back to Scarborough on the roof of the van after a gig in Bridlington!

After a number of months playing around Scarborough and the rest of the North, the band made an executive decision; "Adele Winter was already living in London and the feeling was that if we were ever going to achieve a degree of success, we had to be where the music business was" says Abe Brooks. They started out by playing some gigs there, usually travelling down carrying as much of their equipment as possible on the train!

The first London gig was at the Half Moon, Brixton supporting The Shillelagh Sisters and the following day, they played an illegal warehouse party at The Substation, Bermondsey. The band eventually moved to London in the summer of 1984 and all lived within a couple of miles from each other in Clapham, in various flats and squats.

They would sign on at the Railton Road dole office in Brixton! Adele Winter was now in a relationship with Harry Cooke, a local businessman from Wigan and he became the band's manager. Cooke was a character that had fingers in many pies, aside from managing the band he had involvement with the Soho clothes shop Demob and ran illegal warehouse parties in the capital.

Once they'd arrived in London, the band were on the lookout for a drummer, Anton Hilton takes up the story; "I'd been kicking about in London basically playing drums in my bedroom and Paul Cooke, a mate of mine who'd played with Sade, had been playing with The Friday Club. It wasn't his style of drumming, he was a jazz player and the band were more Northern Soul so he gave me a call and mentioned that I might like to play with them. I rang them up and went to an audition, I played through a few tracks and joined the band there and then". There's some uncertainty about the dates however; "Abe has always said it was 1984 when they came down to London but I always thought it was 1983, I could've got it wrong though".

The Friday Club began to play around London and secured a residency at The Fridge, Brixton. Due to Cooke's connections, they managed to play in a number of underground clubs.

Back of the single cover

The band built up a following in the capital, the underground clubs played soul so they fitted right in.

This was the time of the Miners' Strike and they lent their support, playing a number of benefit gigs. Anton Hilton remembers one particular gig; "We did miner's benefit gigs and there was one in particular where Alexei Sayle was the compere and dressed in a nun outfit! It was quite scary as they were big gigs and I'd look out at the big audience and think oh shit!".

The warehouse gigs led to some in France, including one at La Locomotive in Paris. Horn player Tony Miller remembers; "They were fantastic gigs, the French treated us like royalty and it was just like taking a warehouse party to France!". They also decided to record their own single as Abe Brooks remembers; "We did a limited release single called *What Is Soul?* and we had 100 copies pressed to vinyl which we shopped around all the major record companies. It was the first Friday Club recording to feature Al Elias and Tony Miller as the Boo Bazooka Horns". Elias and Miller had previously been in Zoot and the Roots.

According to Hilton, they recorded other demos during this period; "We did demos for everyone, we even did one for Paul Weller's Target label as he'd expressed an interest and said he liked us". The single was quite effective in gaining interest from the labels and they almost signed with Island Records as Hilton recalls; "We were offered a deal and spent months going through the contract as it was really heavy. The deal was incredible, two or three albums, singles, worldwide tour and even recording in the Bahamas!". However, a disagreement between management and the label didn't end well; "We were close to signing and then something happened between Harry and the guy at Island. They wanted to put one of our songs on a compilation to see how it went down but Harry disagreed. They dropped us like a stone and we were all gutted. It was a massive comedown".

By spring 1985, Stiff Records were interested in signing them and Jerry Dammers was producing one of their bands, The Untouchables. The band were keen to sign with Stiff and submitted a list of producers they'd like to work with, Dammers being the top of the list.

Eventually, the deal fell through and the band continued to ply their trade around London, playing regular live gigs. The Friday Club also played a set at the Rock For Jobs event in Liverpool in September, in aid of the Campaign Against Unemployment.

Having been fans of 2 Tone, they decided to pursue Jerry Dammers and managed to find the squat he was living in at the time, around half a mile away in Stockwell. They posted a demo tape and flyer for an upcoming gig at the Railway Hotel, Brixton through the letterbox and to their surprise he attended with his manager Pete Hadfield.

Abe Brooks recalls the night; "Amazingly Jerry turned up at the gig in Brixton, from memory Jerry, his mate and the barman were pretty much the only audience we had that night". Dammers liked what he'd seen but told them they were the most out of tune band he'd ever heard! Despite this, he said he liked the songs and was interested in releasing *Window Shopping* on 2 Tone. They were happy to accept and were soon in the studio, Brooks says; "As one would expect, we were absolutely over the moon with Jerry's interest and immediately said we'd love to release a record on 2 Tone".

The deal came as a particular relief to Mike Hodges, as he'd been toying with the idea of leaving as the constant gigging and hard work didn't appear to be paying off. Anton Hilton remembers; "Dammers had free reign to try and get bands in to make up for the debt he had with Chrysalis. They almost had Jerry under house arrest in the studio!". As with all 2 Tone bands, The Friday Club were not given a formal contract.

After a few weeks of sorting the arrangements and rehearsing, the single was recorded at Powerplant Studios, North London for around two weeks with Dammers producing and arranging the track.

Some of the band have since observed that they were in the presence of a musical genius and watched while Dammers worked his magic on the track with Abe Brooks commenting; "Jerry Dammers was amazing to work with, we'd always considered him to be a musical genius and working closely with him in the studio only made that more apparent".

Aside from working on the production, Dammers programmed the drums, played the synth strings and hand operated the Wah-Wah pedal on Brooks' guitar track.

The band then moved to Wessex Studios, North London to mix the track with Dammers. On *Window Shopping,* the band were backed by their old friends Al Elias on tenor saxophone and Tony Miller on trumpet and were thanked on the back of the single cover for their efforts.

Miller says Dammers was a "stickler for timing and rhythm" and remembers spending most of the day watching him trying to get the drums right! Miller says; "Don't tell Anton, but I think they ended up using a drum machine on it!". He's also proud of appearing on 2 Tone;" I was into the label originally and to go on and actually appear on it was something else". Miller also remembers Dick Cuthell popping by the studio to complement the horns and considers Powerplant as the best studio he's ever worked in.

Dammers has since said the single was; "a nice little song about being broke" and that The Friday Club were "Scarborough's finest, a pleasant bunch of chaps and chapettes with a nice line in Oxford brogues, bags and blazers. Looked like they came straight from a game of bowls on the bowling green, which was fine by me"1. *Window Shopping* was the final single to be recorded on 2 Tone before it's closure

(although it wasn't the final release), Eddie Eve says; "I think Chrysalis were pissed off with Jerry as he'd given away all the profits for the *Nelson Mandela* single the year before and that was the only time they'd made any money for years!".

In the meantime, Madness were getting ready to embark on their Mad Not Mad Tour and were in need of a support band. Abe Brooks takes up the story; "Jerry Dammers' manager Pete Hadfield had an office in Islington which was located below Madness's management office. We got word via Pete that Madness were looking for a support band for their tour. We played a gig at the Marquee in London and Madness sent some of their guys down to check us out".

The following day, they were offered the support slot on all 28 dates on the tour, which would commence on October 22nd at the City Hall, Cork. "The next day we got word that Madness had offered us the support slot and we gladly accepted". The single *Window Shopping* was rushed out to coincide with the tour and capitalise on the publicity, it was released on October 28th. The band, as well as Dammers, felt this was a mistake as it was almost certain to get caught up in the Christmas market.

Meanwhile, the tour went well and The Friday Club were warmly received by the audiences and now playing with plenty of confidence. The various members have fond memories of the tour including Abe Brooks who says; "Touring with Madness has to be one of the high points of my life, we were so lucky to be playing in support of one of the greatest bands that England has ever produced and also lucky that they were the nicest guys you could ever possibly meet!".

He also remembers the high esteem that Madness held The General in; "I particularly remember a gig that Jerry Dammers attended and to see the respect and affection that the guys from Madness showed to him was truly touching. He had after all launched their careers on 2 Tone".

Eddie Eve says; "All of the Ireland dates were great, they were great gigs. But it was the tour that ended up dividing the band down the middle. There were too many people in the band and that's why we ended up splitting in the end".

Eve also remembers playing in Belfast and being escorted out of the venue by guys with machine guns! Anton Hilton is similarly reflective; "Going on tour with Madness was amazing. I knew Cathal Smyth anyway through his brother Dermot and after doing 28 gigs with the band, we got to know some of them pretty well. Cathal and Suggs were very sociable". Hilton remembers the reception they would get at gigs, particularly up North; "They were really special times, the crowds were so warm to us and it was amazing to see how much Madness were loved. Though we went further South and they weren't as warm! But it was a really special tour". He also remembers those Irish dates; "It was fascinating going over to Ireland though it was pretty scary.

I remember going to the borders and there was a young soldier pointing his gun at the bus! I also remember playing a leisure centre over there and Madness giving away free tickets to the kids. There was a swimming pool there and these were kids breaking through the roof and dropping into the pool!". Tony Miller recalls (along with Al Elias) refusing to go on stage at the final gig at the Hammersmith Odeon as they hadn't been paid!

Window Shopping received some airplay, most notably by Simon Bates at Radio One and Gary Crowley at Capital, and this saw it creep into the Top 100. However, Bates then went on holiday and his replacement wasn't a fan and stopped playing it. It got lost in all the usual rubbish that appears in the charts at Christmas and sunk rather quickly. Anton Hilton remembers; "Chrysalis rushed the single out to coincide with the tour but didn't put any money into the promotion of it. It just got lost in all the Christmas stuff and I think even Jerry hadn't wanted to put it out at that time".

The Friday Club in 1988 (Pic. Abe Brooks)

173

As the deal with 2 Tone was to release just the one single, the band parted ways with the label. Shortly after the tour, the band split down the middle, with Adele Winter, Terri Bateman, Anton Hilton and Graham Whitby all leaving the band. Hilton remembers the split; "The band just fell apart, we just split up. It was a real blow and we worked hard to get where we were. It was a sad moment being on a high from the amazing tour to splitting up soon afterwards". He's proud to have been on the label and was complimentary about it; "2 Tone was an awesome label, talk about homegrown British talent. Jerry is a good old guy and people seem to forget that he wrote most of the early hits".

Despite the split, The Friday Club ended up carrying on and by early 1986, the departed members had been replaced. Clint Golding came in to replace Graham Whitby on bass and Woodie Taylor replaced Anton Hilton on the drums. Golding had been a roadie on the Mad Not Mad Tour and was friends with the band anyway. Abe Brooks also took on singing duties and they briefly recruited a singer in the shape of Julie, although none of the band members can remember her full name and she only lasted a couple of gigs before departing.

While the band were touring with Madness, Red Wedge had been launched in November 1985 by Billy Bragg, Paul Weller, Strawberry Switchblade and Kirsty MacColl. They aimed to raise awareness of left wing policies and campaign for the Labour Party in the run up to the next election with the hope of dislodging Margaret Thatcher.

The Red Wedge Tour was launched in January 1986, with concerts held in Manchester, Cardiff, Birmingham, Leicester, Bradford, Edinburgh and Newcastle. A raft of musicians were involved with Paul Weller (with his band The Style Council), Billy Bragg, The Communards and Junior & Friends headlining, and various other left wing musicians and bands featuring.

The Friday Club joined the tour and played gigs supporting General Public, Billy Bragg and Jerry Dammers. The band were always willing to lend their support to left-wing causes as had been seen during the Miners Strike and also by playing shows for the Campaign Against Employment. Red Wedge ultimately failed after Margaret Thatcher romped to her third successive election victory in June 1987 with Red Wedge quietly ceasing to exist by the end of the decade. Meanwhile, the band continued to be signed to Chrysalis Publishing and spent time recording numerous demos, which ultimately led to nothing, though live performances continued.

It was now 1987 and The Friday Club were struggling on, Mike Hodges left to go to college, something he'd missed out on the first time around. He'd had enough but remains proud to have been involved with what he describes as a "major cultural movement and not just a record label, but something important".

Hodges' departure marked an end of an era for the band as one half of the original songwriting team had now gone. Hodges wrote an article in 2009 detailing in his words "How we killed 2 Tone!". He stated; "Although The Friday Club continued for a while, I left for a life as a toilet cleaner, until college rescued me from Domestos and rubber gloves"[2].

Following Hodges' departure, the band continued to limp on and played regular gigs though most of the original members had gone. It was over two years since the band had been involved with 2 Tone and they realised that their chance at success had probably passed them by and the band went their separate ways in late 1988.

They probably never recovered from the departure of Mike Hodges the previous year as Clint Golding says; "I don't think it was quite the same after the original songwriting partnership broke up" although he looks back fondly of his time in the band simply saying they were "great times".

The final line up of the band consisted of; Andy "Abe" Brooks (guitar/vocals), Eddie Eve (keyboards), Woodie Taylor (drums), Clint Golding (guitar), Steve Hill (bass), Tony Miller (trumpet) and Paco Reed (saxophone).

Anton Hilton says; "The opportunity was there in London and those with their heads screwed on did well out of it. And others didn't!". The final word goes to Abe Brooks; "I am still very proud to have been a part of the 2 Tone family - in my opinion the coolest British record label ever".

Over 30 years after they broke up, a German record label decided to release an EP of unreleased Friday Club tunes in 2020 under the title of *Saturday Night And Sunday Morning*.

Releases on 2 Tone

Window Shopping (1985)
Both 7" and 12" singles.

Where are they now?

Andrew 'Abe' Brooks
Vocals and Guitar, 1984-1988
After the band went their separate ways in 1988, Brooks moved into sales and marketing and worked for Music Lab Limited as sales and marketing manager before he left in 1999. He took the same role at GearBox Sound & Vision and remained there for ten years before his departure in 2009. He moved into business development, joining MediaPros as their business development manager in 2010, remaining at the company for five years before he left to join Jigsaw24 as their head of business development. Since 2019, Brooks has been working as an Apple business specialist for Western Computer and is based in London.

Michael Hodges
Vocals and Congos, 1984-1987
Mike Hodges left the band in 1987 to become a toilet cleaner, later enrolling in college as he looked for a career change.

He ventured into journalism and started out in sports journalism, even penning Kevin Keegan's biography in 1998. Has since written for the New Statesman, Radio Times and Time Out, winning the 2008 Press Gazette Awards Columnist of the Year for the latter and is a published author, winning awards for both his journalism and book writing. Away from journalism, Hodges also ran for London Mayor in 2008 and is currently living in South London with his wife.

Adele Winter
Vocals and Vibes, 1984-1985
Winter remained in the band until the end of the Madness tour. After her departure, she teamed up with Terri Bateman and carried on performing as The Northern Girls. Once the partnership came to an end, Winter went on to teach music in schools but is now sadly suffering from MS. She doesn't let it affect her as she's worked as a sit-down comedian, writer, artist and poet and also volunteers with the Southwark Disablement Association.

Terri Bateman
Vocals and Saxophone, 1984-1985
After leaving the band at the conclusion of the Madness tour in 1985, Bateman carried on with Adele Winter as The Northern Girls. She'd left music by the end of the decade and has since worked at London South Bank University and is still living in London.

Eddie Eve
Keyboards, 1984-1988
Eve remained with the band throughout it's life but moved into techno music afterwards. He'd worked in catering before he joined the band and ended up venturing back into that after he left the music business. He bought a delhi in Clapham, which he ran for six years before selling it and becoming a driver driving DJs to their various gigs. After visiting a friend in Australia, Eve ended up meeting his future wife and remained in the country. He currently resides in Melbourne and runs his own catering firm, specialising in movie catering.

Graham Whitby
Bass Guitar, 1984-1985
Whitby had been a skateboarder and a punk before the Friday Club were formed and was one of the three founder members. He remained in the band until the end of the Mad Not Mad Tour in 1985 before becoming a photographer for Allstar Sportsphoto, where he worked for many years. He is now the official club photographer at Southend United. Away from football, Whitby is a freelance photographer and runs his own business Whitby Boot Photography.

Anton Hilton
Drums, 1984-1986
Hilton joined the band in 1984 and remained until 1985, when he was later replaced in the band by Woodie Taylor and moved to Oxford. He changed careers completely and worked as a tree surgeon and landscape gardener. Hilton later went on to work for Oxford City Council as a community response officer and then later moved on to Oxfordshire County Council working as a community connector for the Learning Disabilities team. He is also Acting Sergeant for the RAF Air Cadets and has held this post since 2017. He also uses his previous experience to teach drums and has a number of students.

Al Elias
Tenor Saxophone, 1984-1985
Elias had been in Zoot and the Roots, with Tony Miller, before he joined the band to record their first single. He also appeared on *Window Shopping,* playing tenor saxophone on the track and is thanked for his contribution on the record sleeve. He now runs his own business Elias Bespoke Guitars where he designs electric guitars, something he has done since 1987.

Tony Miller
Trumpet, 1984-1988
Miller had also been in Zoot and the Roots and first played with The Friday Club on their first single *What Is Soul?* and then on *Window Shopping.* He then became a full-time member of the band and remained until the split in 1988.

He later lived in London before he returned to North Yorkshire and converted his home into a bed and breakfast hotel. Miller is now running The Belmont in Pickering with his wife Anne.

JB's Allstars, Newcastle 1984 - Pic by Graham Pointer

JB's Allstars

John Bradbury had been drumming in The Specials/Special AKA since 1979 but also took a keen interest in Northern Soul music, evident by his cover of *Sock it to Em J.B.* in 1980.

He had wanted to record it as a solo effort but it was eventually included on The Specials' second album. Bradbury later said; "I wanted to put that out as a single under the name of JB's Allstars but politics within The Specials wouldn't permit it".1 By October 1981, The Specials had broken up and re-emerged as The Special AKA, with Bradbury, Jerry Dammers, Horace Panter and Dick Cuthell continuing.

Whilst still in the band, Bradbury formed JB's Allstars in 1983 as a sideline project and he set about putting his own band together. Apart from himself on drums, the nucleus of the band was lifted from The Big Heat, with Drew Barfield and Bill Hurley (vocals), 'Big' George Webley (bass), Chris Parks (guitar), Dick Hanson (trumpet) and John "Irish" Earle (saxophone) all joining. Hanson and Earle were part of the horn section The Rumour Brass and their counterparts Chris Gower (trombone) and Ray Beavis (saxophone) were added to the ranks along with Paul 'Wix' Wickens (keyboards) and Molly & Polly Jackson (vocals). This lineup went into the studio with the producers Ian Guenther and Willi Morrison in the summer of 1983.

Bradbury was still without a record deal at the time of recording and after Chrysalis showed no interest he secured a deal with RCA Victor, most famous for their association with Elvis Presley.

The first single to surface was a cover of John Miles' *One Minute Every Hour*. The single was backed by a JB's Allstars original called *The Theme From 903*, credited to JB's Dub Stars. The single was released in October and despite being a fine tune and a rare example of a cover being better than the original, it failed to reach the Top 40, though it did hit No.78 and remained in the charts for another two weeks before dropping out.

Jason Votier, Dee Sharp, John Bradbury, George Webley

The band were quiet until January 1984 when they released their second single *Backfield in Motion*, a cover of the 1969 song by Mel & Tim. The single was backed by a JB's Allstars original in the form of *Theme From A Beam*, produced by John Bradbury.

Despite the lack of promotion, the single performed well, peaking at No.48 in February. The single achieved the band's highest chart placing and a music video was recorded, where the band were dressed as American football players!

Shortly after the release, Dee Sharp joined the band; "I was introduced to John Bradbury in the mid 80s by my then manager who was working for RCA Records, who I was signed to at the time as a solo artist after my group Buzzz".

Sharp and Bradbury got on well from that initial meeting; "JB's Allstars had released *Backfield In Motion* and *One Minute Every Hour* and Brad and myself struck up an immediate artistic rapport and friendship and he invited me to get involved with his project as lead singer and co-producer".

The two musicians soon became friends; "Brad lived in Hampstead opposite Belsize Tube Station with his wife and young son and I would often visit him there to discuss the project".

JB's Allstars also appeared on *The Tube* in January and this marked Dee Sharp's first involvement with the band; "We went on to perform live on *The Tube* with Paula Yates as the presenter!

I'm not good at remembering the names of the musicians who were involved but Big George was one I never forgot! And the keyboard player played with Paul McCartney I do recall! It was a very memorable performance".

They performed three songs; *One Minute Every Hour, Sign on the Dotted Line* and *Backfield in Motion.* The band now consisted of; John Bradbury (drums), Drew Barfield (vocals), Bill Hurley (vocals), Dee Sharp (vocals), George Webley (bass), Seamus Beaghan (keyboards), Molly and Polly Jackson (backing vocals), Dick Hanson (trumpet), John "Irish" Earle (saxophone), Chris Gower (trombone), Ray Beavis (saxophone), Chris Parks (guitar), Paul "Wix" Wickens (keyboards). The band were also joined by Seamus Beaghen (keyboards) and Graham Pointer (guitar), neither appeared on any of the singles but were part of the live ensemble.

The band was now a 15 piece and there was talk of going on the road in the summer of 1984 as well as plans for an album, dub album and a string instrumental album though this didn't happen. The performance was followed by the release of the single *Sign on the Dotted Line...* in May.

John Bradbury and Dee Sharp (Pic by Dee Sharp)

178

This featured Dee Sharp on lead vocals for the first time. It was backed by another JB's Dubstars number, *And He Was Gone*. The single failed to chart and marked the last involvement of producers Morrison and Guenther. From now on, John Bradbury would oversee production with help from Jon Walls, 'Wix' Wickens and Dee Sharp.

Dee Sharp, John Bradbury, Shezwae Powell, 1984 (Pic. Dee Sharp)

Shezwae Powell and Dee Sharp around the time of the single Ready Willing and Able (Pic. Dee Sharp)

JB's Allstars headed back into the studio to record their fourth single, this time John Bradbury co-produced with Jon Walls and 'Wix' Wickens. It was decided to record a cover of *Reading Willing and Able* and alongside the usual characters, Shezwae Powell was recruited as a guest, sharing lead vocals with Dee Sharp.

Powell was only briefly involved; "my manager at the time who worked at RCA brought me in to be a front person and do some singing. I was never really a band member and *Ready Willing and Able* was the only thing I ever did with them".

Ready Willing and Able, was released in September 1984 and backed by the JB's Dubstars instrumental *Chance Meeting*. The single failed to chart and was their final involvement with RCA before they were dropped by the label. Later member Jason Votier explains; "The Allstars were dropped from RCA, so Brad told me, due to a new A&R donkey. They weren't interested in anything remotely connected with Northern Soul. He was quite cut up by that".

It seems that JB's Allstars played a solitary gig at Hammersmith Palais, young horn player Jason Votier became involved with the band and he takes up the story; "I met Brad in 1985, I had come off a gig playing on cruise ships in the Caribbean. I was offered another contract and said yes. However, on a 2 week break I decided to quit and head for London. To make ends meet I got a job behind the bar at DOME Brasserie in Hampstead. The DOME is where I met Brad, his girlfriend managed the place and we became good friends".

After playing with a number of different bands, albeit unpaid, Votier started to get paid work; "Brad asked me to sort out horns for a headlining gig at the Hammersmith Palais. We rehearsed at John Henry's if I recall, all 12 of us although Steve Nieve and Robert Awhai weren't involved. I think on keyboards was the keyboard player that replaced Mike Barson in Madness". Votier is referring to Seamus Beaghen who also thinks that JB's Allstars played a gig; "I think there was a gig, maybe at Shepherd's Bush but I could easily be getting this mixed up with something else around that time!".

179

Following the disappointment with *Ready Willing and Able* failing to chart and ultimately being dropped by RCA, at some point in 1985, JB's Allstars went back into the studio to record two original tunes, penned by JB himself. The 'A' side was *The Alphabet Army*, Bradbury's attempt to write a song dedicated to teachers and their importance, he also produced it with Dee Sharp. The song had extra meaning as Bradbury had been a teacher in the days before The Specials.

The band looked slightly different by now and although John Bradbury, Dee Sharp and 'Big' George Webley remained, they were now joined by Jason Votier on horns. The rest were made up of session musicians, Steve Nieve (piano), Robert Awhai (guitar) and Mark Hughes (harmonica). Despite certain publications claiming that Awhai, Hughes and Nieve were members of JB's Allstars, they simply played on the record.

Robert Awhai doesn't even have any recollection of playing on the record or his involvement with JB's Allstars! In contrast, Jason Votier remembers the time well; "I only overdubbed on *Alphabet Army* at a studio in Camden Mews owned by Paul Hardcastle". The single saw a change in musical direction for the band as they moved away from their Northern Soul sound to a new funkier soul sound.

Dee Sharp, George Webley, John Bradbury, Jason Votier
(Pic. Dee Sharp)

The 'B' side *Al.Arm* was another Bradbury original and in keeping with the tradition across the previous four singles, it was an instrumental produced by Bradbury. The single was granted a release on both 7" and 12" formats, with the 12" version containing a "string mix" and a "radio version" alongside the original version of the song.

Despite recording their final single before The Friday Club recorded *Window Shopping* in August 1985, JB's Allstars became the final band to feature on 2 Tone when they released *The Alphabet Army* in January 1986. The single failed to chart, despite the admirable message as Jason Votier says; "The song had too much of a political message and just wasn't a hit. It didn't have a hook like *Nelson Mandela*!".

There was never an official word on the band's breakup but they never released another single before the death of John Bradbury in 2015. The single also marked the end of an era for the label as shortly after the release, Chrysalis called time on 2 Tone and closed it down.

Releases on 2 Tone:

The Alphabet Army (1986) - 7" and 12"

Where Are They Now?

The band contained a number of permanent members and a number of session musicians between 1983 and 1985. They are all detailed here and are in the order that they appeared with the band on the records or otherwise.

John Bradbury
Drums & Backing Vocals, 1983-1985
See The Specials.

'Big' George Webley
Bass Guitar, 1983-1985
'Big' George had been playing in The Big Heat when he was recruited by JB in 1983. After his involvement with JB's Allstars, Webley became the musical director at EMI

Records and also composed a number of television theme tunes including *Have I Got News For You, Room 101* and *The Graham Norton Show* as well as classic shows *One Foot in the Grave* and *The Office*. He also composed theme tunes for radio shows, ballet and the National Theatre. Webley also forged a successful broadcasting career on GLR but suffered a heart attack on air in 1996 and despite finishing the show, he wouldn't set foot in the studio again for three years. He continued to present various radio shows throughout the 2000s on BBC London. Webley played with his own band The G Spot in 2010 before his death from a heart attack in 2011 after taking the legal drug Meow Meow.

Drew Barfield
Vocals, 1983-1984
Barfield had been playing with The Big Heat before he joined JB's Allstars and remained with the band after ceasing to be in JB's Allstars. He also worked with Bill Hurley on his solo record *Double Agent* in 1985 and became a songwriter, writing songs for Joe Jackson, Paul Young and Go West. Barfield has continued to work with Paul Young and currently plays alongside him in Los Pacaminos, having been in the band since its formation in 1992.

Bill Hurley
Vocals, 1983-1984
Hurley was another recruit from Big Heat in 1983 and featured on the first three singles before his involvement ceased in 1984. In 1985, he recorded a solo LP *Double Agent* and then returned to his old band The Inmates in 1986, having left in 1981 due to illness. He later recorded a second solo album in 1996, *Angel To Memphis* which was popular in France and Spain. Bill Hurley & The Inmates later reformed in the 2000s and were still touring into the 2010s but Hurley is now believed to be in an institution for the mentally ill.

Paul 'Wix' Wickens
Keyboards, 1983-1984
Aside from playing keyboards with JB's Allstars, Wix was also involved on the production side.

After his involvement with the band he went on to play with Tracey Ullman, Boy George and The Damned before he joined Paul McCartney's touring band in 1989, a role he continues in to this day. Wix has occasionally worked on production for other artists such as Tasmin Archer and Melanie Garside and performed at Douglas Adams' memorial in 2001, Adams had been an old school friend. Wickens also composed the music for the radio productions of *The Hitchhiker's Guide to the Galaxy* in the early 2000s.

The Rumour Brass
The Rumour Brass began their life supporting Graham Parker in 1976 and they consisted of John "Irish" Earle (saxophone), Chris Gower (trombone), Dick Hanson (trumpet) and Ray Beavis (saxophone). They started playing with The Big Heat and it was through this association they became involved with JB's Allstars in 1983. As a collective, they toured with Shakin' Stevens between 1982 and 1990 and also played with The Boomtown Rats and Katrina and the Waves.

Chris Gower
Trombone, 1983-1984
Gower joined JB's Allstars with the rest of the Rumour Brass in 1983 and has remained musically active. He's played with Shakin' Stevens, the BBC Radio Big Band and the Syd Lawrence Orchestra and is currently playing with Digby Fairweather's Half Dozen, Ian Bateman's Bone Supremacy and Suzi Quatro.

John "Irish" Earle
Saxophone, 1983-1984
Irish Earle was an accomplished saxophonist having played with Kirsty Maccoll, Jona Lewis, Mike and the Mechanics and The Clash. He was perhaps most famous for playing on Thin Lizzy's *Dancing In The Moonlight,* The Boomtown Rats' *Rat Trap* and Katrina and the Waves' *Walking on Sunshine*. By the 1990s, Earle had returned to Dublin blowing his sax with the International Blues Band, The Chaps and the Thin Az Lizzy. He passed away in May 2008 at the age of 63.

Dick Hanson
Trumpet, 1983-1984
Hanson has had a wide and varied career in music and aside from his involvement with JB's Allstars has played with Shakin' Stevens between 1982 and 1990, Graham Parker in the 1990s and Richie & The Lowdown Milton from the 1990s to the mid 2000s. He is now playing in Suzi Quatro's live band and has played with her since the 1990s.

Ray Beavis
Saxophone, 1983-1984
Aside from his involvement with JB's Allstars, Beavis has worked incessantly as a session musician, with artists such as Elvis Costello, The Temptations, Cliff Richard, U2 and The Boomtown Rats. He is now playing with Suzi Quatro and also works as a freelance session player, horn section arranger, soloist and saxophone teacher.

Chris Parks
Guitar, 1983-1984
Parks was another musician pinched from The Big Heat and after he played with JB's Allstars he worked on Bill Hurley's solo record *Double Agent* in 1985 and Drew Barfield's solo project Deep Water Terminal in 2004. He also played with Clive Gregson, Doky Brothers and Sulo, and in 2007 reunited with his former bandmates from Any Trouble for a reunion tour. They have occasionally reunited since for touring and recording, the last occasion was in 2015 with the release of *Present Tense*.

Molly & Polly
Backing Vocals, 1983-1984
See The Special AKA.

Dee Sharp
Vocals, 1983-1985
Dee Sharp had been in Buzzz and worked with Nick Heyward before he joined JB's Allstars at the request of John Bradbury. Sharp worked on production as well as providing vocals on the final three releases. He went on to have a solo career, releasing the single *Moon Dance* in 1987 and the LP *Gone Digital* in 1992. Sharp has since worked for Diamond Dub Sounds as a recording engineer, arranger, producer, composer and a manager and is currently in the process of compiling an online archive of his work and remastering JB's Allstars recordings.

Seamus Beaghen
Keyboards, 1984
Beaghen joined JB's Allstars for the live performance on *The Tube* in January 1984. He was familiar with a number of the members as he'd played with them in the band Big Heat. He later played keyboards with Madness in 1986 during their live shows and was involved with the sessions for their seventh album. However, the band broke up before they completed it though he did play on the album *The Madness* in 1988. He has played with Iggy Pop since 1990 and has also played with Morrissey, Paul Weller, Death In Vegas, Squeeze, Tom Jones and The Blockheads along with Terry Edwards from The Higsons and Lee Thompson's Ska Orchestra in an accomplished and successful career which shows no sign of stopping.

Graham Pointer
Guitar, 1984
Pointer was another member that'd played with Big Heat before he joined JB's Allstars for *The Tube* performance. He almost became part of Lee Parry's band, along with John Bradbury, Seamus Beaghen and Mick Green but this didn't end up happening, much to the disappointment of all those involved. After being involved in live music for over 25 years, Pointer began to concentrate on recorded work. He's since been the musical director of a theatre company, worked with dance companies and performance artists, worked in advertising for radio and TV and has worked on documentaries and films. He combines this with teaching guitar, digital music making and composition from his base in Glasgow.

Shezwae Powell
Vocals, 1984
Powell was a brief member of the band in 1984 when she sang on the single *Ready Willing and Able*. By her own admission,

she was brought in for the song and went on to enjoy a wide and varied career as a singer, actress, director and a producer. She is currently working as an Instructor in the Theatre department at Mt. San Jacinto College in Houston, Texas.

Mark Hughes
Harmonica, 1985
Mark "Harpdog" Hughes had been in the rhythm and blues band Split Rivitt and delighted the audiences with his unique and impressive harmonica playing. He later featured on the final JB's Allstars single, playing harmonica. After leaving the music business, Hughes sadly passed away in 2002 after a long battle with depression.

Jason Votier
Trumpet & Flugel Horn, 1985
Votier had been a part of the Norwich punk band Screen 3 in the early 1980s before he was approached to join JB's Allstars for their final single. After that fleeting appearance, Votier worked with The Stranglers on their 1988 single *All Day And All Of the Night* as well as appearing on their live album *All Live And All Of The Night*. He worked with John Bradbury again in 1990 when, as 2 To The Power, they released the acid house tune *The Flasher*. His association with Bradbury continued when he joined Special Beat on tour in the early 1990s. Votier has since left the music business and became a restaurant owner in St. Ives, Cornwall. He doesn't seem to have hung up the trumpet either as he is featured on the St. Ives Jazz Club Roll of Honour which details every musician that's played there since 1998.

Robert Ahwai
Rhythm Guitar, 1985
Ahwai had played with Chris Rea, Hummingbird, Linda Lewis, Wham and Lenny Zakatek before he featured on *Alphabet Army* in 1985. Ahwai was a session player rather than a full-time member of JB's Allstars and after the single, he continued session work, famously playing on George Michael's *Faith* in 1987. He has also continued his association with Chris

Rea but now works as a music teacher, teaching guitar and bass from his home in Surrey.

Steve Nieve
Piano, 1985
See Elvis Costello and The Attractions.

Neol Davies, Neville Staple and Sugary Staple open John Coles' photo exhibition at the 2 Tone Village in 2019

The End, Reflection and Beyond

So there it was, the final curtain came down in early 1986 and Chrysalis eventually pulled the plug and closed the place down.

Only Jerry Dammers can truly say whether he intended 2 Tone to change the world or not, but it's fair to say that it made a difference. The movement brought black and white people together and changed attitudes along the way. The influence that it had in the early days was unbelievable and it wasn't just a style of music but a movement, it influenced a change in fashion with much of the nation dressing like rudies!

The music also helped to bring black and white people together, for the first time, people were witnessing multi-racial bands preaching unity and it rubbed off on the youths of the day. Although racist organisations such as the National Front are still in existence, their powers were ultimately limited by the 2 Tone bug that swept the nation from 1979 onwards and it gave a lot of youths a sense of belonging and something to hang on to and it represented something different, showing them that they didn't have to fight, they could dance instead.

Unfortunately, the label started to wane after *Ghost Town* as people moved on from ska. Jerry Dammers had witnessed the changing styles in music and ska was no longer the 'in' thing, he set about recruiting some new talent and decided to sign The Higsons and The Apollinaires, two bands that certainly weren't ska but funk bands.

Dammers had also put together a new line up for The Specials, now known as The Special AKA, and they started to release some new music on the label as well as two singles each from The Higsons and The Apollinaires. Most of the releases between 1982 and 1983 failed to chart and when they did, they were in the low 30s at best.

The Higsons and The Apollinaires soon ceased to be on the label, leaving The Special AKA as the sole band on the label.

The Special AKA fizzled out by 1985 but Dammers ploughed on and signed The Friday Club to the label in late 1985. Their association with the label didn't last more than their first single and they had parted ways by the end of the year.

John Bradbury's band JB's Allstars had also found themselves without a record deal and their final single was released on the 2 Tone label in January 1986, although it had been recorded prior to The Friday Club's single *Window Shopping*. The JB's Allstars single was *The Alphabet Army*, a song which called for an army of teachers, even to the end, 2 Tone was releasing highly charged political music, it's just a shame that only the diehards were listening by this point.

The label had done its job in its first couple of years and achieved something to be proud of. It would have been interesting to see if any of the bands would have played Live Aid if they'd still been together, Madness were the only ones that were still around at the time and they turned down the invitation to play.

Go to any ska gig in this country, whether it's in the local working men's club or at a big arena, you will see scores and scores of rudies, some are black, some are white, some are fat, some are bald but they all have one thing in common - love of the music!

Dammers created a movement that has actually grown as generation after generation are exposed to the music and in the current climate where racism is being used as a political football, maybe 2 Tone is needed once again? Well, it's already there, look around you. For a movement that was powerful for just two years, and in existence for just seven, the popularity it still enjoys is simply incredible.

Office door at the 2 Tone Village full of signatures
Pic by Mark Harrison

The popularity has continued to grow and this saw the launch of the 2 Tone Village in Coventry in 2010. Run by a healthy band of volunteers, it contains a lot of memorabilia and is Coventry's best kept secret.

The label has since been reactivated to release albums and the occasional single. Just two years after it's closure, *Nelson Mandela* was remixed and released as *Free Nelson Mandela (The Whole World Is Watching Dance Mix)* for his 70th birthday.

In 1991, *Ghost Town (Revisited)* was released and credited to The Specials/Special Productions which saw the original *Ghost Town* appear on the 'A' side and a new remix on the 'B' side. Out of interest, the 'B' side was on Tone Records whereas the 'A' side was on 2 Tone. The label also released *The Specials Singles*, another compilation featuring all the singles released by The Specials and The Special AKA, along with a select number of 'B' sides. Interestingly it missed out *The Boiler* and *Jungle Music* which were both 'A' sides. This was followed by the release of *Live At The Moonlight Club* in 1992, a live recording of a gig by The Specials though it'd been released as a bootleg back in 1979.

The compilation *Best of 2 Tone* was released in 1993 along with *The 2 Tone EP*. The EP is still sought after and quite a rarity whereas the album has been re-released in recent years on vinyl. It was followed by *The Compact 2 Tone Story* which included George Marshall's book *The Two Tone Story*. Jerry Dammers was scornful of the boxset in a later interview. Then for over 20 years, the label once again remained dormant until 2014 when a single was released on the label. *Sock It To Em J.B. (Dub)* was credited to The Specials.

Vinyl Treasures was released in 2019 and saw the re-issue of 12 singles from the label's heyday and also contained a signed card from Jerry Dammers. A re-release of *Dance Craze* and *This Are Two Tone* was released in September 2020 also saw the re-release of every album that was released on the label between 1979 and 1986, including some released on CD for the very first time.

UK Discography

Between 1979 and 1986, 2 Tone Records released a total of 29 singles and 8 albums, as well as a free single. Since 2 Tone closed down there have been further releases with 4 more singles and 7 more albums being released in the meantime. Releases, release dates, and charting positions are included here.

Singles

The Special AKA vs The Selecter - Gangsters
Released: March 1979, re-released July 1979
Catalogue number: TT1/TT2
Chart position: No.6
Weeks on Chart: 12
The single was a double 'A' side with Gangsters on side one and the instrumental track The Selecter on the flip side. Re-released in July 1979 when Chrysalis licensed 2 Tone.

Madness - The Prince
Released: August 1979
Catalogue number: CHS TT3
Chart position: No.16
Weeks on Chart: 14
Only release by Madness on the 2 Tone label. Prince Buster is given a songwriting credit but as Colin and not his actual name Cecil.

The Selecter - On My Radio
Released: October 1979
Catalogue number: CHS TT4
Chart position: No. 8
Weeks on Chart: 9
First release by The Selecter as a proper band, also their highest charting single on the label.

The Specials featuring Rico - A Message To You Rudy/Nite Klub
Released: October 1979
Catalogue number: CHS TT5
Chart position: No. 10
Weeks on Chart: 14
Double 'A' side, The Special AKA are now known as The Specials and credit Rico's appearance on the sleeve along with Dick Cuthell. Some copies were mispressed with Nite Klub on both sides.

The Beat - Tears of a Clown /Ranking Full Stop
Released: December 1979
Catalogue number: CHS TT6
Chart position: No. 6
Weeks on Chart: 11
The Beat's only 2 Tone release and the label's joint-highest charting single at the time. Released as a double 'A' side.

Elvis Costello & The Attractions - I Can't Stand Up For Falling Down
Released: January 1980 (pulled)
Catalogue number: CHS TT7
Chart position: N/A
Weeks on Chart: N/A
Pressed but was subject to an injunction so pulled and given away at Costello gigs in early 1980. Distributed in a plain white sleeve rather than the usual black and white one featuring Walt Jabsco. One of 2 Tone's best kept secrets!

The Special AKA - Too Much Too Young
Released: January 1980
Catalogue number: CHS TT7
Chart position: No.1
Weeks on Chart: 10 (2 at No.1)
Live EP released by The Specials, though they reverted to the name The Special AKA for the release. This was 2 Tone's first No.1 and first single release to be granted a picture sleeve.

The Selecter - Three Minute Hero
Released: February 1980
Catalogue number: CHS TT8
Chart position: No.16
Weeks on Chart: 6
Lowest charting single on the label since The Prince. Paper label pressings contain the words EP, despite this being a single.

The Bodysnatchers - Let's Do Rock Steady/Easy Life
Released: February 1980
Catalogue number: CHS TT9
Chart position: No.22
Weeks on Chart: 9
First release on the label by The Bodysnatchers and released as a double 'A' side. Side 1 is mispressed as People Do Rocksteady.

The Selecter - Missing Words
Released: March 1980
Catalogue number: CHS TT10
Chart position: No.23
Weeks on Chart: 8
The Selecter's final release on the label before their departure in June 1980. Some copies were mispressed as Nissing Words.

The Specials - Rat Race/Rude Buoys Outa Jail
Released: May 1980
Catalogue number: CHS TT11
Chart position: No.5
Weeks on Chart: 9
The first and only Roddy Radiation song to be released as a single by The Specials. A double 'A' side with Rude Buoys Outa Jail on the flip.

The Bodysnatchers - Easy Life/Too Experienced
Released: July 1980
Catalogue number: CHS TT12
Chart position: No.50
Weeks on Chart: 3
Final release on the label by The Bodysnatchers and lowest charting 2 Tone single to this point.

The Specials - Stereotype
Released: September 1980
Catalogue number: CHS TT13
Chart position: No.6
Weeks on Chart: 8
The first release from the album More Specials. The band's first single to be censored due to the word "pissed". First 2 Tone single not to feature a cover on either side.

Swinging Cats - Mantovani/Away
Released: September 1980
Catalogue number: CHS TT14
Chart position: No.96
Weeks on Chart: 1
Only release on the label by the Swinging Cats, didn't get anywhere near the Top 40, although it did hit No.96.

Rico - Sea Cruise
Released: October 1980
Catalogue number: CHS TT15
Chart position: N/A
Weeks on Chart: N/A
Rico's only solo single release on the label although it became the first 2 Tone single not to chart at all.

The Specials featuring Rico with The Ice Rink String Sounds - Do Nothing/ Maggie's Farm
Released: December 1980
Catalogue number: CHS TT16
Chart position: No.4
Weeks on Chart: 11
Do Nothing appeared on More Specials originally before it was repackaged and had a synthesiser added to it. Some copies were mispressed as The Specials featuring Rico with The Ice Rirk Strirg Sourds.

The Specials - Ghost Town
Released: June 1981
Catalogue number: CHS TT17
Chart position: No.1
Weeks on Chart: 14
Final release by The Specials in their original form, released on both 7" and 12" with a picture sleeve and the usual paper sleeve. Interestingly, it was released with a 12" paper sleeve, the only 2 Tone release to be granted such a thing. Also the final No.1 single on 2 Tone.

Rhoda & The Special AKA - The Boiler
Released: January 1982
Catalogue number: CHS TT18
Chart position: No.35
Weeks on Chart: 5
Rhoda gets a credit here on the first release from the post-Specials Special AKA. Featured a guest appearance on bass from former Bodysnatcher Nicky Summers.

Rico & The Special AKA - Jungle Music

Rico & The Special AKA - Jungle Music
Released: March 1982
Catalogue number: CHS TT19
Chart position: N/A
Weeks on Chart: N/A
Rico's final single release on the label and the last single to feature Walt Jabsco in the label's original life form. Released on 7" and 12" formats.

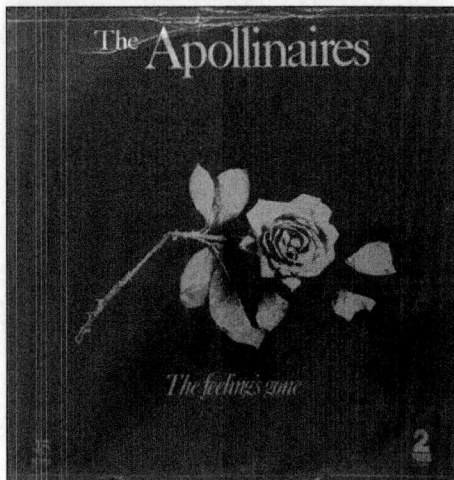

The Apollinaires - The Feeling's Gone
Released: June 1982
Catalogue number: CHS TT20
Chart position: N/A
Weeks on Chart: N/A
Released on 7" and 12" with a picture sleeve, The Apollinaires' first release on the label and produced by Jerry Dammers.

The Higsons - Tear The Whole Thing Down
Released: October 1982
Catalogue number: CHS TT21
Chart position: N/A
Weeks on Chart: N/A
Released on 7", 1st release by The Higsons on the label but their 4th overall.

The Apollinaires - Envy The Love
Released: November 1982
Catalogue number: CHS TT22
Chart position: N/A
Weeks on Chart: N/A
Final release from The Apollinaires on 2 Tone, released on 7" and 12".

The Special AKA - War Crimes
Released: November 1982
Catalogue number: CHS TT23
Chart position: No.84
Weeks on Chart: 2
First release by The Special AKA with the new lineup, released on 7" and 10" with a picture sleeve.

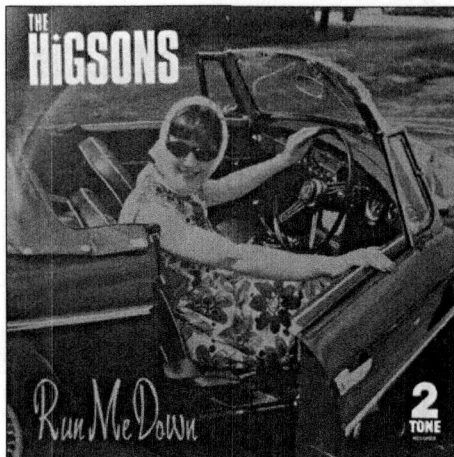

The Higsons - Run Me Down
Released: January 1983
Catalogue no: CHS TT24
Chart position: N/A
Weeks on Chart: N/A
Released on 7" and 12", the final release by The Higsons on 2 Tone.

The Special AKA - Racist Friend /Bright Lights
Released: September 1983
Catalogue number: CHS TT25
Chart position: No.60
Weeks on Chart: 3
Released as a double 'A' side and on both 7" and 12" formats, the highest charting single from The Special AKA since The Boiler.

The Special AKA - Nelson Mandela /Break Down The Door
Released: March 1984
Catalogue number: CHS TT26
Chart position: No.9
Weeks on Chart: 10
Highest charting single on 2 Tone since Ghost Town in 1981. Released on both 7" and 12" formats and later charted at No.96 following the death of Nelson Mandela in 2013.

The Special AKA - What I Like Most About You Is Your Girlfriend
Released: September 1984
Catalogue number: CHS TT27
Chart position: No.51
Weeks on Chart: 5
Released on 7" and 12" with a special 7" picture disc also available. The final release by The Special AKA on the label.

The Friday Club - Window Shopping
Released: October 1985
Catalogue number: CHS TT28
Chart position: N/A
Weeks on Chart: N/A
Released on both 7" and 12", the only release by the band on 2 Tone. Also has the distinction of being the final single to be recorded on 2 Tone.

JB's Allstars - The Alphabet Army
Released: January 1986
Catalogue number: CHS TT29
Chart position: N/A
Weeks on Chart: N/A
The final release on 2 Tone and the only release by JB's Allstars on the label. This single was released on both 7" and 12" formats. John Bradbury had the distinction of appearing on both the first and last single on 2 Tone Records.

The Specials/Special Productions - Ghost Town (revisited)
Released: June 1991
Catalogue number: CHS TT30
Chart position: N/A
Weeks on Chart: N/A

Single released on the 10th anniversary of Ghost Town, which featured on the 'A' side, and a remix of the single entitled Ghost Dub '91. This was also released on 12".

Various - 2 Tone EP
Released: January 1993
Catalogue number: CHS TT31
Chart position: No.30
Weeks on Chart: 3
EP released in conjunction with The Best of 2 Tone and contained a track from each of The Specials, The Selecter, The Beat and Madness. Last single/EP release from 2 Tone to chart.

The Specials - Sock it to Em' J.B. (DUB)/ Rat Race (DUB)
Released: April 2014
Catalogue number: CHS TT32
Chart position: N/A
Weeks on Chart: N/A
Double 'A' side containing dub versions of Sock It To Em J.B. and Rat Race released in aid of Record Store Day 2014 complete with Walt Jabsco sleeve.

The Specials - Dubs
Released: October 2020
Catalogue number: CHS TT33
Chart position: N/A
Weeks on Charts: N/A
Released in aid of Record Store Day 2020 complete with Walt Jabsco sleeve. Delayed release due to the coronavirus pandemic.

Albums

The Specials - Specials
Released: October 1979
Catalogue number: CDL TT 5001
Chart position: No.4
Weeks on Chart: 45
Debut album by The Specials, also released on cassette. Highest charting album on the label.

The Selecter - Too Much Pressure
Released: February 1980
Catalogue number: CDL TT 5002
Chart position: No.5
Weeks on Chart: 13
The Selecter's debut album on the label, also released on cassette. Highest charting album for The Selecter throughout the band's life.

The Specials - More Specials
Released: October 1980
Catalogue number: CHR TT 5003
Chart position: No.5
Weeks on Chart: 20
Second album from The Specials, released with a free 7" single and a jumbo sized poster.

Various - Dance Craze
Released: February 1981
Catalogue number: CHR TT 5004
Chart position: No.5
Weeks on Chart: 15
Compilation album to accompany the film containing live tracks from The Specials, The Selecter, Madness, The Beat, The Bodysnatchers and non 2 Tone band Bad Manners.

Rico - That Man Is Forward
Released: March 1981
Catalogue number: CHR TT 5005
Chart position: N/A
Weeks on Chart: N/A
Rico's first album on 2 Tone. Also released on cassette. Contained a version of Walt Jabsco playing the trombone on the label.

Rico - Jama Rico
Released: May 1982
Catalogue number: CHR TT 5006
Chart position: N/A
Weeks on Chart: N/A
Final release on the label for Rico, cassette version was also released.

Various - This Are Two Tone
Released: November 1983
Catalogue number: CHR TT 5007
Chart position: No.51
Weeks on Chart: 9
Compilation released by Chrysalis to claw back some money spent on the album by The Special AKA. Tracks by The Specials, Madness, The Selecter, The Beat, The Bodysnatchers, The Swinging Cats and The Special AKA.

The Special AKA - In The Studio
Released: June 1984
Catalogue number: CHR TT 5008
Chart position: No.34
Weeks on Chart: 6
The final album of original material to be released on 2 Tone Records and perhaps the most expensive!

Various - The 2 Tone Story
Released: 1989
Catalogue number: CHR TT 5009
Chart position: N/A
Weeks on Chart: N/A
Double album compilation released for the 10 year anniversary of the label. Contained tracks by The Specials, The Special AKA, Madness, The Beat, The Selecter, The Bodysnatchers and Rico, although The Higsons, The Swinging Cats. The second album included live performances by all the previously mentioned bands as well as Bad Manners which had previously featured on Dance Craze.

The Specials - Singles
Released: May 1991
Catalogue number: CHR TT 5010
Chart position: No.10
Weeks on Chart: 9
Album that contains every 'A' side from singles by The Specials and The Special AKA. Also released on CD, cassette and VHS containing music videos for the songs on the release.

The Specials - Live at the Moonlight Club
Released: 1992
Catalogue number: CHR TT 5011
Chart position: N/A
Weeks on Chart: N/A
A live recording of a gig from May 1979 just before the band hit the big time. The band demonstrate their raw fusion of punk and ska and an early insight into the style of the music that swept the nation just months later.

Various - Best of 2 Tone
Released: 1993
Catalogue number: CHR TT 5012
Chart position: N/A
Weeks on Chart: N/A
Vinyl release containing 16 tracks considered to the best of the lot. Released in conjunction with The 2 Tone EP.

Various - The Compact 2 Tone Story
Released: 1993
Catalogue number: CHR TT 5013
Chart position: N/A
Weeks on Chart: N/A
CD box set containing 4 discs featuring the 'A' and 'B' sides from every single release on the label. Also came with a copy of the book, The Two Tone Story by George Marshall.

Two Tone 7" Treasures
Released: November 2019
Catalogue Number: CHR TT 5014
Chart position: N/A
Weeks on chart: N/A
Set of 12 singles that were released on the label chosen by Jerry Dammers. These vinyls came in a special box which also contained a signed art card from Dammers himself and a seven-inch slipmat featuring Walt Jabsco.

Various - Dance Craze
Released: September 2020
Catalogue Number: CHR TT 5015
Chart position: N/A
Weeks on chart: N/A
Remastered 40th anniversary release originally meant to be released early in 2020 but was delayed due to the coronavirus pandemic.

Various - The Albums
Released: September 2020
Catalogue Number: CHR TT 5016
Chart position: N/A
Weeks on chart: N/A
A CD re-issue of every 2 Tone album released between 1979 and 1983, including Dance Craze and This Are Two Tone.

Notable mentions:

The Specials - Braggin & Tryin' Not To Lie
Released: October 1980
Catalogue number: CHS TT999
Chart position: N/A
Weeks on Chart: N/A
Free single released with More Specials. Contains Braggin' & Tryin' Not To Lie credited to Roddy Radiation and The Specials (featuring Paul Heskett on saxophone) and Rude Boys Outa Jail credited to Neville Staples AKA Judge Roughneck.

The Special AKA - Nelson Mandela (Special 70th Birthday Remake)
Released: July 1988
Catalogue Number: FNMX1
Chart position: No.93
Weeks on chart: 2
Released on Tone Records and featured a remix of the original song featuring new vocals from Ndonda Khuze and Jonas Gwangwa, with the 'B' side containing the original.

Related Bands

This section details bands that are related to the 2 Tone label, either by association or featuring former members of 2 Tone bands.

NiteTrane
1975-1976

Neol Davies and Ray King formed the band in 1975 and put an advert out to recruit a keyboard player. Jerry Dammers responded to the advert and joined. NiteTrane gigged for around a year but split after a short tour of Tunisia that was particularly disastrous. The band is prominent in the 2 Tone story thanks to the involvement of Dammers and Davies. They recorded some demos on Davies's recording system. The Tunisian trip has a particular significance as Dammers bought an American bowling shirt out there with the words Walt Jabsco on them!

Transposed Men
1977-1979

Shortly after leaving The Automatics, Neol Davies formed his own band to showcase the songs he'd written. The band consisted of Davies, Desmond Brown, John Bradbury, Steve Wynne and Kevin Harrison. They attracted some interest from Virgin but this ultimately came to nothing and they split when Bradbury joined The Special AKA in 1979. After the success of the *Gangsters/The Selecter* single, Davies formed The Selecter, of which Desmond Brown joined, Steve Wynne joined Swinging Cats and Kevin Harrison later joined Urge.

Pharaoh's Kingdom
1970s

Pharaoh's Kingdom was a Ray King band formed in the mid 1970s, its lineup boasted Lynval Golding, Aitch Bembridge, Desmond Brown and Silverton Hutchison at one point. Golding left the band to join The Automatics in 1977.

Hard Top 22
1970s-1979

Reggae band from Coventry that consisted of Charley Anderson, Compton Amanor and Charley "Aitch" Bembridge as well as Amos Anderson and Chris Christy. Jerry Dammers also played keyboards with them for a while. Once Neol Davies was instructed to put a band together after the success of *The Selecter* track, he invited Charley Anderson, Aitch Bembridge and Compton Amanor to join his band.

Dexy's Midnight Runners
1978-1986, 2003-present

Led by Kevin Rowland, Dexy's Midnight Runners were formed in 1978 and were soon on the Birmingham scene alongside The Beat and UB40. When Madness left the 2 Tone Tour halfway through in 1979, Dexy's Midnight Runners replaced them. Despite the obvious connections, Dexy's never appeared on the label and went their own way in the music business. Dammers is said to have approached them to sign to 2 Tone but they declined. Originally, they had their roots in ska but they went down the commercial route and are best known for their 1982 hit *Come On Eileen*. They broke up in 1986 but have since reformed as Dexy's and since 2003 they've recorded numerous albums of new material. Steve Wynne from Swinging Cats played with the band for a short time in 1981.

The People
1980-1982

The People were formed by Charley Anderson and Desmond Brown from The Selecter after they left the band in 1980. Anderson played bass and took on the vocals, Brown played keyboards and they were joined by Chris Christie (bass) and John Hobley (drums).

They released one single *Musical Man* on John Bradbury's Race Records in 1981, Lynval Golding helped produce the single along with Dave Jordan. The People later broke up in 1982.

The Belle Stars
1980-1986
When The Bodysnatchers broke up in late 1980, five of the seven members went on to form The Belle Stars. Sarah-Jane Owen, Stella Barker, Judy Parsons, Miranda Joyce and Penny Leyton were joined by Lesley Shone (bass) and Jennie Mathias (vocals). They enjoyed some chart success with songs such as *Sign of the Times* and *The Clapping Song*. Three years after they broke up, The Belle Stars achieved a hit record on the Billboard 100 when *Iko Iko* reached No.14 in 1989 after it appeared in the film *Rain Man*.

Fun Boy Three
1981-1983
Fun Boy Three were formed by Terry Hall, Lynval Golding and Neville Staple at the tail end of 1981 when they left The Specials. They had been recording demos together and after they'd had enough with The Specials, they broke away and formed their own band. The band's first release came out in November 1981 when *The Lunatics Have Taken Over The Asylum* hit the charts. The band enjoyed considerable chart success throughout 1982 and 1983 before Terry Hall left the band in late 1983.

General Public
1983-1987, 1994-1995
Formed by Dave Wakeling and Ranking Roger in 1983 shortly after they left The Beat, Horace Panter from The Specials soon joined and the rest of the band was made up of Mickey Billingham (keyboards), Kevin White (guitar), Stoker (drums) and Mick Jones (guitar). Jones left shortly after the recording of the first album *All The Rage* in 1984. They recorded one more LP, *Hand To Mouth* in 1986 before breaking up in 1987. Dave Wakeling and Ranking Roger later reunited to record the soundtrack to the film *Threesome* in 1994, resulting in the hit single, *I'll Take You There* and an album in 1995 before they broke up.

The Go-Gos
1978-1985, 1990, 1994, 1999-present
The Go-Gos were an American female punk band formed in 1978 and by 1980 they found themselves in the UK after they'd supported Madness in the US. They joined The Specials on their Seaside Tour of 1980 and also appeared as backing vocalists on their *More Specials* album. They have gone on to have a very successful career both here and in the US, with one of their most successful releases being *Ours Lips Are Sealed*, co-written by Jane Wiedlin and Terry Hall. They have continued to record and tour the world and after breaking up in 1985, and reunions in 1990 and 1994, they reunited in 1999 and despite announcing a farewell tour in 2016, they have since toured twice more and are still active.

Fine Young Cannibals
1984-1992, 1996
Having been left in the lurch when Ranking Roger and Dave Wakeling broke up The Beat, David Steele and Andy Cox formed a new band, recruiting Roland Gift and emerging with the single *Johnny Come Home* in 1984. This launched a successful charting career which saw them hit the big time in 1989 with the album *The Raw & The Cooked,* which topped the charts in the UK and the US. They hadn't previously made an impact in the US but this album changed things for them as it sold over 4 million copies worldwide. They broke up in 1992 but reformed briefly in 1996 to record a new single for the release of their Greatest Hits album, *The Finest.*

Sunday Best
1984
Following the breakup of Fun Boy Three, Neville Staple and Lynval Golding teamed up with Pauline Black to form Sunday Best. They recorded a one-off single called *Pirates on the Airwaves*, released in 1984. The rest of the band were made up of Wayne Lothian (bass), Phil Graham (drums) and Jeremy Edwards (keyboards and guitar) although this was very much a one-off project. The single peaked at No.93.

The Colourfield
1984-1987

Terry Hall formed The Colourfield with Toby Lyons from The Swinging Cats and Karl Shale in 1984 shortly after he'd left the Fun Boy Three. The band first surfaced with the single *The Colour Field* in January 1984 and this was followed with the album *Virgins and Philistines* in 1985, spawning the No.12 hit *Thinking of You*. The band released a further album, *Deception* in 1987, shortly before they broke up.

Robert Wyatt with The SWAPO Singers
1985

After penning the anti-apartheid tune *Nelson Mandela* in 1984, Jerry Dammers turned his attentions to Namibia, deciding to record a single to raise awareness and funds for the Namibian resistance movement, South West Africa People's Organisation (SWAPO). Dammers teamed up with Robert Wyatt & SWAPO in 1985 to record *Wind of Change*, another anti-apartheid tune in the mould of *Nelson Mandela* and extremely danceable. Dammers produced and arranged the single, as well as playing piano, guitar and synth. The single also featured a vast array of musicians including Lynval Golding (guitar) and Dick Cuthell (cornet) though only reached No.86 in the charts - a forgotten classic.

Starvation
1985

With famine relief a hot topic in 1984, the idea to record a charity single was mooted by a Madness fan that walked into their studio and suggested they cover *Starvation*, an old Pioneers number. They soon had Jerry Dammers on board and he recruited a number of former 2 Tone stars to record the single and managed to recruit Lynval Golding, John Bradbury, Dick Cuthell, Dave Wakeling and Ranking Roger and they were also joined by members of UB40 and The Pioneers. The single took time to record and mix and by the time it was released, Band Aid had already beaten them to it. It still performed okay in the charts, reaching No.33, but it was a bit of a missed opportunity in the end.

Special Beat
1989-1993

Formed by Neville Staple, John Bradbury, Horace Panter and Ranking Roger to capitalise on the third wave of ska boom in America towards the end of the 1980s. After a number of tours of the US, Horace Panter left the band although Lynval Golding joined. To make up for the lack of original material, a number of live releases surfaced. The band continued until around 1993 before they split as the Specials members reformed to record with Desmond Dekker.

2 To The Power
1990

John Bradbury and Jason Votier teamed up to release an acid-house single in 1990. They'd been working on ideas and Pete Waterman allowed them to use his studio and given free rein. They ended up releasing *The Flasher* on Lisson Records but nothing else came of it.

The Cosmics
1991

Not to be confused with a band that John Shipley played with, The Cosmics were formed in 1991 to play a benefit show for The Tic Toc Club which faced closure. Jerry Dammers, Lynval Golding, Roddy Radiation, Neol Davies and Aitch Bembridge joined in. The club survived too!

Big 5
1992-1997

Big 5 were formed in 1992 by Nick Welsh and Jennie Mathias, after having a chat at a gig one night. Martin Stewart and Perry Melius, his bandmates in The Selecter at the time, were drafted in on keyboards and drums respectively. Melius was quickly replaced by John Bradbury. They performed numerous tours and released three albums before disbanding in 1997.

Neol Davies Box of Blues
1998-2002

Neol Davies and Horace Panter teamed up in 1998 and formed Box of Blues, they performed live in a number of pubs and clubs around Coventry and released an album.

3 Men + Black
2001-2005
Pauline Black teamed up with Jake Burns, JJ Burnel and Nick Welsh in 2001 for a tour. Toured again in 2002 and 2003 before they reconvened in 2004 for an album featuring Burns, Burnel and Welsh along with former bassist from The Jam, Bruce Foxton. A tour followed in 2004 and a one-off performance occurred in 2005 which saw the band consist of Black, Welsh, Wakeling, Roddy Radiation and Rhoda Dakar.

Roddy Radiation & The Skabilly Rebels
2003-present
Roddy Radiation formed his own band The Skabilly Rebels in 2003 to indulge his love of rockabilly. After gigging for a number of years, they released the album *Blues Attack* in 2009. Radiation joined the reformed Specials in 2009 so gigs were limited. Once he departed in 2013, he threw himself into gigging with the Scabs and released the EP, *Fallen Angel* in 2016. They followed this up in 2018 with the EP *Losing Control*, which featured a guest appearance from Neville Staple on a new version of *Hey Little Rich Girl*. The Skabilly Rebels continue to tour the world delighting audiences wherever they go and shared a bill with The Neville Staple Band in 2019 to celebrate the 40th anniversary of 2 Tone.

From The Specials - The Neville Staple Band
2004-present
Neville Staple formed The Neville Staple Band in 2004 when he returned to the UK after a spell in California. They have released a number of albums and have continued to tour, even when Staple rejoined The Specials between 2009 and 2012. Staple's wife, Christine 'Sugary' Staple joined the band in 2017. They released the album *Rude Rebels* in 2017 which featured Roddy Radiation. They also toured the UK in 2019 with Roddy Radiation & The Skabilly Rebels and select dates saw Jerry Dammers and Neol Davies join them on stage. They became From The Specials in 2019 and released *The Rude Boy Returns* in 2020 and then the single *Lockdown* during the coronavirus pandemic.

Skaville UK
2006-2009
Skaville UK was formed in 2006 by Nick Welsh and he was joined by Al Fletcher and Martin Stewart and Louis Cook from Bad Manners. They would play a mixture of Bad Manners songs and some originals and later recorded the album *1973* in 2007. Rhoda Dakar and Jennie Mathias guested on the album. This was followed by another album in 2008, *Decadent*, which once again featured Dakar. Skaville UK released one more album, *Devil Beat*, in 2009 with a different line-up but soon split.

Jerry Dammers' Spatial AKA Orchestra
2006-2014
Jerry Dammers formed his own orchestra in 2006 as a tribute to Sun Ra. In the early days, the orchestra played Sun Ra tunes but this was later extended to include covers of Specials songs. The orchestra contained a raft of musicians including Rico and Terry Edwards and embarked on a tour in 2010. They last surfaced in 2014 when they played a show in London.

Near Jazz Experience
2010-present
Formed by Terry Edwards, Simon Charterton and Mark 'Bedders' Bedford as a sideline project to indulge their love of jazz. They perform frequently and have released some original material, the last of which was *The NJE* in 2019.

Ruder Than U
2014-present
The musical *Three Minute Heroes* was launched in October 2014 and the stage show was set in the late 1970s, 2 Tone's heyday, and saw a backing band featuring Aitch Bembridge. Once the theatre run was over, some of the actors decided to keep going and formed Ruder Than U. They are popular around Coventry and often play further afield. The band consists of Elizah Jackson (vocals), Conor Nolan (vocals), Sarah Workman (guitar) and Aitch Bembridge (drums). Ruder Than U have also featured guest appearances from John Shipley, Lynval Golding and Neol Davies and released an EP, *Phat Cat*, in 2015.

Two Tone Trail

The Two Tone Trail's roots can be traced back to 2005 when Pete Chambers wrote a brilliant book about prominent places in Coventry that were vital to the 2 Tone story after being disappointed that none of this had been previously documented.

With the 30th Anniversary celebrations upcoming in 2009, Chambers decided to launch the Two Tone Trail where 11 plaques would be unveiled throughout the year at a selection of locations that had appeared in the book. Each plaque was unveiled by someone relevant to the story and some of those involved included; Roddy Radiation, Horace Panter, Paul Heskett, Pauline Black, Neville Staple, Buster Bloodvessel, Neol Davies and Charley Anderson.

Coventry University
Lanchester Polytechnic, as it used to be known, is the first step on the trail, Pauline Black, Jerry Dammers, Horace Panter all studied here and the student union bar was where Roddy Radiation first came up with the idea for *Rat Race*. The Specials later recorded the video for the single in the Main Hall in 1980 with some of the students appearing as extras in it, they also played live later in September 1980. Perhaps more importantly though, this was where Horace Panter would first meet Jerry Dammers in 1972 while they were art students and the plaque was unveiled by Sir Horace Gentleman himself in October 2009.

The Hand & Heart
The Hand & Heart pub was a major venue in the city for the emerging music scene and had played host to The Specials, The Selecter and The Swinging Cats in the late 1970s. The plaque was unveiled on the site of the former pub by Steve 'Cardboard' Eaton who had featured on The Selecter's *Too Much Pressure* album cover and was a prominent Coventry ska DJ. The unveiling was followed by a gig at The Dog & Trumpet which saw John Shipley and Paul Heskett play as The Swinging Cats, Cardboard Eaton joined them along with his wife Linzi, Dom Hazell on bass and Terry Downes on drums.

The Binley Oak
The Binley Oak was the location for The Selecter's first rehearsal as a band and where Pauline Black effectively joined back in 1979. The Specials had also rehearsed here in the past and they later played a live gig in the venue. The plaque was unveiled by the Deputy Lord Mayor Councillor Jack Harrison, Neol Davies and Pauline Black in February 2009. The unveiling was followed by a live show by The Allskas. As of 2020, the plaque has vanished and its whereabouts unknown.

The Selecter also recorded *Celebrate The Bullet* in the studio and Bad Manners recorded their albums *Ska 'N' B* and *Loonee Tunes!* here, all under the watchful eye of the legendary Roger Lomas. The plaque was unveiled by Buster Bloodvessel and Neville Staple in May 2009. As Horizon was later demolished and the plaque was situated across the road at The Rocket pub. Following the demolition of The Rocket, the plaque has vanished and its whereabouts are unknown.

The Canal Basin

The Canal Basin in Coventry was the location of the photograph sessions for the album covers of *Specials* and *More Specials*. The plaque was unveiled in January 2009 by Horace Panter and Roddy Radiation. The unveiling was followed by the launch of a photo exhibition featuring photographs from the legendary 2 Tone photographer John Coles.

51 Albany Road

This is the most important place on the 2 Tone Trail as this is where it all began, the birthplace of 2 Tone, Jerry Dammers lived at 51 Albany Road in the upstairs flat and it was here where he formed the label. Once 2 Tone was licensed by Chrysalis, this is where the office was located. A bit of trivia: Joe Reynolds from The Selecter actually lived here in the early 1970s, long before the crazy days of 2 Tone! The plaque was unveiled by Lynval Golding and Charley Anderson with Gaps Hendrickson and Aitch Bembridge also appearing at the unveiling in March 2009.

Horizon Studios

Horizon Studios was a recording studio in Coventry and this is where The Specials and The Selecter recorded much of their work that was released on the 2 Tone label. The Specials recorded *Gangsters* and *More Specials* here and The Selecter recorded *Too Much Pressure* at the studio. Although they weren't released on 2 Tone,

Holyhead Youth Club

The Holyhead Youth Club was once run by the famous Coventry singer, Ray King. Neol Davies had attended in his younger days and the basement of the building was later the host of jam sessions between Charley Anderson, Aitch Bembridge, Lynval Golding, Gaps Hendrickson and Silverton Hutchison along with Davies and King. Neville Staple also operated the Jah Baddis sound system from here along with his friend and later roadie of The Specials, Trevor Evans. It is poignant that the graffiti that featured on the walls of the youth club is still preserved on the basement walls. The plaque was unveiled by Ray King and Neol Davies in September 2009 and the launch saw King, Davies, Paul Heskett and 'Gaps' Hendrickson perform with The Allskas at The Caribbean Centre, Coventry. Paul Williams' 2009 book, *You're Wondering Now* was also launched and he was on hand to sign copies.

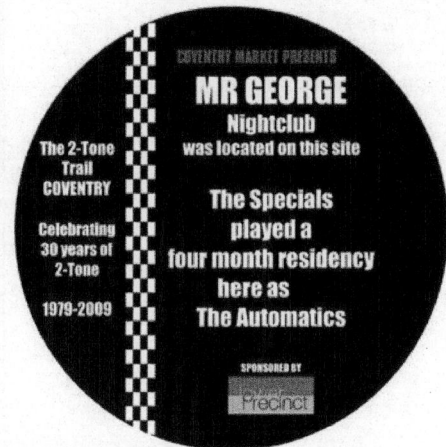

COVENTRY MARKET PRESENTS

MR GEORGE
Nightclub
was located on this site

The 2-Tone Trail COVENTRY

Celebrating 30 years of 2-Tone

1979-2009

The Specials played a four month residency here as The Automatics

SPONSORED BY
Precinct

Mr. George

The Mr. George nightclub was where The Automatics secured a four month residency in the early days in 1978 before they became The Specials and before 2 Tone was launched. The plaque was unveiled by Felix Hall, son of Terry, and Trevor Evans a former roadie with The Specials in August 2009 and after the ceremony they both played a DJ set at The Warehouse.

Tiffany's

Tiffany's was a popular nightclub in Coventry during the 2 Tone days and it played host to The Specials, The Selecter, The Beat, Madness, The Bodysnatchers and The Swinging Cats during their heydays. This is where The Specials recorded *Longshot Kick The Bucket*, *Liquidator* and *Skinhead Moonstomp* for the *Too Much Too Young* live EP in 1979.

It was also known as the Locarno and is referenced by Terry Hall in The Specials song Friday Night Saturday Morning. Now the site of Coventry Library, the plaque was unveiled in July 2009 by Ranking Roger, Everett Morton, Aitch Bembridge and Paul Heskett.

Virgin Records

This plaque was unveiled at the site of Virgin Records in Coventry, John Bradbury, Tim Strickland and Chris Long all worked here at some point before they became involved with 2 Tone. The plaque was unveiled by Pete Waterman, John Bradbury, Horace Panter and Neville Staple in December 2009 and was followed by a performance by Special Brew with Silverton Hutchison on drums.

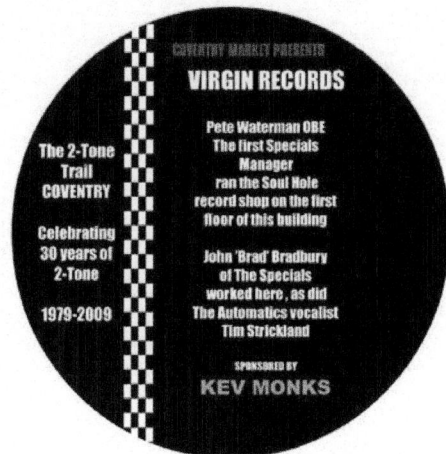

COVENTRY MARKET PRESENTS

THE HEATH HOTEL

The 2-Tone Trail COVENTRY

Celebrating 30 years of 2-Tone

1979-2009

In October 1977 history was made when The Specials played their very first gig here as The Automatics

SPONSORED BY
SPECIAL BREW
Coventry ska band since 2006

The Heath Hotel

The Heath Hotel is one of the most important places on the list as it is the venue that first played host to The Specials, but back when they were known as The Automatics. This was the band's first ever gig and they supported The Wild Boys, Certified, Urban Blight and Squad. The plaque was unveiled by the original Specials drummer, Silverton Hutchison and Neol Davies in November 2009. The unveiling was followed by a gig at the General Wolfe which saw Neol Davies guest with Dub Jam Force and also featured a DJ set from Steve 'Cardboard' Eaton.

COVENTRY MARKET PRESENTS

VIRGIN RECORDS

The 2-Tone Trail COVENTRY

Celebrating 30 years of 2-Tone

1979-2009

Pete Waterman OBE
The first Specials Manager ran the Soul Hole record shop on the first floor of this building

John 'Brad' Bradbury of The Specials worked here, as did The Automatics vocalist Tim Strickland

SPONSORED BY
KEV MONKS

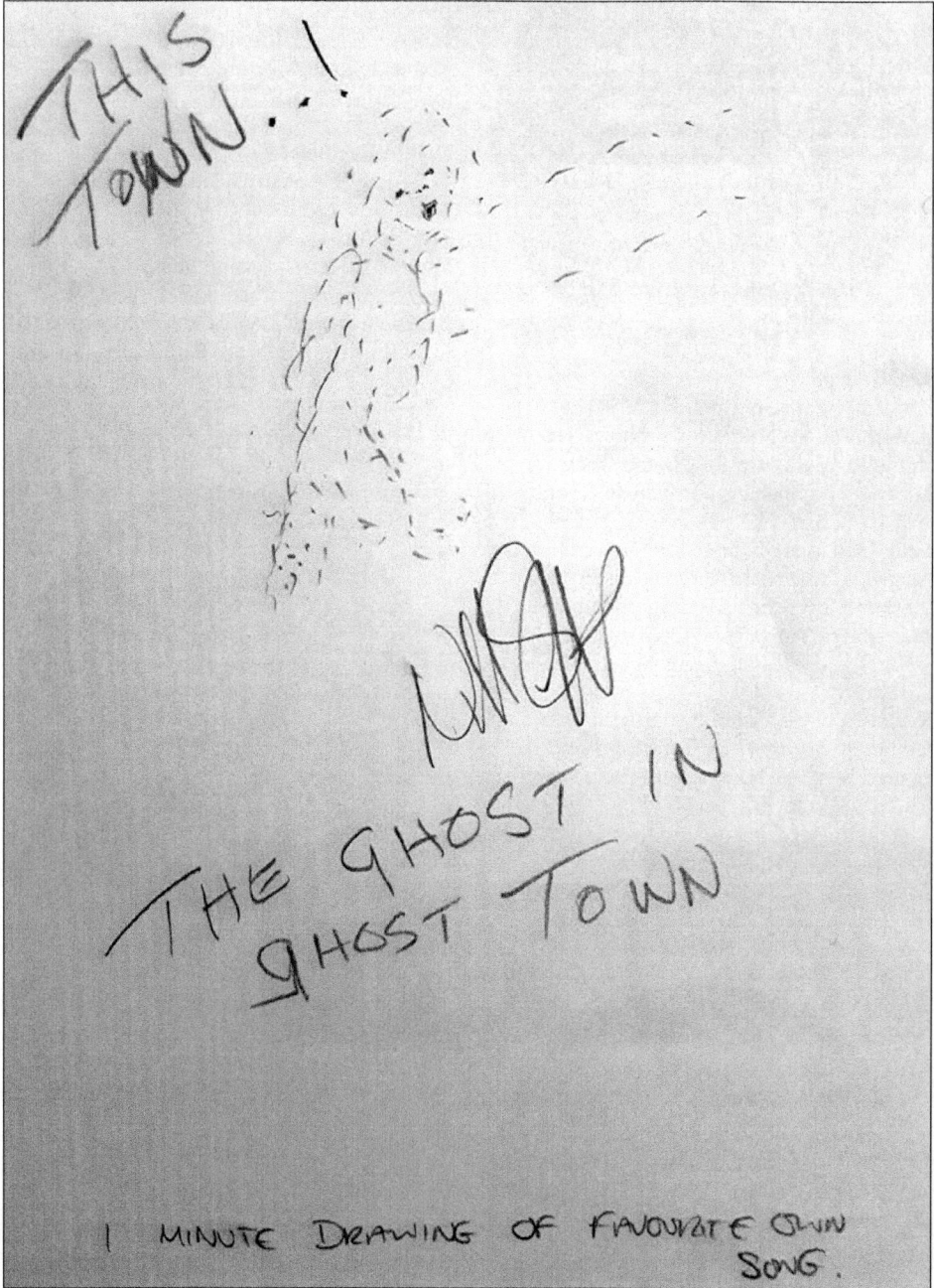

Artwork by Neville Staple depicting the ghost in Ghost Town and auctioned for charity in July 2020

Acknowledgements

I'd like to use this section to thank everybody that I spoke to who provided previously unknown information about themselves, the bands they played with or otherwise;

Terry Edwards, Stuart McGeachin, Joe Reynolds, Simon Charterton, Anthony Wimshurst, Chris Long, Steve Wynne, Dave Cummings, Jane Bom-Bane, Bruce Thomas, Stephen Leonard-Williams, Abe Brooks, Laurence Wood, Anthony Miller, Pete Thomas, Paul Heskett, John Shipley, Clint Golding, Dee Sharp, Ray Beavis, Dick Hanson, Seamus Beaghen, Gaz Birtles, John Barrow, Alan Sayag, Paul Hyman, Martin Stewart, Louis Cook, Mike Hodges, Peter Millen, Simon Kirk, Anton Hilton, David Heath, Eddie Eve, Nick Parker, Charlie Higson, Graham Pointer, Shezwae Powell, Jason Votier, Glen Da Costa.

Special thanks go to:

John Coles, Pete Chambers, Michael Boucher, Mike Pearsall, Dominic Hazell, Mark Harrison, Joe Kerrigan, Yve Paige, Simon Bennett, Tracey Salford, Alan Dargue, Gillian Flanagan-Jones, Gwyn Jones, Josh Haworth.

Bibliography

A lot of the information in this book has been provided from conversations with band members and others that were involved in the 2 Tone story and beyond. However, the book couldn't have been completed without help from a number of books and articles.

Books that have been particularly helpful;

George Marshall, *The 2 Tone Story* (ST Publishing, 1993)

Paul Williams, *You're Wondering Now - History of The Specials* (ST Publishing, 1995)

Tony Clayton-Lea, *Elvis Costello: A Biography* (Andre Deutsch Ltd, 1998)

Horace Panter, *Ska'd For Life: A Personal Journey with The Specials* (Pan Macmillan, 2007)

Neville Staple, *Original Rude Boy: From Borstal to The Specials* (Aurum Press, 2010)

Heather Augustyn, *Ska: An Oral History* (McFarland & Co, 2010)

Pauline Black, *Black By Design* (Serpent's Tail, 2011)

Suggs, *That Close* (Quercus, 2013)

John Reed, *House of Fun: The Story of Madness* (Omnibus Press, 2014)

Elvis Costello, *Unfaithful Music & Disappearing Ink* (Viking, 2015)

Nick Welsh, *The Life and Times of a Ska Man* (New Haven Publishing, 2017)

Ranking Roger, *I Just Can't Stop It: My Life in The Beat* (Omnibus Press, 2019)

John Barrow, *How Not To Make It In The Pop World* (Trafford Publishing, 2020)

The articles, interviews and books that were helpful are referenced below by band.

The Specials
1 Davies, N. Interview with Wolfman Radio Show, 2009.
2 Panter, H. Interview with Pete Mitchell, 2019.
3 *Uncut*, July 1998.
4 Chambers, Pete. *Coventry Observer*, 16 February 2019.

The Selecter
1 Davies, N. Interview with Wolfman Radio Show, 2009.
2 Davies, N. Interview with Rocker's Revolt, 2009.
3 Black, P 2011, *Black By Design*, Serpent's Tail, London.

4 Black, Pauline. Interview with Secret Records, 2003.

Madness
1 *NME,* November 24 1979.
2 *Sounds,* November 24 1979.

The Beat
1 *NME,* March 8 1980.
2 Charlery, R. Interview with Secret Records Limited, 2004.

Elvis Costello
1 *NME,* January 12 1980
2 *Record Collector,* Issue 91, March 1987
3 *Record Collector,* Issue 363, June 2009
4 Bruno, F 2005. *Elvis Costello's Armed Forces: 21 (33 ⅓).*Bloomsbury Continuum, London.
5 Crandall, B. (2003). Rock and Roll Hall of Fame: Elvis Costello. https://www.rollingstone.com/music/music-news/rock-and-roll-hall-of-fame-elvis-costello-176284/

The Bodysnatchers
1 *NME,* January 26, 1980
2 *Record Mirror,* February 2, 1980
3 *Smash Hits,* 1 May 1980
4 Nicky Summers Blog, 2017.

Swinging Cats
1 *NME,* July 27 1980.

Rico
1 Panter, H, 2007. *Ska'd For Life,* Pan Macmillan, London.

Bad Manners
1 Lomas, R. Interview with Pauline Black, 1999.
2 *NME,* April 26, 1980.
3 Record Mirror, October 30, 1982.
4 Trendle, D. Interview with John Shearlaw, unknown source, 1982.

The Special AKA
1 *Record Collector* Issue 363, page 37.
2 Panter, H, 2007. *Ska'd For Life,* Pan Macmillan, London.
3 *NME,* January 8, 1983.
4 *Sounds*, January 19, 1985

5 *Sounds,* September 17, 1983.
6 Dammers, J. Interview. Source unknown.

7 *Record Mirror,* April 7, 1984
8 *Melody Maker,* January 19, 1985

The Apollinaires
1 Barrow, J, 2020. *How Not To Make It In The Pop World,* Trafford Publishing.
2 *Leicester Mercury,* July 2 1982.
3 *NME,* December 11, 1982.
4 *Record Mirror,* April 7, 1984
5 *Record Collector* Issue 363, page 37.

The Friday Club
1 *Record Collector* Issue 363, page 37.
2 Hodges, M. New Statesman. (2009). *How I Killed Two Tone.* Retrieved from https://www.newstatesman.com/music/2009/07/tone-dammers-single-specials

JB's Allstars
1 *The Face,* March 1984.

Photographs

All the photographs that appear in this book are from my own collection except;

2 - Brett Jordan - https://www.flickr.com/photos/x1brett/11706163635

3, 5-6, 64, 66, 72-75, 77, 86 - Gillian Flanagan-Jones

8 - Wonker - https://commons.wikimedia.org/wiki/File:The_Special_Concert.jpg

14, 33, 47, 54, 76, 78-79, 97 - Joe Kerrigan

16 - Paurclarke - https://commons.wikimedia.org/wiki/File:John_Bradbury_Drummer.jpg

24 - Miles Gehm - https://commons.wikimedia.org/wiki/File:Pauline_Black.jpg

28 - Don Wright - https://www.flickr.com/photos/8374568@N07/32561087220

31 - Michael Baxter

32 - Karl Overend

34, 37 - Livepict.com -https://commons.wikimedia.org/wiki/File:Madness_(band)_2008.06.20_013.jpg

https://commons.wikimedia.org/wiki/
File:Madness_(band)_2008.06.20_006.jpg

36, 38 - Tracey Salford

39 - Ian James

42 - Simon Bennett

48 - Darin Barry - https://commons.
wikimedia.org/wiki/File:The_English_
Beat,_Truckee,_California.jpg

50 - Mykal Burns - https://commons.
wikimedia.org/wiki/File:The_English_
Beat_1.jpg

55 - Braunov - https://commons.wikimedia.
org/wiki/File:Elivis_Costello_1980_1.jpg

56 - Robman94 - https://commons.
wikimedia.org/wiki/File:Elvis_
Costello_2012.JPG

60 - Stuart Sevastos - https://commons.
wikimedia.org/wiki/File:Elvis_Costello_
and_The_Imposters_@_Fremantle_Park_
(17_4_2011)_(5648205875).jpg

61 - Shayne Kaye - https://commons.
wikimedia.org/wiki/File:Elvis_Costello_
and_Diana_Krall.jpg

62, 63 - Robman94 - https://commons.
wikimedia.org/wiki/File:Steve_Nieve.JPG

https://commons.wikimedia.org/wiki/
File:Pete_Thomas2.JPG

82 - OC Roy - https://commons.wikimedia.
org/wiki/File:RicoRodriguez.jpg

87-88 - TimDuncan - https://commons.
wikimedia.org/wiki/File:MikeyChung1979.
png

https://commons.wikimedia.org/wiki/
File:RobbieLyn1979.png

89-90 - Schorle

91 - Joakim Westerlund

94 - John Coles

96 - Skibz777 - https://commons.wikimedia.
org/wiki/File:BadMannersLive.jpg

103 - Yve Paige

106-115 - Stephen Leonard-Williams

116 - John Barrow

122 - Christopher William Adach - https://
commons.wikimedia.org/wiki/File:Charlie_
Higson_2013.jpg

125-127 - Abe Brooks

128 - Graham Pointer

129-133 - Dee Sharp Archives

135 - Mark Harrison

143 - DRJazz.ch - https://commons.
wikimedia.org/wiki/File:Dexys_Midnight_
Runners_(1982).png

144-150 - Pete Chambers

Printed in Great Britain
by Amazon